MW00511600

FRANCE

Published by Thomas Cook Publishing
A division of Thomas Cook Holdings Ltd
PO Box 227, Thorpe Wood
Peterborough PE3 6PU
United Kingdom

Telephone: 01733 503571
E-mail: books@thomascook.com

Text: © 2000 Thomas Cook Holdings Ltd
Maps prepared by Polly Senior Cartography
Maps © 2000 Thomas Cook Holdings Ltd
Transport maps © TCS Ltd

ISBN 1 841570 69 9

Distributed in the United States of America by the Globe Pequot Press,
PO Box 480, Guilford, Connecticut 06437, USA.

Distributed in Canada by Whitecap Books, 351 Lynn Avenue,
North Vancouver, British Columbia, Canada V7J 2C4.

Distributed in Australia and New Zealand by Peribo Pty Limited,
58 Beaumont Road, Mt Kuring-Gai, NSW, 2080, Australia.

Publisher: Donald Greig
Commissioning Editor: Deborah Parker
Map Editor: Bernard Horton

Series Editor: Christopher Catling

Written and researched by: Eric and Ruth Bailey, Christopher Catling,
Mike Gerrard, Brent Gregston, John Harrison, Christopher and Melanie Rice,
Andrew Sanger and Gillian Thomas.

Although every care has been taken in compiling this publication, and the
contents are believed to be correct at the time of printing, Thomas Cook
Holdings Ltd cannot accept responsibility for errors or omissions, however
caused, or for changes in details given in the guidebook, or for the consequences
of any reliance on the information provided.

The opinions and assessments expressed in this book do not necessarily
represent those of Thomas Cook Holdings Ltd.

Readers are asked to remember that attractions and establishments may open,
close or change owners or circumstances during the lifetime of this edition.
Descriptions and assessments are given in good faith but are based on the
author's views and experience at the time of writing and therefore contain
an element of subjective opinion which may not accord with the reader's
subsequent experience. We would be grateful to be told of any changes or
inaccuracies in order to update future editions. Please notify them to the
Commissioning Editor at the above address.

Cover photograph: Michael Busselle

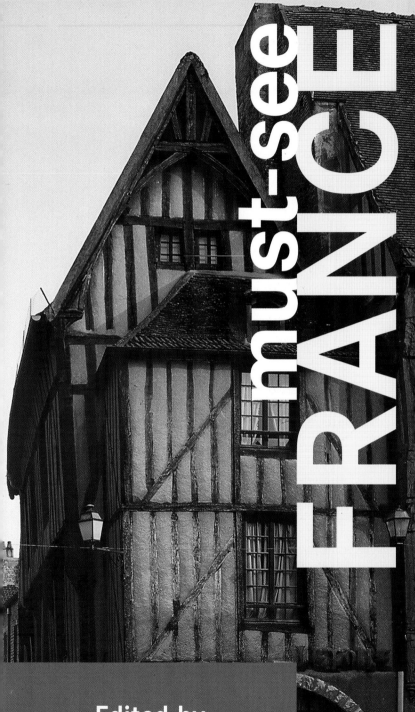

must-see FRANCE

Edited by
CHRISTOPHER
CATLING

Getting
to know
France

Discovering France

France is one of the most diverse countries in the world but also one of the easiest in which to travel. The biggest drawback is the difficulty in deciding where to go: there are Gothic cathedrals in the north, Mont-St-Michel in the northwest, Renaissance châteaux on the Loire, megaliths to the west, Strasbourg in the east, Roman monuments and beaches in the south – and a little north of centre lies Paris.

Many of the 70 million-odd foreign tourists who visit France each year seek something more: a way of living that celebrates the good things in life – art, love, food, drink, fashion – and elevates their enjoyment to an *art de vivre* ('art of living'). And the French themselves share in this aspiration. Eighty per cent of the French holiday in their own country.

> *Every man has two nations, and one of them is France.* **Benjamin Franklin**

France is **diverse** geologically as well as culturally. It is, in fact, a microcosm of Europe, encompassing the continent's characteristics within its borders while touching upon most of western Europe's natural features. The Atlantic, the North Sea and the Mediterranean – along with the Alps, the Pyrenees and the River Rhine – form the sides of 'L'Hexagone'. Although France has the fourth-largest economy in the world, a surprisingly large part of it is still rural. The French call their countryside *La France Profonde* ('deep France') and regard it as their ancestral realm, from which many of them apparently want to escape and to which they regularly return.

The spectrum of **restaurants and hotels** in France is perhaps wider than anywhere else in Europe and there are multiple ways of getting around. The country has an outstanding network of trains, and motorways that are quick and efficient; there are leisurely alternatives as well – from drifting along waterways in canal boats, to walking or cycling along country lanes.

Even in hectic Paris (and despite the reputation), **courtesy** is the rule rather than the exception, and French people are almost always polite to visitors. But the visitor has to return the politeness. Start every conversation with a cheery *Bonjour!*, whether you are buying a loaf of bread, a bus ticket or a Prada handbag, and all should be well. Address everyone – even buskers and beggars on the street – as *Monsieur* or *Madame*. Remember the old adage that when you are in a foreign country, *you* are the one with the peculiar habits.

Life in France

*The English-speaking world has had a **love-hate relationship** with the French for many centuries, and clichés have filled many books. Probably the most critical Francophobe of all was Tobias Smollet, who visited France in 1763 and wrote: 'A Frenchman lays out his whole revenue upon tawdry suits of clothes, or in furnishing a magnificent repas of fifty or a hundred dishes, one-half of which are not eatable or intended to be eaten. His wardrobe goes to the fripier, his dishes to the dogs, and himself to the devil.' The Francophiles, by contrast, envy the French simply for, well, being French.*

Vive Le Look

The French **sense of style** is not simply a question of clothes, as commercialised in *haute couture* or ready-to-wear items, but also of beauty and lifestyle. It influences the way French people set a table, arrange flowers or furnish a house. Appearances matter a lot in France to just about everyone, from middle-aged people in suits to teenagers on rollerblades. Ironically, the French have borrowed the English word 'look' and use it to describe not only a person's wardrobe but also his or her 'style'.

Sacred mealtimes

The French are punctual when it comes to **food** (just try to find a table in a popular restaurant at 1330 or 2030). Their attitude, despite some inroads by *le fast food*, has changed little since Brillat-Savarin wrote over a century ago that 'the way in which mealtimes are passed is most important to what happiness we find in life'.

Social action

Somewhere in France someone is **on strike** almost every day of the year. The French strike can involve many groups – transportation workers, teachers, sanitation workers, lorry drivers, air traffic controllers, hospital staff, and so on, and so on. These 'social actions' might also involve farmers dumping tomatoes on the road or traditional cheesemakers protesting against EU regulations that threaten to put them out of business. The strike can be interpreted in the grand French context of 'the people' rising up, as is their right, but it is also something rather more banal: a national sport, in which foreigners are unwilling spectators, if they happen to be on a French road or trying to board a French train, bus or plane.

" A sociologist has suggested that the French should be divided not into three social classes, but into sixty-three, to do full justice to all the nuances of culture, experience, possessions, and forms of esteem that they can acquire. "

Theodore Zeldin,
The French **(1983)**

Yesterday and tomorrow

Human history began in France 100,000 years ago. The **cave paintings in Lascaux** *– the 'Sistine Chapel' of prehistory – are perhaps 15,000 years old. Someone erected the first of 3 000 menhirs in* **Carnac** *in 10,000 BC. However, most textbooks on French history begin around 1200 BC with the* **Celts**, *who called their territory Gaul or Gallia. Julius Caesar arrived in 58 BC and annexed it to the rapidly expanding Roman empire.*

France acquired its name in the 9th century; it meant 'country of the Franks' (from the Latin word *Francia*) in reference to a Germanic people who conquered the region after the fall of the western Roman empire. Various rulers followed, including ones whose name the French still honour, such as **Charlemagne**, and the ones the French would rather forget – like the **British**, who ruled parts of France for several centuries and even Paris, briefly, from 1420 to 1436. One name that resonates down the centuries is **Cardinal Richelieu**, the power behind the throne of the under-age Louis XIII and responsible for such buildings as the Palais Royal and the Sorbonne.

Revolution and the triumph of the bourgeoisie

One of the long-term consequences of the **French Revolution** in **1789** was to put the bourgeoisie – the middle classes – firmly in charge of France. This is reflected in both the national and the regional government of the country. French intellectuals, from Flaubert to Sartre, have sometimes objected to this state of affairs, feeling that they should really be the ones in charge, but it is the case now more than ever, with the decline of the farming population and the diminishing influence of the working class.

Catastrophic wars and a new Europe

France was **invaded three times in 70 years** between 1870 and 1940. Two of the wars ended quickly in defeat and occupation. The First World War ultimately ended in victory but at a price that left France a crippled nation. Today, France, as much as any country in the **European Union**, is reinventing itself and looks favourably upon the creation of a pan-European bloc that can rival the United States in economic power.

❝ *No historian I know has ever adequately explained the basic reasons that move a people to become great or why it ceases to be so, nor the impetus, positive or negative, that lies behind a country's growth or decline.* ❞

François Mitterrand, *The Wheat and the Chaff* (1975)

People and places

*The idea of France as a single country and the **French as a single people** has been evoked with semi-religious power by Joan of Arc, Napoleon and de Gaulle. It is certainly a force in the minds of the French and even in the imagination of the non-French. However, beneath the passion and eloquence lies the more elemental world of **French tribalism**. The millennia-long history of invasion and settlement has introduced many peoples and cultures to French soil: Celts, Greeks, Romans, Franks, Normans, Arabs, Huns … They have shaped the identity of people in the French provinces – their beliefs, folklore, traditional dress and festivals.*

> " *France is … France.* "
>
> **Charles de Gaulle**

Except for the Île de France, the north and the Loire Valley, just about all of France's territory is divided between diverse **regions with their own culture and language**: Provence, Languedoc, Catalan, Basque and Brittany. Indeed, over 20 languages are spoken on French soil, from Alsatian to Zaphartic.

Roots and racism

French cities today are a **racial *pot au feu***, with large populations from the overseas territories and former colonies. Indeed, one-third of France's population has its roots outside of France. The country has the largest Muslim population in Europe and Europe's largest Jewish minority outside of Russia. The situation has moved unscrupulous politicians to play the 'race card' in their search for votes. However, one striking statistic is largely ignored by right-wing extremists: only 6 per cent of the people living in France are actually foreign.

Ironically, **football** has recently come to symbolise France's **multiracial identity**. In the World and European cups, the French squad stood out for being the most ethnically mixed, with players from Africa, North Africa, the Caribbean and Pacific islands – all areas where France still has territories or strong links to its past as a colonial power. The team's leader – Marseilles-born **Zinedine Zidane** – is a *beurs*, a French-born North African, who grew up in an impoverished *quartier difficile* with 50 per cent unemployment. After France's victories he was depicted on national magazine covers draped in the French flag. What a difference a goal can make.

Getting around

" *'They order,'* Mr Yorick said, *'this matter better in France.'* He thereupon climbed into the early stagecoach to Dover, took the nine o'clock boat to Calais, and by three had got sat down to dinner upon a fricassee'd chicken. "

Laurence Sterne, *A Sentimental Journey* (1768)

Air

Travelling by air within France is usually much more expensive than using the railways and not that much faster. **Air Inter** (*tel: 01 45 46 90 00*) has flights between Paris and all major cities.

Rail

The French train service (*www.SNCF.fr*), provided by the state, is fast, efficient and almost always on time. There are more than 12,000km (7 500 miles) of electrified track. The French railway network has pioneered the use of a superfast train, the *TGV* (*Train à Grande Vitesse*, or 'high speed train'), which reaches speeds of 300km/h (186mph).

Driving

You are allowed to drive in France with a UK or US driving licence. There are two kinds of driving in France. The *autoroute* is boring and stressful but efficient. However, it is also relatively expensive because of the *péages* ('tolls'). The second kind of driving, of course, is for pleasure, either on the old main roads (*routes nationales*, or 'N' roads) or, better still, the 'D' roads (*départmentales*). Wherever you drive in France, be careful. The French drive very fast and have almost three times as many fatal traffic accidents per year as the British.

Driving conditions
The *Centre d'information ASF* provides practical information on traffic conditions on the *autoroutes*, as well as maps and suggested routes. Their offices can be found by the toll booths at the beginning of every *autoroute*.

Rest areas (*aires*) are provided roughly every 10km (6 miles) along *autoroutes*. Facilities may include a café, toilets, telephones, even picnic and play areas. You'll also find petrol stations, restaurants and snack bars along the way.

Many roads on the edges of towns have **cycle lanes**, and, as cycling is a popular national sport, you'll need to be on the look out for cyclists wherever you travel.

Autoroutel (*tel: 08 36 68 10 77* or *www.autoroutes.fr*) offers information (also in English) on traffic and road conditions for all of France.

Speed limits and fines
The speed limits on French roads are 130km/h (80mph) on the *autoroute*, 110 (68mph) on dual carriageways and 90 (56mph) on other roads. In towns, the speed limit is 50km/h (31mph). Fines for speeding are high (up to several thousand francs) and you will

be expected to pay on the spot in cash. The legal blood alcohol limit in France is lower than in the UK, at 0.5 per cent. Drink-driving fines may also be payable immediately.

Car hire

The major international rental companies are all represented in France, as are a range of European firms. Shop around before you leave and pre-book, if necessary with the help of a travel agent. Resolve the question of insurance, too. Many credit cards offer free supplementary car rental insurance, which might allow you to save money. It is also a good idea to get breakdown cover. **European Motoring Assistance** (*tel: 0800 550055*) and **AA Five-Star Europe** (*tel: 0800 444500*) both offer it.

Auto Europe (*www.autoeurope.com*)
Tel: 0800 899 893

Avis *Tel: 0990 900 500*

Budget *Tel: 0800 181181*

Dollar UK *Tel: 0990 565 656*

Europcar *Tel: 0345 222 525*

Hertz *Tel: 0990 996 699*

National Car Rental
Tel: 0990 365365

Parking

In towns and cities there are zones where parking is restricted to certain times and charged – tickets, obtainable from machines, should be displayed on the windscreen on the driver's side. The sign for car parks is a blue 'P'. In larger towns underground car parks are easiest for parking, but if you want to be near a particular sight, look for

COMMUNE

D'EUROPE

Jumelée avec

LES ANGLES
66.210

SETTLE
ANGLETERRE

République Tchèque
KRALUPY

N 114

BANYULS S/ MER

BANYULS DE LA MARENDA

the *stationnement payant* areas. In some towns you will see short-stay blue parking zones (maximum $1^1/2$–$2^1/2$ hours), indicated by a blue line on the pavement and a blue 'P' sign. Here you must display a **parking disc**. Buy the disc (*disque de stationnement*) in supermarkets or petrol stations. Parking meters take two-franc coins; ticket machines will also require coins, so have a selection ready.

A yellow line on the kerb means that parking is forbidden. There are also additional parking restrictions in the centre of towns on market days. Illegal parking may result in on-the-spot fines, clamping or even your vehicle being towed away – and the police are eagle-eyed.

Seat belts
Seat belts must be worn at all times in both the front and the back of the car, except in older vehicles that do not have seat belts fitted. Children under ten are not allowed to travel in the front seats (except for babies up to 9 months weighing under 9kg (20lb) and seated in a rear-facing baby seat). Even in rear seats, all children must use seat belts.

What to take
You must have a red warning triangle or hazard warning lights in case of accident. Your car's headlights must be adjusted to avoid dazzle when driving on the right: you can buy stick-on headlight deflectors. You'll also need a GB sticker, a first-aid kit, a torch, a petrol container and spare headlight bulbs. Spectacle wearers are advised to carry a spare pair.

Information
Road maps are published by the motoring organisations. Michelin produce clear regional maps (scale 1:200,000). Information points at the end of motorways provide maps showing *Bison Futé* (routes avoiding traffic build-ups), as well as restaurants, hotels and petrol stations.

Inter Service Route (*tel: 01 48 58 33 33*) is a 24-hour telephone service (in French) that updates motorists on road works, weather hazards, and so on.

Caravans and camper vans
Although camping in unauthorised areas is permitted, there are numerous restrictions. To avoid a lot of inconvenience, look for an official site. There are no additional customs formalities for bringing a caravan into France, unless you intend staying for more than six months. Camper vans and cars towing caravans have to pay higher *autoroute* tolls. A useful guide is the Michelin *Camping Caravaning France*.

By river and canal
France has a vast network of navigable rivers and canals, and boating holidays are a slow, serene alternative to driving. Brittany, Burgundy, Picardy, Alsace and Champagne can all be explored by boat. Contact the **French Government Tourist Office** or one of the following companies:
Hoseasons *Tel: 01502 500 555*
Crown Blue Line *Tel: 01603 630 513*
Abercrombie & Kent
Tel: 020 7730 9600

Don't miss

1 Beaune

If you like wine, you'll love Beaune, capital of burgundy the drink, not Burgundy the region. Wander round its narrow cobbled streets, seek out one of its great restaurants and don't forget to look up to admire its fabulous Flemish-Burgundian multicoloured roof tiles. **Pages 96–7**

2 Chartres

See Strasbourg cathedral for its spire, Reims for its rose window, Bourges for its chapels, Laon for its eccentric life-size bestiary in stone. However, if you are in the unfortunate position of having to choose just one French cathedral, make it Chartres, the 'French Parthenon', according to Rodin. **Page 202**

3 Côte Provençale

Some of the best coastline in France is rocky, like this relatively undeveloped strip of *calanques* ('inlets'), cliffs, pine-covered headlands and miniature port towns. **Pages 128 and 130**

4 Gorges du Tarn

If you're brave enough, take your car on steep, twisting roads and follow the limestone cliffs rising steeply from the River Tarn. Or get out of the car, and risk life and limb on spectacular cliff paths, or underground in fascinating cave systems. **Page 155**

5 Loire Valley châteaux

France is full of châteaux, the results of a thousand years of aristocratic building. The Loire region has played an essential part in the country's history, and all along the river's length stands a succession of Renaissance palaces – some grand, some grim, all evocative and a few straight out of a fairytale. **Pages 192–215**

6 The Louvre

The eighth wonder of the world, the Louvre is not only the most monumental art museum, but also the most rationally organised. Despite the crowds, many of its corridors remain blissfully serene. **Pages 30–1**

7 Mont-St-Michel

The Normans were the masters of western Europe in architecture as well as in arms in the 11th century. Wander through eight centuries of architecture in the abbey-church of Mont-St-Michel, then climb to the top to look across sea, sand and a landscape that still recalls their way of life.
Pages 244–5

8 Paris

The fascination of Paris is eternal, from Gothic Notre-Dame cathedral to 19th-century boulevards and designer window-shopping. The city is always a spectacle and a *fête* but particularly so now that it is booming after a glum spell in the 1990s. **Pages 20–49**

9 Versailles

Throughout history, the powerful have used culture for their own ends but few examples are more striking than Versailles, where the Sun King (Louis XIV) employed an army of architects, artists and artisans to build him the ultimate château and garden. **Pages 214–15**

10 War memorials in Flanders and Normandy

No single monument can do justice to either of the 20th century's world wars, but the bunkers of Verdun in Flanders, and Omaha Beach and the Caen Memorial in Normandy, offer moving and meaningful lessons.
Pages 81, 85 and 228

Paris

Everyone knows Paris, the City of Light, even those who have never been there. A place of romance, sex, art and protest, of haute couture *and* haute cuisine, *the French capital is one of the great cities of the world. Sometimes it seems that every building is beautiful, every street elegantly designed. Paris is so uniquely itself that it never disappoints the visitor, who discovers it to be exactly as he or she had imagined – only more so.*

PARIS

Paris

Getting around: In Paris, **RER** trains are faster than the Métro but less frequent. For most central journeys it is usually simpler to stick to the **Métro**, which is the biggest, most efficient system in the world, and also extremely good value. Note the number of your line and the name of the end station in the direction you wish to travel, and follow signs for that number and name. Tickets can be bought individually or more economically in a carnet of ten. The same tickets can be used on the **bus** network; longer journeys may require two tickets.

① The Left Bank

For some, St-Germain and the Latin Quarter are the most quintessentially 'Parisian' of all the areas of the city. Everything is here: cafés, bars, nightlife, bookshops, food, drink, galleries, little parks, grand boulevards, the Seine.
Pages 24–5

② Centre Beaubourg (Pompidou Centre)

Great monument or great monstrosity? Well, almost eight million people a year come to see for themselves, making it the world's most visited cultural site. Page 26

③ Eiffel Tower

Paris's unique city symbol dominates the skyline, and as corny as it sounds, no visit is complete without a journey to the top. Spend a little time in Paris and the tower on the skyline starts to become an old friend. Page 27

④ The Louvre

The largest palace in Europe contains the greatest art collection in the world. It is breathtaking, but attempting it all in a single visit is likely to leave you exhausted and footsore. Pages 30–1

⑤ Place des Vosges (the Marais)

At the other Parisian extreme from Pompidou brashness is this graceful 17th-century square framed by four rows of arcades. It is not a precious place, though – its central gardens attract local children who play there and its benches are a favourite spot for the old folk of the neighbourhood.
Page 32

Tourist information

French Tourist Office, 178 Piccadilly, London W1V 0AL. Tel: 0891 244123; fax: 020 7493 6594.

⑥ Musée d'Orsay

The second great art museum in the world's art capital. Many prefer it to the Louvre for its light, its space, its layout and, of course, its incomparable collection of Impressionist paintings. If only all cities could convert their old railway stations with such *élan*.
Pages 36–7

⑦ Musée Picasso (Picasso Museum)

A monument to a monumental artistic talent, set in a beautiful Parisian townhouse. His breadth of ability was astonishing, so what he chose to do with his gift is fascinating. Page 38

⑧ Musée Rodin (Rodin Museum)

The best work of one of the world's best sculptors – including *The Kiss* and *The Thinker* – displayed inside and outside the home in which he died. Many of the pieces are here because the artist paid his rent with them.
Page 39

⑨ Notre-Dame

One of the world's great cathedrals is built on the island in the Seine where Paris was born. It manages to encompass both sublime stained glass and gruesome gargoyles within its architectural variety. Even without Victor Hugo's 'Hunchback' adding to its fame, it would be an essential stop on any trip. Page 40

Tip

See many of Paris's finest buildings from the Seine on one of the river's bateaux-mouches, either by day, or on a night-time dinner cruise. The Pont Neuf is a convenient embarkation point.

23

Boulevard St-Germain

To many visitors – and many residents – the area of St-Germain and its neighbouring Latin Quarter simply are Paris. This is the Paris of Hemingway and Scott Fitzgerald, of Jean-Paul Sartre and Simone de Beauvoir, and of the oldest café in the world.

There are entertaining diversions all along the length of the boulevard St-Germain. For up-market shopping, turn off into rue du Bac, or head south down boulevard Raspail (Japanese designer **Kenzo** is at number 17). Turning west into rue de Grenelle, just beyond the **Fontaine des Quatres Saisons** (Four Seasons Fountain), is the **Musée Maillol** (*open: Wed–Mon 1100–2000; £; basement café*), devoted to the work of sculptor and painter Aristide Maillol (1861–1944).

> " *It is said that the world's first café opened in Istanbul … in 1550. Paris got its first one in 1686, when a Sicilian named Francesco Procopio dei Coltelli opened an establishment called Le Procope on the Left Bank, on what is now the rue de l'Ancienne Comédie.* "
>
> **Angela Mason, 'Café Society',**
> ***Los Angeles Times* magazine**

Further down the boulevard Raspail, and off to the left, is the bread shop of **Lionel Poilâne** (*8 rue du Cherche-Midi*). Poilâne's bread is considered to be the finest in France, and is made in 24 wood-fired ovens by 24 bakers.

Halfway along boulevard St-Germain are the legendary **Café de Flore** and **Aux Deux Magots**. Have a (wildly overpriced) coffee and watch the passing parade. Further on, to the left, is the 12th-century church of **St-Germain-des-Prés**, which gives the street and district its name. (In Roman times, this was an area of meadows, or *prés*.)

Just beyond the church, a left turn takes you into **rue de Buci**, where there is an excellent street market (*daily except Mon*). Beyond here, the street continues into the Latin Quarter; the boulevard St-Michel more or less marks the border.

Boulevard St-Michel

In the middle of the 19th century, Napoleon III ordered urban planner Georges Eugène Haussmann to redesign Paris on a huge scale, with long, wide boulevards and more parks. **Boulevard St-Michel** was one of the newly created streets.

St-Mich', as it's known, runs as straight as a Roman road, and covers many different aspects of Paris's history. **Rue de la Harpe** and **rue de la Huchette**, which branch off **place St-Michel** to the east, are among the oldest streets in Paris. In medieval times, rue de la Huchette was filled with barbecue pits. In 1795 Napoleon Bonaparte lived at number 10.

Number 12 **rue de l'Odéon** was the site from 1921 until 1940 of the most famous bookstore in Paris, **Shakespeare and Company**. It was run by American Sylvia Beach, and was a second home to writers such as Ezra Pound, Scott Fitzgerald and Ernest Hemingway. Beach was the first to publish James Joyce's controversial novel *Ulysses*, in 1922. Shakespeare and Company is now in rue de la Bûcherie in the Latin Quarter.

West of rue de l'Odéon, **place St-Sulpice** is a pleasant place for a break. Its huge church was begun in 1646 and took 134 years to complete. In a side chapel to the right are some murals by Delacroix.

Jardin du Luxembourg (Luxembourg Gardens)

Between boulevard St-Michel, rue d'Assas, rue de Vaugirard. Open: in summer daily 0730–2130; Nov–Mar daily 0815–1700.

These 24 hectares (60 acres) of formal gardens, stretching south of the **Palais du Luxembourg** (Luxembourg Palace), were set out in the early 17th century in Florentine style by Marie de' Medici. The park is a perennially popular spot with strolling couples, chess and boule enthusiasts, and anyone who just wants to get away from the noise of the city. Its avenues are lined with statues, and there are tennis courts, a puppet theatre, a children's playground, pony rides, and a pear orchard, the fruit of which can be bought during the **Expo-Automne** (*annually, last week Sept*).

Centre Beaubourg (Pompidou Centre)

*Centre national d'art et de culture Georges Pompidou, place G Pompidou.
Tel: 01 44 78 12 33; www.centrepompidou.fr. Metro: Rambuteau, Hôtel de
Ville. RER: Châtelet/Les Halles. Open: Wed–Mon 1100–2200; museum and
exhibitions 1100–2100. Closed 1 May. Centre free but admission charge
(£–££) to exhibitions.*

With its 'inside-out' architecture,
incorporating highly visible, coloured
service pipes, the *Centre Beaubourg*
(or Pompidou Centre, as it is more
popularly known in English) has
become a Paris landmark. There is
no other building in the world like it
– 'thank goodness', its critics would
say – and it is the most visited place
in Paris.

The idea for a multi-purpose modern
art centre was set in motion by
President Pompidou in 1969, but not completed until 1977,
three years after his death. The **building** was designed by
the English architect Richard Rogers and Italian Renzo Piano.
The theory is that having water, electricity and other pipes
outside the building frees up more space inside for exhibitions.

The Centre has recently undergone extensive renovation,
and the superb **Musée National d'Art Moderne** (National
Museum of Modern Art) has been re-housed in new galleries.
The Centre also contains the largest public library in Paris,
providing access to half a million books as well as videos,
films, magazines, photographs and CD-ROMs. The **Grande
Galerie** is used for temporary exhibitions. The transparent
escalator tubes provide great free views of the city.

Outside

There's always something going on in the piazza in front of
the building, from street theatre to impromptu bongo sessions.
To the side, the colourful **Fontaine de Stravinsky** is a
fantasy fountain inspired by the ballet *The Firebird*, designed
by Niki de Saint-Phalle and Jean Tinguely. To the north of
the centre, the futuristic sculpture *The Defender of Time*
comes crashing to life on the hour, every hour.

Eiffel Tower (La Tour Eiffel)

Parc du Champ de Mars, on Avenue Gustave Eiffel. Information: tel: 01 45 51 22 15. Métro: Trocadéro, unless the weather is really bad, in which case go to Bir-Hakeim or École Militaire. RER: Champ de Mars Tour Eiffel. Open: daily 0930–2300. ££.

The Eiffel Tower, built by over 300 workers to commemorate the centenary of the storming of the Bastille, was the tallest building (300m, or 984ft) in the world at the time of its construction. The designer, Gustave Eiffel (1832–1923), was the winner from among 700 entries in a controversial open competition.

Vital statistics

Work began in 1884, and the bulk of the two and a half million rivets were put in place from 1887 to 1889. The structure expands in extreme heat by up to 155mm (6in), but the top hardly sways at all – by no more than 120mm ($4^1/2$ in) on even the windiest of days. The tower weighs in at about 7 110 tonnes (7 000 tons), and is kept stable by a complex criss-cross network of girders. It is said that on that elusive 'clear day' you can see not quite for ever but for about 70km (45 miles).

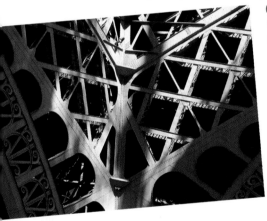

Going up

Visitors can go as high as the third level of the tower, almost at the very top, by taking the lifts, or climbing the steps. At the very top, there is space for up to 800 people. The queues for the lifts can be quite long, so go early or late in the day.

A lick of paint

It takes a team of 25 painters 18 months to give a new lick of paint to the Eiffel Tower – and the 'lick' requires about 50 tons of paint. Then they wait seven years and start again.

Île de la Cité

*The two islands in the Seine are the heart of Paris, where the very first settlers made their homes. The larger Île de la Cité is much visited by tourists, who come to see Notre-Dame (*see page 40*), the less well-known but unmissable Sainte-Chapelle (*see below*) and Point Zéro, the spot from which all distances from Paris are measured. The smaller Île St-Louis has a few quiet side streets alongside lively restaurants, great galleries and fashionable shops.*

The Conciergerie

1 quai de l'Horloge. Tel: 01 43 54 30 06. Métro: Cité, Châtelet. Open: daily, Apr–Sept 0930–1800; Oct–Mar 1000–1600. ££.

Located in the complex containing the law courts, and opposite the police headquarters of Maigret fame, this grim building was the city's main prison during the French Revolution.

The visitor's first view is of the enormous underground 14th-century **Salle des Gens d'Armes** ('Hall of the Men at Arms'), still used today for occasional concerts. The main curiosity for most people, though, is the fact that this is the site of the oldest prison in Paris. About 2 600 prisoners were held here and condemned to death at the guillotine, most notably Marie-Antoinette. Her cell and others have been restored to their original state, to give an impression of conditions at the time – worse for some than for the Queen. Those who died are all listed around the walls.

Sainte-Chapelle

4 boulevard du Palais. Tel: 01 53 73 78 51. Métro: Cité. Open: daily, Apr–Sept 0930–1830; Oct–Mar 1000–1700. ££.

Around the corner from the Conciergerie is the unique twin-chapelled **Sainte-Chapelle**. Try to get here as early as possible, as the chapel's genuinely glorious yet intimate nature is best appreciated when there are few other visitors.

The double-decker chapel was built by Louis IX in 1248 to house the religious relics he had collected, including most notably the alleged Crown of Thorns and a fragment of the True Cross.

The lower chapel was reserved for royal servants and other commoners, while the king and royal family said their prayers in the chapel above. When you step into the upper chapel you are entering one of the most revered buildings in western architecture, once referred to as the 'Gateway to Heaven'. It is only tiny – the size perhaps of a small parish church – yet it is lined with 15 stained-glass windows containing incredible colour and detail. There are over 1 000 separate religious scenes depicted in all. Some 720 pieces of the glass are original, making them the oldest surviving stained glass in Paris (the chapel pre-dates Notre-Dame by almost a hundred years).

" *And the stained glass! Narrow ribs of soaring stone separate band after band of illumination – what seems like more glass than all of Notre-Dame in a space one-tenth the size.* "

Tim O'Reilly, *'Illumined in Sainte-Chapelle'*

PARIS

The Louvre

The greatest art collection and museum in the world is housed in a sumptuous former royal palace – the biggest building in Paris – and won't you know it after walking around! One trip will not be enough to see everything here. The average visit lasts just over three hours.

Beating the queues

Arrive about 20 minutes before opening time, wait until later in the afternoon, or go to one of the mid-week evening openings. The main entrance is through the pyramid, but there is a less frequented entrance on rue de Rivoli, near rue de Rohan; alternatively, go into the underground Carrousel du Louvre shopping complex, and access the museum from there.

Highlights

Beneath the pyramid, the visitor is faced with three entrances to the different wings of the Louvre: Denon, Sully and Richelieu. The wings all link up inside the building. To see the highlights, most people opt for the Denon wing. On the first floor in room number 6 is the surprisingly tiny *Mona Lisa*; beyond room number 1, on the large staircase down to the ground floor, is the huge *Winged Victory of Samothrace*. From here, enter the Sully wing and follow the signs for the *Venus de Milo*, displayed at the end of a corridor of antiquities.

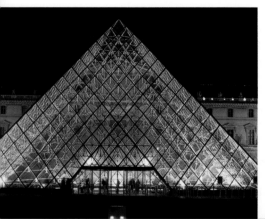

The pyramid

The idea of a sheet-glass and stainless-steel pyramid in front of the ancient Louvre seemed an affront to architectural traditions. However, the bold and simple design by Chinese-American architect Ieoh Ming

Pei, which was opened in 1989, is a triumph of the imagination. It is also functional, allowing light into the huge underground reception area.

Collections

Until you have seen the Louvre's collections, it is hard to appreciate their size and quality. There are over 200 rooms on three floors in its three wings, with a new wing opened for the Millennium. It has over 400,000 items, although only a fraction of these are displayed at any one time. Its collection of European painting from 1400 to 1900 includes work by Rubens, El Greco, Leonardo da Vinci, Turner, Van Dyck, Vermeer, and many other great names. Its collection of antiquities is breathtaking, and it is hard to know where to begin … or to end. The vast Egyptian collection ranges from the hugely impressive – an enormous sphinx, and complete crypts – to the tiny and intimate, such as children's toys or fishermen's nets.

Getting there: Rue de Rivoli. Tel: 01 40 20 53 17. Métro: Palais-Royal/Musée du Louvre. Open: Thu–Sun 0900–1800; Mon and Wed 0900–2145. £££ to 1500; ££ after 1500 and Sun.

Number **107 rue de Rivoli**, part of the Louvre, houses the **Musée des Arts Décoratifs** (Museum of Decorative Arts), the **Musée de la Publicité** (Poster and Advertising Museum) and the **Musée de la Mode et du Textile** (Costume and Fashion Museum).

Beyond the Louvre's eye-catching pyramid stands the **Arc de Triomphe du Carrousel**, completed in 1808 to celebrate Napoleon's 1805 military victories at Austerlitz and elsewhere. On top of the arch are replicas of the bronze horses from San Marco in Venice; Napoleon captured and used the originals, but they were returned in 1815 and replaced with copies.

66 *Even recent civic 'improvements' such as dropping a glass pyramid into the lap of the Louvre – Europe's most romanticised museum – appear intentionally designed to stimulate passionate argument.* 99

Thom Elkjer, *'Vive l'Argument'*

The Marais and the Bastille

Today the Marais is one of the most fashionable areas of Paris, but it wasn't always the collection of classical buildings and glitzy galleries that it is now. The French word marais *means 'marsh', and that's exactly what it was until the 13th century, when the Knights Templar, who had occupied the north of this district, began draining the swamps.*

Henry IV took a shine to the area at the start of the 17th century, ordering the creation of the oldest square in Paris, the beautiful and symmetrical **place des Vosges**, originally called the place Royale. Of its 36 harmonious buildings, none is more than three floors high and all are linked with galleried arcades. The elegant **Maison de Victor Hugo** (*6 place des Vosges; open: Tue–Sun 1000–1740; £*), where the writer lived from 1833 to 1848, has his desk, letters and other documents, and a lovely view of the square from the upstairs windows. **Madame de Sévigné** (1626–96) was born at number 1. Her published collection of over 1 500 letters was a literary triumph. **Cardinal Richelieu** lived at number 21 from 1615 to 1627; the writer **Molière** moved in later.

The main street of the Marais is **rue St-Antoine**, which has many first-class food shops. The other street you should not miss is the **rue des Francs-Bourgeois**. Its many fine old houses include the **Palais Soubise**, home of the Archives de France, which contains six billion documents, including letters by Joan of Arc and Voltaire, and Napoleon's will.

The **Jewish Quarter**, with its kosher butchers, delis, bakers and bookshops, centres on the **rue des Rosiers** (Street of the Rosebushes). It suffered terrible losses during the Second World War, was regenerated by the arrival of North African Jews after the war, but has suffered again more recently at the hands of France's right-wing Front National.

Getting there: Métro: Place de la Bastille, St-Paul.

Place de la Bastille

The Bastille Prison, which stood in the centre of the huge **place de la Bastille**, was torn down in the revolutionary storming of 14 July 1789. Today, a bronze column commemorates Parisians who died in the prison.

> " *Now, hip Paris has descended* en masse *into the Bastille, once a poor, working-class neighbourhood.* "
>
> **John Brunton, *The Daily Telegraph* (1998)**

The area around the *place* is now being regenerated. On its north side, the relatively new **Opéra-Bastille** is the largest opera house in the world. The building is hated by many for being too overblown, although it has no doubt played its part in the regeneration of this area.

North from place de la Bastille, the wide **boulevard Richard-Lenoir** is the site for one of the city's best and most irresistible produce markets (*Thu and Sun mornings*). There are cheese stalls, honey stalls, stalls specialising in shellfish, bread and wine, or in produce from different regions of France. Three markets also cluster together around **place d'Aligre**, just off the rue du Faubourg St-Antoine (*every morning except Mon*). A smart and expensive covered market sells fine wines and cheeses, game, and even truffles; outside there is a cheaper food market and a bric-à-brac market.

Montmartre

The touristification of Montmartre, with dozens of artists touting to paint visitors' portraits, shouldn't overshadow its cultural past. The ghosts of artists such as Picasso, Dalí and Utrillo still haunt its streets and houses. The name 'Montmartre' derives in part from the Mount of the Martyrs – three local martyrs were beheaded here in the 3rd century AD.

Sacré-Coeur

Rue Chevalier de la Barre. Tel: 01 42 51 17 02. Metro: Abbesses. Basilica: open: daily 0700–2330; dome and crypt daily 0900–1900; Oct–Mar daily 0900–1800. ££.

This white basilica, begun in 1876, is one of the handful of images that say 'Paris', but up close it looks rather like a jigsaw puzzle that hasn't quite been put together properly.

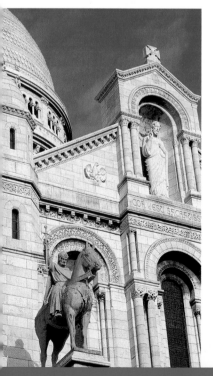

The church owes its origins to the disastrous Franco-Prussian War of 1870, when some 58,000 citizens lost their lives. A group of Catholics determined to create a church to the Sacred Heart on Paris's highest point, as a memorial. The French state stepped in to help in 1873, and building began three years later, to designs drawn up by Paul Abadie. When Abadie died, in 1884, only the foundations were in place. The hill was on the site of an old quarry and the time-consuming sinking of pylons had been necessary.

The church was completed in 1914 for a total cost of 40 million francs. For a spectacular view, make your way to the top of the church's dome, where you can look down on the interior of the church and, from an external gallery, look over the Paris skyline for several miles. The gallery is almost at the same height as the Eiffel Tower.

Several places around Sacré-Coeur are named after artists from the area; rue Maurice Utrillo is to the east and place Suzanne Valadon (Utrillo's daughter, also an artist) is at the foot of the funicular.

Sacré-Coeur is not the only church here. The **Église St-Pierre**, just across the street to the west, is thought by some to be the oldest church in Paris. It dates back to the early 12th century, making it a few years older even than the grand Notre-Dame.

Montmartre village

The Montmartre that visitors expect to see, the **place du Tertre**, below the Sacré-Coeur, is a square bustling with cafés and with people, especially artists with easels doing lightning sketches. Around the corner is the **Espace Montmartre Salvador Dalí**. This impressive basement gallery contains a large collection of the Spanish artist's sculptures, paintings, prints and engravings. To the west of the area, the densely packed **Cimetière de Montmartre** (Montmartre cemetery) displays a map near the entrance in case you wish to pay homage to Degas, Berlioz, Dumas, Offenbach, Nijinsky, Stendhal and film director François Truffaut, all of whom are buried here. Down the road, in contrast, are the world-famous **Moulin Rouge** cabaret, where the modern striptease was born, and the **Musée de l'Érotisme**, which houses a global collection of erotic arts and crafts.

Getting there: Métro: Anvers for the funicular, Blanche for the cemetery or Lamarck-Caulaincourt to start near the top. Funicular: from place Suzanne Valadon up to place du Parvis-du-Sacré-Coeur all day, every day, for one Métro ticket.

Fruit of the vine

Montmartre has one of only two vineyards that survive in Paris. The best time to be there is on one of the first two Saturdays in October, when a festival is held to celebrate the start of the new harvest.

Musée d'Orsay

The bright new Musée d'Orsay, with its compact but high-quality collection, particularly from the Impressionists, will disappoint no one. From the outside, it looks unusual, as you appear to be entering a glass-arched railway station – which, of course, it once was. Inside, however, the station building has been transformed into a breathtaking and innovative display area.

To avoid too much queuing at this incredibly popular museum, aim to arrive at least 15 minutes before opening time. Later, the queues can be enormous. Another advantage of early arrival is that you might have some of the galleries almost to yourself. When the coach parties start to arrive, scrums can form in front of the most popular works, particularly in the Impressionist galleries, which are located on the upper level. (Turn right as you enter the main doors to find the up escalators.)

Van Gogh

The museum has a good collection of works by Van Gogh (1853–90), some of which will be familiar – such as the

Portrait of Doctor Paul Gachet and the painting of the artist's own room in Arles – and some of which will not. There are some strong and mesmerising self-portraits, glimpses into the painter's tortured soul. Van Gogh began painting in 1880, and was dead by his own hand ten years later. From 1886 to 1888 he lived with his brother Theo in Paris, where he became familiar with the exciting new work of the Impressionists.

Impressionists

There are too many great artists represented in these galleries to do them all justice here, but highlights include paintings, pastels and sculptures by **Edgar Degas** – notably his statues and paintings of graceful dancers – and the unflinching *Absinthe Drinker*. Several works by **Renoir** include tender portraits of bathing nudes and the *Bal du Moulin de la Galette*, with its wonderful handling of light and shade. **Claude Monet** is also well represented, as is **Manet**: his controversial *Le Déjeuner sur l'Herbe* is a huge and arresting canvas. There are also other fine works by **Pissarro**, **Sisley** and **Cézanne**.

Post-Impressionists and Neo-Impressionists

A room devoted to **Gauguin** includes not only some of his pastels and paintings from the South Seas, but sculptures too and even his own design for the front of his house there. Another room is dedicated to the work of **Toulouse-Lautrec**, from portraits of prostitutes and dancers to a tender scene of two boys asleep in a huge bed. Other artists represented include **Rousseau**, **Bernard**, **Seurat** and **Matisse**.

> *There is but one Paris and however hard living may be here, and if it became worse and harder even – the French air clears up the brain and does good – a world of good.*

Vincent Van Gogh (1853–90) in a letter of 1886 to an English artist considering a move to Paris

Other works

The middle level of the museum is given over to paintings, sculptures and fine-art objects from the late 19th and early 20th centuries, including work by **Rodin** and **Burne-Jones**, while the ground level covers the period 1848–70, including photography and the decorative arts as well as paintings and sculptures.

Getting there: Quai d'Orsay. Tel: 01 40 49 48 14 or for recorded information on 01 45 49 11 11. Métro: Solférino. RER: Musée d'Orsay station. Open: Tue–Wed, Fri–Sat 0900–1800 (from 1000 in winter); Thu 0900–2145 (from 1000 in winter) and Sun 0900–1800; closed Mon. Restaurant, cafeteria, and large bookshop. £££.

Musée Picasso

5 rue de Thorigny. Tel: 01 42 71 25 21. Métro: Chemin Vert. Open: Thu–Mon 0915–1715; Wed 0915–2200. ££.

The **Musée Picasso** (Picasso Museum) is also sometimes called the Hôtel Salé after the mansion that houses it, which was built between 1656 and 1659 for a salt tax collector. It was an art school until 1969, when it was closed and refurbished to open as this splendid museum, dedicated to the work of long-time Paris resident Pablo Picasso (1881–1973).

Picasso, born in Málaga in Spain, lived at 7 rue des Grands Augustins in St-Germain from 1936 until 1955. When he died, his heirs gave parts of his huge private collection to the French state in lieu of death duties. The museum now has almost 4 000 pieces, including 200 paintings, sculptures, ceramics, over 3 000 drawings, collages, prints and sketchbooks, enhanced by photographs of Picasso – including many light-hearted personal ones – and video displays of the artist at work.

The work is arranged chronologically, and illustrates the artist's energy as well as his ability to diversify into many different fields. His Blue Period is well represented, and the basement area contains a large collection of his lesser known sculptures. There are large numbers of nudes and Cubist works, a tender portrait of his son Paul dressed as a harlequin, and his first-ever collage, *Still Life with Chair Caning* (1912). An excellent little gift shop sells fairly tasteful artistic souvenirs of work by Picasso and other artists.

Musée Rodin

77 rue de Varenne. Tel: 01 47 05 01 34. Métro: Varenne. Open: Tue–Sun 1000–1745; closes 1700 in winter. ££.

The prosperous area around Les Invalides has some splendid houses. The **Musée Rodin**, one of the most popular small museums in Paris, stands in the immediate vicinity of the Hôtel itself.

The collection is housed in the Hôtel de Biron, built in 1730 and bought in 1753 by the wealthy Maréchal-Duc de Biron, who lavished money on the gardens before meeting his end at the guillotine. By the time the sculptor Auguste Rodin (1840–1917) moved in in 1908, it had been converted to a collection of artists' studios. Rodin lived there for the rest of his life, alongside some illustrious neighbours such as Isadora Duncan and Henri Matisse. Although Rodin is now regarded as one of the greatest sculptors of all time, there were periods when he was unable to pay his rent and many of the statues on display were handed over in lieu of money.

Born in Paris in 1840, Rodin achieved notoriety in 1877, when his statue *The Age of Bronze* was exhibited at the Paris Salon. It outraged many people with its powerful physicality. Some of his greatest creations are on display in the house and in the attractive and tranquil gardens. Outside are *The Thinker* and *The Burghers of Calais*, while the best-known work inside the house must be his magical and sensuous representation of *The Kiss*.

Notre-Dame

Place du Parvis Notre-Dame. Tel: 01 42 34 56 10. Métro: Cité, St-Michel. Cathedral and towers open: daily 0900–1930, but closed Sat 1230–1400. Crypt open: daily Apr–Sept 1000–1730; Oct–Mar 1000–1630. Cathedral free; crypt ££.

La Cathédrale de Notre-Dame de Paris, the Cathedral of Our Lady of Paris, or just plain **Notre-Dame**, is a masterpiece of medieval architecture, which has stood solidly alongside the banks of the Seine for 600 years.

The foundation stone of the cathedral was laid in 1163, but the building was not completed until 1345. During the Revolution, its statues were decapitated, and it later fell into disrepair. Partly as a result of Victor Hugo's 1831 novel *The Hunchback of Notre-Dame*, an order was made in 1841 for the cathedral to be restored. The renovation was magnificent, and in recent years it has been thoroughly cleaned again.

To see the oldest (Gallo-Roman) remains in the foundations, visit the **Crypte Archéologique** and its museum. To get to the top of Notre-Dame, climb the 255 steps up the North Tower, and take a peek at the famous gargoyles. A further 125 exhausting steps takes you to the top of the South Tower, which contains the 13-ton Emmanuel Bell, and provides splendid views.

Inside is the largest organ in France, used for recitals on Sunday afternoons. Some of the stained glass is glorious, particularly the three famous rose windows, in the north, south and west walls, and the fine window in the north wall, which retains its original 13th-century glass.

Sorbonne University

47 rue des Écoles. Tel: 01 40 46 22 11. Courtyard and buildings open:
Mon–Fri 0900–1630. Admission free.

The **university** dates back to 1253, when Robert de Sorbon (a Parisian canon originally from the village of Sorbon in the Ardennes) founded a college of theology for 16 poor students. The Sorbonne established itself as the centre for theological study in France and became, and remains, the seat of the University of Paris. The first printing houses in France were established here in 1469, when Louis XI brought three printers from Mainz.

The church overlooking the main courtyard is the **Église de la Sorbonne**, built between 1635 and 1642. Cardinal Richelieu's white marble tomb is in the chancel; the red hat hanging above it is reputed to be his, and it is said that it will fall to the ground when his soul is released from Purgatory.

Not far from the Sorbonne's main entrance is the **Musée National du Moyen-Âge** (National Museum of the Middle Ages) (*6 place Paul-Painlevé; tel: 01 53 73 78 00; open: Wed–Mon 0915–1745; ££*), formerly known as the **Musée de Cluny**. Its extensive collection of medieval tapestries and stained glass is housed in one of the oldest private residences in Paris, first built in 1330.

The Sorbonne is at the centre of Paris's famous and revolutionary Rive Gauche, the **Left Bank**, where the 1968 student uprisings were based. Student life is predominant here, particularly in the bars, cafés and clothes shops around the lively **rue Mouffetard**. Stalls lining the Seine along the **quai de Montebello** and the **quai de la Tournelle** sell second-hand books and prints. These *bouquinistes* have been here for centuries.

St-Honoré

This is the glitzy Paris of the Hôtel Ritz, former palaces and designer shops whose names are a roll-call of haute couture. A shop-window stroll round place

de la Madeleine will show why this area also appeals to the gourmet, while the President of France lives round the corner, at the Palais de l'Élysée.

Place de la Madeleine

Métro: Madeleine.

The Église Ste-Marie Madeleine, known as **La Madeleine**, dominates this square in Paris's main financial district. It is a strange construction and had a lengthy and complex gestation period. Building began in 1764, but the church was only consecrated in 1842 – after it had been considered as a possibility for Paris's first railway station!

Gourmets will find foodie heaven at **Fauchon** (*26 place de la Madeleine; tel: 01 47 42 60 11*), where the window displays are a work of art. **Hédiard** grocery at number 21 (*tel: 01 43 12 88 88*) has been here since 1854 and rivals Fauchon in its worldwide exotic produce and its fine French wines.

Rue du Faubourg St-Honoré

Métro: Madeleine.

The eastern end of this fashionable road has become one of the most chic shopping streets in the world, from Gucci's four floors of marble and mirrors, all the way to Christian Lacroix, via Catherine Deneuve's hair stylist, Hermès' shop and private museum (containing Napoleon's stirrups), two Yves Saint-Laurent shops (one for clothes and one for beauty products) and the classic names of Christian Dior, Sonia Rykiel, Ungaro, Pierre Cardin *et al.*

Palais Royal

Métro: Palais Royal-Musée du Louvre.

The **Palais Royal** (Royal Palace) was first commissioned in 1632 by Cardinal Richelieu, the effective ruler of France at the time. In 1643, Louis XIII's widow, Anne of Austria, moved here from the Louvre, and the Cardinal's palace became the Royal Palace.

Louis-Philippe, Duke of Orléans, redeveloped the site to raise some much-needed money, and built shop arcades and offices around three sides of the palace gardens. Today, the buildings house the Ministry of Culture and a number of private residences. The gardens are open to visitors and contain modern sculptures.

Place de l'Opéra

Métro: Opéra.

The building that dominates the **place de l'Opéra**, the **Opéra-Garnier**, was first conceived as long ago as 1820, before its eventual architect had even been born. In 1860, Charles Garnier won the competition for the design of the new opera house. His first problem was how to cope with flooding from an underground spring; he transformed it into an artificial lake, from which the Paris fire brigade still draws water.

When the theatre finally opened, in 1875, it was the biggest in the world, with a stage large enough to hold 450 people. The elaborate design was the architect's reaction against classical architecture, and his grand foyer and staircase are a dazzling display of gilt, mirrors, mosaics and paintings.

Across from the Opéra-Garnier is another Paris institution: the **Café de la Paix** (*12 boulevard des Capucines; tel: 01 40 07 30 20; open: daily 1000–0130, food 1200–0100; £££*). Its interior was designed by Garnier, and it is officially classed as a historic landmark. General de Gaulle celebrated the liberation of Paris on 25 August 1944 with a takeaway from the café; other famous patrons have included Oscar Wilde, Salvador Dalí and Maria Callas.

Eating and drinking

*The Parisians have thousands of good places to eat, from the cheapest neighbourhood bistro to Michelin-picked restaurants. Inevitably, tourist hotspots suffer from poor-quality, over-priced cafés and restaurants – best avoided. On the other hand, in the **Latin Quarter** and **St-Germain**, the **Marais** and around the **place de la Bastille**, it's the norm to find good food and drink, by day or by night, and a great atmosphere. For authentic Parisian ambience, try the **Île St-Louis** in the evening.*

Cafés and bars

St-Germain and the Latin Quarter

Café de la Mairie
8 place St-Sulpice. Tel: 01 43 26 67 82. Open: Mon–Sat 0700–0200; food 1100–0200. £. Popular young hang-out and people-watching spot, handy for the Jardin du Luxembourg.

Le Mouffetard
116 rue Mouffetard. Tel: 01 43 31 42 50. Open: Tue–Sat 0715–2200, Sun 0715–2000; food all day; closed July. £. Busy café that reflects the Mouffetard market atmosphere, with cheap and hearty *plats du jour*, and croissants and bread baked on the premises.

The Eiffel Tower

Café le Dôme
41 avenue de la Bourdonnais. Tel: 01 45 51 45 41. Open: daily 0700–0200. ££. A good non-touristy café/bar/brasserie, with a view of the Eiffel Tower from one side, and a simple menu. Or you can just sit and sip a coffee.

Le Royal Tour
23 avenue de la Bourdonnais. Tel: 01 47 05 04 54. Open: daily 0600–2400. ££. Within short walking distance of the Eiffel Tower, this immaculate café also serves meals from noon onwards, with simpler snacks and pastries available too.

> " *The Closerie des Lilas, a bar-restaurant at the junction of boulevard St-Michel and boulevard Montparnasse … When I sat waiting at the bar my elbow touched a plaque marking the spot where Hemingway used to drink. I moved away in scorn to a corner table.* "
>
> **Peter Lennon, *Foreign Correspondent* (1994)**

> *Another American professor ... observed couples taking meals in different countries, and counted the number of times they touched each other in the space of a single hour: the result for London was none, for Jacksonville (Florida) eight, for San Juan (Puerto Rico) twenty, for Paris 110.* **"**

Theodore Zeldin, *The French* (1983)

Île de la Cité and Île St-Louis

Le Bar du Caveau

17 place Dauphine. Tel: 01 43 54 45 95. Open: Mon–Fri 0830–2000 and Sat 1000–1900 in May–July; food all day; closed two weeks in Aug and one week in Dec. ££. A great place to sit and have lunch or while away an evening. Offers a *plat du jour* and light snacks such as *charcuterie* and cheeses.

Berthillon

31 rue St-Louis-en-l'Île. Tel: 01 43 54 31 61. Open: Wed–Sun 1000–2000. £. For the best ice cream in Paris, over 70 flavours (including kiwi fruit, whisky, rhubarb and fig) in cones or tubs, to take away or eat on the little terrace.

Taverne Henri IV

13 place du Pont-Neuf. Tel: 01 43 54 27 90. Open: Mon–Fri 1200–2100, Sat 1200–1600; food all day; closed Aug. ££. Long-established wine bar near the western tip of the Île de la Cité, usually packed with local workers. Plenty of choice of wines by the glass, a regular *plat du jour*, *charcuterie* and regional cheeses.

The Marais and the Bastille

Café des Musées

49 rue de Turenne. Tel: 01 42 72 96 17. Open: Mon–Sat 0700–2300; Sun 0800–2000; food from noon. £. Well located for the place des Vosges, a smart corner café that also serves sandwiches, salads and simple meals.

St-Honoré

Harry's Bar

5 rue Daunou. Tel: 01 42 61 71 14. Open: daily 1045–0400; food 1200–1500. £££. The prices are elevated but so is the history; customers since it opened in 1911 have included Scott Fitzgerald and George Gershwin.

Ma Bourgogne

133 boulevard Haussmann. Tel: 01 45 63 50 61. Open: Mon–Fri 0700–2200; hot food 1200–1430 and 1900–2200. ££. Award-winning and relaxing wine bar with a wide and affordable selection. Also serves simple but good dishes such as steak, *coq au vin* or the house speciality, *oeufs en Meurette* (eggs and bacon cooked in red wine).

Restaurants

St-Germain and the Latin Quarter

L'Épi Dupin
11 rue Dupin. Tel: 01 42 22 64 56. Open: Mon–Fri 1200–1430 and 1930–2330; closed most of Aug. ££. Much sought after by discriminating Parisians and visitors; book three weeks ahead for Friday night. Bright and bustling smart-casual place that bakes its own bread, serves imaginative dishes and won't break the bank.

L'Huître et Demie
80 rue Mouffetard. Tel: 01 43 37 98 21. Open: daily 1200–1430 and 1900–2330. £–££. A good choice for seafood lovers, with lobster, langoustines and bouillabaisse. Spend a lot in the evenings, or stick to one of the fixed-price menus: lunchtime's is a great bargain.

The Eiffel Tower

Altitude 95
Eiffel Tower. Tel: 01 45 55 20 04. Open: daily 1130–1500 and 1830–2200. ££. Surprisingly good and not-too-expensive bistro on the first floor of the Eiffel Tower. Book a table near the windows well in advance.

Au Bon Accueil
14 rue Monttessuy. Tel: 01 47 05 46 11. Open: Mon–Fri 1200–1430 and Mon–Sat 1930–2215; closed Aug. ££. A short walk from the Eiffel Tower, this is one of the best bistros in the district. Exceptional food, market-fresh, is offered at affordable prices. Booking essential.

Île de la Cité and Île St-Louis

Restaurant Paul
15 place Dauphine. Tel: 01 43 54 21 48. Open: daily 1215–1430 and 1930–2230. ££. In a wonderful setting in a classical house, this bustling bistro serves inexpensive and good-standard bistro grub: lobster salad, rack of lamb, chicken in tarragon sauce. A dessert speciality is *baba au rhum flambé*.

The Marais and the Bastille

Les Sans-Culottes
27 rue de Lappe. Tel: 01 48 05 42 92. Open: Tue–Sun 1200–1445 and 1900–2400. ££. Relaxed bistro atmosphere, with an authentic old feel, equally popular with tourists and young Parisians for its fixed-price menu and à la carte options, such as duck in raspberry sauce and grilled salmon with garlic and basil sauce.

Montmartre

Le Moulin à Vins
6 rue Burq. Tel: 01 42 52 81 27. Open: Tue–Sat 1800–2400; also Wed–Thu 1200–1500; closed Aug. ££. Unpretentious little back-street place serving wholesome country cooking from the French regions. Lots of local people come here to eat, and to drink in the popular wine bar at the front. Book first and come with a healthy appetite.

Clubs and nightlife

St-Germain and the Latin Quarter

Caveau de la Huchette
5 rue de la Huchette. Tel: 01 43 26 65 05. Open: Mon–Fri 2130–0200; Sat–Sun 2130–0400. £. In the cellar of a building on one of the oldest streets in Paris, everything from swing to be-bop, with a few jazz-rock bands.

La Closerie des Lilas
171 boulevard Montparnasse. Tel: 01 43 54 21 68. Open: daily 2200–0100. ££. Classic jazz piano-bar venue just south of the Jardin du Luxembourg.

Restaurant origins

It is claimed that the first private restaurant in the world opened in rue Bailleul, between the Louvre and Les Halles, in 1765. An innkeeper named Boulanger began serving cooked meals in his tavern, in defiance of a previous government monopoly on the provision of food to travellers. His main dish was sheep's meat in a white sauce, described as a restorative: a restaurante.

The Marais and the Bastille

China Club
50 rue de Charenton. Tel: 01 43 43 82 02. Open: Mon–Thu 1900–0200; Fri–Sat 1900–0300; food 1930–0030. £££. Absolutely *the* place to see and be seen around the Bastille. Have a pre- or post-dinner drink in one of the several bars.

Shopping

Food, fashion and art are all on sale in vast quantities in this city. Take gifts and souvenirs home from the daily produce markets and specialist food shops – look out for beautifully packaged cheeses, chocolate, specialist jams, olive oils, vinegars, mustards, *foie gras*, teas, truffles ... **place du Tertre** in **Montmartre** is the place to buy art works whose paint is still drying, or a portrait of yourself. All of the main museums and art galleries have wonderful shops – for something a bit risqué, try the outlet at the **Musée de l'Érotisme**.

> Mrs Allonby: *They say, Lady Hunstanton, that when good Americans die, they go to Paris.*
> Lady Hunstanton: *Indeed? And when bad Americans die, where do they go?*
> Lord Illingworth: *Oh, they go to America.*

Oscar Wilde, *A Woman of No Importance*

Café culture

Cafés in Paris are like cafés should be, and as unlike the archetypal British 'caff' as you can imagine. To begin with, they also serve alcohol and usually food too, so whether you want an espresso, a beer, a glass of wine, a sandwich, a salad, a brandy or a cup of tea, you can get them all in the typical Paris café. One thing they have in common is that

your drinks are cheaper if you sit or stand at the bar, more expensive when the waiter serves you at a table.

But cafés are more than just somewhere to sit and have a drink; they are part of the culture of Paris and have always provided a retreat for writers, artists, intellectuals and political thinkers. Some have gone there to work, some to talk, some to think about sorting out the world's social problems, some even for a glass of wine and a snack.

Parisians frequent them from dawn till, well, almost round till dawn again, as many cafés open very long hours. With an estimated 12,000 of them in the city, you're sure to find one that suits you. Few will move you on or make you feel uncomfortable if you want to sit there a while with your paper, nursing a drink.

Writers and philosophers

'Simone de Beauvoir and I more or less set up house in the Flore', Sartre wrote of the Café de Flore on boulevard St-Germain. 'We worked from 9am till noon, when we went out to lunch. At 2pm we came back and talked with our friends till 4pm, when we got down to work again until 8pm'.

Another writer, the Irish journalist Peter Lennon, observed that, 'In Paris bars and cafés, the proximity of a celebrity gave no right of contact, one of the factors which helped [Samuel] Beckett preserve his privacy. When he gave up the Falstaff, eight years and about five hundred *steaks au poivre* later, I still hadn't exchanged a word with Sartre'. That the winner of the Nobel Prize for Literature, and two of the world's greatest writers and philosophers, could all sit in cafés unbothered by anyone, is a testimony to the importance that cafés play in the life of all Parisians, both famous and unknown.

The Northeast

Northern France's seemingly under-populated wide plains and its centres of industry are hardly the stuff of tourist brochures. Turn off the A26 or the A1, though, and you'll find both history and hedonism. The region has always been the gateway for invaders; the First World War battlefields and cemeteries are a harrowing testimony. Alsace-Lorraine is a difficult-to-define blend of Gallic and Teutonic culture, whose attractions are equal parts food, wine and folklore.

THE NORTHEAST

Getting there: Strasbourg and Mulhouse-Basel are international airports. **Air France** *(tel: 020 8742 6600)* flies to the former; **British Airways** *(tel: 0345 222 111)* and **Crossair** *(tel: 020 7434 7300) fly to the latter. Trains from Paris Est station serve the Northeast. Calais, about two hours by car from Reims, is the best Channel port for reaching the Northeast.*

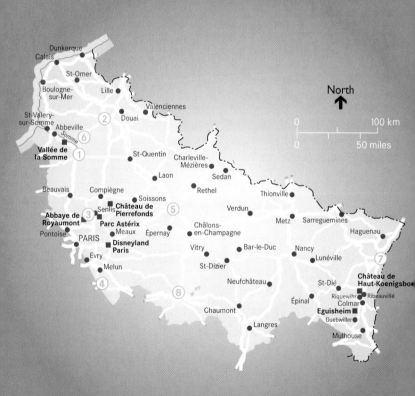

North

0 ——— 100 km
0 ——— 50 miles

Dunkerque
Calais
St-Omer
Boulogne-sur-Mer
Lille
Valenciennes
St-Valery-sur-Somme
Abbeville ② Douai
Somme ⑥
Vallée de la Somme ①
St-Quentin
Charleville-Mézières
Laon
Sedan
Beauvais
Compiègne
Rethel
Thionville
Soissons
Château de Pierrefonds ⑤
Abbaye de Royaumont ③
Senlis
Verdun
Metz
Sarreguemines
Parc Astérix
Pontoise
Châlons-en-Champagne
Haguenau
PARIS
Meaux
Épernay
Disneyland Paris
Nancy
⑦
Evry
Vitry
Bar-le-Duc
Lunéville
Melun
St-Dizier
Château de Haut-Koenigsbo
④
Neufchâteau
St-Dié
Riquewihr Ribeauvillé
⑧
Épinal
Colmar
Chaumont
Eguisheim
Guebwiller
Langres
Mulhouse

① Amiens

Come to the capital of Picardy, and lose yourself in France's largest cathedral, follow in the footsteps of Jules Verne, then take a punt on the town's delightful water gardens. **Page 55**

② Arras

Known for its magnificent tapestries – indeed, giving its name to a heavy embroidered curtain in Shakespeare's *Hamlet* – and for its Franco-Flemish architecture, Arras has two perfect arcaded squares and a bustling atmosphere. **Pages 56–7**

③ Chantilly

It has lent its name to a type of lace, and to fluffy whipped cream, but in Chantilly it's the horse that reigns supreme. The château's stables date from the 18th century, while the racecourse is from the 19th, and is the scene for one of the social events of the season – the Prix du Jockey-Club in June. **Pages 62–3**

④ Fontainebleau

Close enough to Paris to have been a favourite weekend hunting haunt of French kings, yet far enough away to have a wild, game-filled forest. Benvenuto Cellini was one of the Italian craftsmen who worked on transforming a hunting lodge into the opulent late Renaissance palace that visitors see today. **Pages 72–3**

⑤ Reims

Its great cathedral witnessed the crowning of the kings of France over more than a thousand years, but two world wars took their toll on the building. Restoration is ongoing, however, and the famous smiling angel on the west front has got her grin back – perhaps it's the champagne? **Pages 78–9**

⑥ The Somme

The veterans are almost all dead and the terrain around the former trenches has softened, but the memories remain. The Great War battlefields and cemeteries of the Somme are compelling examples of *tourisme du souvenir* ('remembrance tourism'). **Page 81**

⑦ Strasbourg

Taste Alsatian white wines, hear the region's German-based dialect being spoken, and see Germanic-style half-timbered houses along the River Ill – but remember that you're still in France. Climb the tower of the city's magnificent Gothic cathedral only if you don't suffer from vertigo – the view straight down to the square below is quite dizzying. **Pages 82–3**

⑧ Troyes

With its old quarter shaped like a champagne cork, vast expanses of medieval stained glass and a close association with courtly love, once-English Troyes is a town with a lived-in feel that does little to hide its great age. **Page 84**

Abbaye de Royaumont

Fondation Royaumont, Asnières-sur-Oise, Val-d'Oise. Tel: 01 30 35 59 00.
Open: daily. £.

Shortly before his death, Louis VIII ordered the construction
of a monastery here. His son, although only 14, finished the
project in 1228. The Cistercian abbey is well preserved and
its park is still crossed by the canals dug by the monks
centuries ago to power their mill and workshops. As with all
Cistercian abbeys, the layout follows the model of Clairvaux,
with a cloister in the centre giving access to all its parts. Only
a tower remains of the original Notre-Dame church to the
north. The east wing, heavily restored in the 19th century,
was once the dormitory. The early Gothic splendour of the
refectory, on the south side, is still evident.

Amiens

Tourist information: 6 bis, rue Dusevel. Tel: 03 22 71 60 50; fax: 03 22 71 60 51; www.amiens.com.

Amiens' massive **Notre-Dame cathedral**, begun in 1220, is the largest in France in terms of surface area. Its elegant nave is, at 42.5m (140ft), the highest in the country. Its west front, with three highly decorated doorways, is strongly reminiscent of Notre-Dame in Paris. The sculptures are particularly fine examples of Gothic work.

In other respects, the town is less inspiring, although it's bound to be of interest to readers of **Jules Verne**, its most famous native. The house (*2 rue Dubois*) where he lived for 18 years is now a museum with some curious features, including a small tower where he used to entertain guests and a model of the *Nautilus* from *Twenty Thousand Leagues Under the Sea*.

The **hortillonnages** of Amiens are a series of charming water gardens – fruit and vegetable gardens among the canals on a stretch of land that also attracts migratory birds. These ancient, man-made waterways criss-cross 245 hectares (605 acres) of flowers and vegetables and overgrown cottages. There are inexpensive one-hour guided tours on them in traditional punt-like vessels.

> " *In 1206, the citizens of Amiens, Picardy's proud and prosperous capital, already a commune for a hundred years, acquired a piece of John the Baptist's head. As a fitting shrine for the relic, they determined to build the largest church in France, 'higher than all the saints, higher than all the kings'.* "
> **Barbara Tuchman, *A Distant Mirror* (1978)**

Arras

Blending French and Flemish styles of architecture and urban planning, Arras is the capital of the historic Artois region. It was promoted to an episcopal see in the 6th century, and then became a wealthy centre for banking and trade in the Middle Ages, achieving fame for its magnificent tapestries.

Arras was all but destroyed in the 15th century as it was fought over by France and Burgundy. Eventually, the Treaty of Arras (1482) created the northern boundaries of modern France. The Spanish arrived soon after, however, in 1492, and remained until 1630, when Arras became a possession of the French king. The town suffered badly in major encounters during the two World Wars, but today its fortunes have been restored, and it is a transportation hub and industrial centre.

At the core of Arras, two arcaded and gabled squares – the **Grand' Place** and the **Petite Place** – are the finest ensembles of Flemish architecture in France. The 16th-century Gothic Hôtel de Ville is on the Petite Place, while the town-hall belfry (*viewing platform open: Mon–Sat 1000–1200 and 1500–1800, Sun 1000–1200 and 1500–1830*) towers over the Grand' Place, the place de Héros and the rue de la Taillerie. This style of square became common in the villages of the Northeast during the late Middle Ages. Its town hall would have had shops on the ground floor (including a butcher's), mayoral conference rooms on the first floor and a gibbet from which to suspend criminals. A magnificent belfry was a must-have and, if the budget allowed (as it did here), it was built, impiously, just a bit higher than the cathedral tower.

The former cloister of Arras's cathedral is now the **Musée des Beaux-Arts** (*22 rue Paul-Donnier; open: Apr–Sept Mon and Wed–Sat 1000–1200 and 1400–1800, Sun 1000–1200 and 1500–1800, Oct–Mar Mon and Wed–Fri 1000–1200 and 1500–1700*), which houses notable medieval statues, porcelain from Arras and Tournai and some fine Arras tapestries.

Tourist information: Hôtel de Ville, place des Héros. Tel: 03 21 51 26 95; fax: 03 21 71 07 34.

Parc Astérix

Plailly, 35km (22 miles) north of Paris. Tel: 03 36 68 30 10; www.parcasterix.com. Open: Apr–mid-July daily 1000–1800 (0930–1900 weekends May–mid-July, but closed some Mons and Fris in May and June – phone to check); mid-July–end Aug and weekends in Sept 0930–1900; Sept–Oct Wed, Sat and Sun 1000–1800. July and August are the busiest months, but the park closes its gates once 25,000 people are inside. £££.

Parc Astérix is an entertainment complex based on the adventures of French national cartoon hero *Astérix*. France's third most popular theme park, it attracts two million visitors a year – and some say it's more fun than Disney. The park has its own hotel, Hôtel des Trois Hiboux ('Three Owls Hotel'), and six children-friendly restaurants.

There are rides suitable for all age groups, including some miniature ones for toddlers. The maximum queuing time is about one hour; waiting times are displayed on all rides. The **Croisière d'Epidermais**, a boat that winds its way through scenes from Asterix cartoons, is the longest and gentlest ride in the park. The **Tonnerre de Zeus** ('Thunder of Zeus') wooden rollercoaster, on the other hand, will satisfy speed freaks of all ages. It is classed as one of the top two in the world. The park also has ten water rides, including **L'Oxygenarium**; riders are transported on over-sized tyres to the treetops via a large conveyor belt, and then descend a 400m (1 312ft) serpentine water toboggan.

The shows are easy to follow, even for non-French speakers. Acrobats flip-flop around in the Roman Arena, the **Mona Lisa Caper** is a whodunnit – the spectators help to search for the stolen masterpiece – and D'Artagnan and his Musketeers perform duels. You can also check out the dolphins at the **Théâtre de Poseidon**, or the **Druid Forest**, with its log slides, climbing walls and stone swings.

Beauvais

Tourist information: 1 rue Beauregard-Espace Piéton. Tel: 03 44 45 30 30; fax: 03 44 45 30 31.

Beauvais would be of no more interest to the world than the flat farmland that surrounds it were it not for its legendary **cathedral**. It is a glorious example of medieval one-upmanship triggered in 1225 by the megalomaniac Bishop of Beauvais, who felt that the best way to honour St Peter was by building a cathedral higher than the one in nearby Amiens. Its vaults quickly reached 48m (157ft) but collapsed twice in the 13th century.

In 1539, the people of Beauvais erected the highest tower in France but it, too, came tumbling down. The parts of the cathedral that didn't fall down are still awe-inspiring, particularly the Renaissance sculpture on the south portal and the stained-glass windows, which are the finest in northern France. An astronomical clock tower rings out the hours.

The **church of St-Étienne** has a Romanesque nave, and a Jesse window on the north side of the choir that is well worth a detour for its luminous colours and fine transparency.

Boulogne-sur-Mer

Tourist information: Forum Jean Woël, quai de la Poste. Tel: 03 21 31 68 38; fax: 03 21 33 81 09.

Boulogne has been an important cross-Channel port since the days when the Roman emperor Claudius embarked on the conquest of England. Today, the hordes travel in the opposite direction. Of all the Channel ports, Boulogne is the one with the most to offer besides cut-price shopping. It has first-class restaurants, a walled Old Town with a view, a quirky cathedral and a museum full of Napoleonic Egyptian booty.

The **Ville Basse** ('lower town') is foodie heaven and the reigning cheese shop is **Philippe Olivier** (*43–45 rue Thiers; closed Mon*), where you can take a long narrow olfactory tour of France's cheeses at various stages of ageing. The **Ville Haute** ('upper town') was built on top of the remains of a Roman fortress. The 13th-century ramparts are still mostly intact. The **Basilique Notre-Dame** (*closed for two hours at lunchtime except during July and Aug*) is a pompous pastiche put up by a 19th-century vicar who was also an amateur architect. The **crypt** (*open: Tue–Sat 1400–1700 and Sun 1430–1700*), by contrast, is from the Romanesque church that preceded it and displays tantalising bits of a Roman temple to Diana.

> *Study a packed cross-Channel ferry if you want to see a modern ship of fools.* 99
>
> **Julian Barnes, *Flaubert's Parrot***

The château (*rue de Bernet; tel: 03 21 10 02 20; open: Mon and Wed–Sat 0930–1230 and 1400–1700, Sun 1000–1230 and 1430–1730; ££*) of the counts of Boulogne makes a suitably imposing museum – the **Château-Musée** – with an impressive drawbridge. Built in 1227–31 by a son of Philippe Auguste and renovated by François I during the Renaissance, it was transformed into a barracks in 1767–91.

Châlons-en-Champagne

Tourist information: 3 quai des Arts. Tel: 03 26 65 17 89; fax: 03 26 21 72 92.

Châlons was once the capital of the entire Champagne region and remains an important administrative centre today, manufacturing products as diverse as electrodes and musical instruments. Although, like so many other cities in the Champagne province, Châlons suffered badly in both world wars, its greatest treasure, the 13th-century **Cathédrale de St-Étienne**, survived.

The cathedral is magnificently endowed with its original medieval and Renaissance stained glass, depicting all sorts of images, from scenes from Genesis to medieval tanning practices. The medieval glaziers achieved fame far and wide for their use of a range of extraordinary green hues. Among several medieval Gothic churches in Châlons, the **Notre-Dame-en-Vaux** is the most interesting. It has more of the greenish stained glass on show in the cathedral, a quirky Gothic ambulatory and fine sculpture in its Romanesque cloisters.

Chantilly

Tourist information: 23 avenue du Maréchal Joffre. Tel: 03 44 57 08 58; fax: 03 44 57 74 64.

Chantilly has long been identified with the good life, and is associated with the princes of Condé, whipped cream, lace and pure-bred horseflesh. The forest of Chantilly, its château, park and racecourse all attract numerous Parisian day-trippers.

Chantilly's **château** (*23 avenue du Maréchal Joffre; tel: 03 44 57 08 58; open: Mar–Oct daily except Tue 1000–1800, Nov–Feb Mon and Wed–Fri 1030–1245 and 1400–1700, Sat and Sun 1030–1700*) has a heavyweight art collection. The *Très Riches Heures du Duc de Berry,* usually referred to as 'the king of the illuminated manuscripts', can be found in the château's library. Commissioned by Jean, Duc de Berry, in 1413, it was painted by the Limbourg brothers, who left it unfinished at their (and the duke's) death in 1416. The Duc Charles I de Savoie commissioned Jean Colombe to complete the painting of the manuscript between 1485 and 1489. The fine-art collections of the château include works by Raphael, Van Dyck, Botticelli, Watteau, Ingres and others.

" *Chantilly resembles a long lane in Versailles. You must see it in summer, in splendid sunshine, walking noisily on the fine resounding pavement. All is ready and waiting for princely splendours and for the privileged hunting and horse-racing circle. Nothing is as strange as the vast portal that opens on to the château green and resembles an arc de triomphe or the monument next to it, which looks like a basilica but is just a stable.* "

Gérard de Nerval, *Les Filles du Feu* (1854)

The celebrated 18th-century **stables** (in a château annexe) were built to house 240 horses and 400 hounds. They now house the **Musée Vivant du Cheval** (horse museum) (*Grandes Ecuries du Prince de Condé; tel: 03 44 57 40 40; open: Apr–Oct Mon and Wed–Fri 1030–1730, Sat and Sun 1030–1800, May and June also open Tue 1030–1730, July and Aug also open Tue 1400–1730, Nov–Mar Mon–Fri 1400–1700, Sat and Sun 1030–1700; ££*), which puts on frequent equestrian shows. Chantilly remains one of France's premier horse-training centres and the 19th-century racecourse is still going strong. The annual races of the French Jockey Club are run in June.

Château de Haut-Koenigsbourg

St-Hippolyte. Tel: 03 88 92 11 46. Open: daily 0900–1200 and 1300–1800; shorter hours in winter; closed 5 Jan–5 Feb. ££.

The château is the highest castle in Alsace, at 757m. Destroyed in 1633, it was rebuilt at the turn of the 20th century with little regard for historical accuracy. The French often refer to the castle of Haut-Koenigsbourg as 'William's folly'; it was the German Kaiser Wilhelm II who financed the reconstruction of what had been Alsace's most impressive ruin. He did it to honour his ancestors and to demonstrate the 'Germanity' of Alsace. Ironically, the province would be French again only ten years after the building was finished.

The restorers smothered the massive original hulk – part medieval and part Renaissance – in neo-Gothic fantasy. However, they also added furniture and armour that is mostly authentic and the castle works wonders on the imagination. The panorama of the surrounding countryside alone is worth the trip.

Vive la gastronomie

The Northeast offers great gastronomic variety and abundance. It is the source of several of the world's best cheeses, including maroilles, brie de Meaux and brie de Melun, of steamed mussels (Lille), sausages (Troyes), quiche Lorraine (where else?) and madeleines, the French cakes that inspired Marcel Proust. Alsace provides pretzels, Flammekueche *(Alsatian pizza),* choucroute, Munster cheese and Kougelhopf *– one of Marie-Antoinette's favourite desserts. Last, but not least, the Northeast is the source of those bottles of celebration and sophistication – champagne.*

Château de Pierrefonds

Pierrefonds, Oise. Tel: 03 44 42 72 72. Open: May–Aug daily 1000–1800; Mar, Apr, Sept and Oct Mon–Sat 1000–1230 and 1400–1800, Sun 1000–1800; Jan, Feb, Nov and Dec Mon–Sat 1000–1230 and 1400–1700, Sun 1000–1730. ££.

The towers of Pierrefonds bristle above the treetops of the forest of Compiègne, recalling the times of medieval knights and chivalry. If they seem just too good to be true, it is because they are not. A château *was* built here in the 14th century by Louis d'Orléans, the brother of Charles VI, but it was knocked down in 1617 on the express orders of Louis XIII, who disliked the people living there (whom he called *mécontents*, or 'malcontents').

Like the French Romantics, Napoleon III had a passion for all things medieval. In 1857, he invested heavily in the château's reconstruction, hiring the architect **Viollet-le-Duc**, who had already restored the Ste-Chapelle and Notre-Dame in Paris. What the visitor sees today is Viollet-le-Duc's fantasy.

A few authentic elements remain, including the ducal latrines. The rectangular *enceinte* (ramparts) and its towers are true to the original floor plan, as are the private apartments. The great hall, chapel and barracks are pure 19th century. Interestingly, some of the details of Viollet's 'medieval' architecture – particularly the ironwork – anticipate the art-nouveau style that would emerge 50 years later. Much of the iron, copper and lead details were created by the Monduit workshop, which was also responsible for New York's Statue of Liberty.

> " 'Restoration': the word and phenomenon are modern. To restore a building is not maintenance, repair or remodelling, it is establishing a perfect state that could never have existed at any given moment. "

Viollet-le-Duc, *Dictionnaire raisonné de l'architecture française du XI au XVI siècle*

Colmar

Tourist information: 4 rue d'Unterlinden. Tel: 03 89 20 68 92.

The factories on the outskirts of Colmar will remind you that Alsace is not just full of quaint villages and vineyards but is, in fact, an industrial powerhouse. However, the town's medieval core soon returns you to the past.

Colmar's streets and alleyways are right out of the Middle Ages. Churches, cloisters, half-timbered houses, balconies, façades with ornate wood sculpture, paintings and carved gables are all part of the picture, many of them reflected in the waters of the Lauch river, which drifts through the city. The medieval **leathermakers' district** has been aggressively restored and dubbed *La Petite Venise* ('Little Venice'). Many of the ancient houses are illuminated at night so that the shadows play across their façades, creating an unofficial *son et lumière* effect.

The **Musée d'Unterlinden** (*1 rue d'Unterlinden; tel: 03 89 41 89 23; open: Apr–Oct daily 0900–1800, Nov–Mar except Tue 1000–1200 and 1400–1700; £*) occupies a 13th-century Dominican monastery. Its star attraction is the Isenheim altarpiece painted by Matthias Grünewald, which was unfolded only on special days, when the congregation could view the Annunciation, Resurrection, Virgin and Child or the saints Anthony, Augustine and Jerome. Now, museum visitors can study Grünewald's universe of demons, angels, saints and madonnas all year. Works by Picasso and Léger hang in the basement.

Compiègne

The forest around Compiègne has been a haunt of the French aristocracy for many centuries. Most of France's leaders have lived in its château, from the Capetian kings to Napoleon III. Today, the forest provides a network of walking trails within easy striking distance of Paris.

The forest was a war zone during the Hundred Years War, and Burgundians – allies of the English against the king of France – captured Joan of Arc here on 23 May 1430, and pawned her to the English. They in turn had her tried and … well, everyone knows the fate that awaited her in Rouen a year later.

The present château, or **Palais National** (*place du Général de Gaulle; tel: 03 44 38 47 00; interiors open daily except Tue, only by guided tour; open: Apr–Sept 0915–1815, Oct–Mar 0915–1630, last tour 45 minutes before closing time; ££*), was commissioned by Louis XV at the beginning of 1751, based on plans by the architect Ange-Jacques Gabriel, who would later design the Place de la Concorde and École Militaire in Paris. It was completed in 1788 under

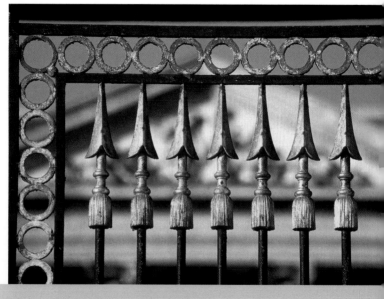

Louis XVI. Napoleon III spent much time here, often throwing huge parties. The **Museum of the Second Empire** is a unique evocation of his life and times, with displays of furniture, painting, sculptures and souvenirs of the imperial family.

The **Musée de la Voiture** (Motor Museum) traces the story of horse-drawn and motorised transport up to the First World War. There are displays on the history of the bicycle, a collection of ornate 18th- and 19th-century coaches, and an electric car (the *Jamais Contente*, or 'Never satisfied') that was the first vehicle to reach 100km/h (62mph).

The First World War ended on 11 November 1918, with the signing of an armistice at 0515 in a railway carriage 8km (5 miles) east of Compiègne. The Battle of France ended in June 1940 at the same spot when Hitler insisted that the French delegation surrender in a replica railway carriage. Today, there is a small museum here, the **Musée Wagon de l'Armistice** (*Clairière de l'Armistice, signposted to the RN31, 5km (3 miles) from Compiègne; tel: 03 44 85 14 18; open: daily, except Tue, 0900–1200 and 1330/1400–1730/ 1830; ££*), which has many more exhibits about First World War victory than about Second World War defeat. Pride of place is given to Maréchal Foch, the general of the 'Miracle of the Marne', France's greatest First World War victory.

Tourist information: place de l'Hôtel de Ville. Tel: 03 44 40 01 00; fax: 03 44 40 23 28; www.compiegne.com.

Disneyland Paris

*In the early 1990s, Disney transformed a 1 945-hectare (4 806-acre) site east of Paris into an approximate replica of its other amusement parks in California, Florida and Japan. When **Euro Disneyland** (its original name) opened in 1992, it had six hotels, a campsite, apartments, 29 restaurants and a golf course. There*

are now 40 restaurants inside, and a picnic area outside; no 'non-Disney' food is allowed inside.

Planning ahead

Disneyland Paris (its new name) is divided up into five areas – **Main Street USA, Adventureland, Discoveryland, Fantasyland** and **Frontierland** – and a little advance planning will definitely improve your visit. Check train times and current opening hours, and arrive there just as they open the doors, if at all possible. Queues build up quickly outside, and inside too, for each and every attraction; at least you get signs indicating how long you might expect to wait according to the length of the queue. Take careful note of these signs –

rides such as Small World can take a lot of people on each trip, so a long queue doesn't always mean a long wait. A big innovation at Disneyland is the possibility of reserving a place (*for information, tel: 01 60 30 60 30*) for certain attractions, including Indiana Jones, which has just been remodelled. Heart-stopping *frissons* are guaranteed thanks to a 360-degree loop and cars that go backwards.

Rides for big and small

If you have toddlers with you, head for Fantasyland first; the simpler rides such as **Small World** seem to appeal to them most. In fact, they appeal so much that you may need to pack an extra dose of patience. Older children will want the big-thrills rides, and these are divided up among Adventureland, Discoveryland and Frontierland.

If you get to Disneyland early, head for **Space Mountain**, by far the fastest ride in the park, and a thrilling experience as you hurtle through pitch darkness at speeds of up to 75km/h (45mph). Those who don't make the entry requirements – 1.4m (4ft 3in) tall or over ten years old – can watch from round the back. Other 'white-knuckle' rides include **Indiana Jones and the Temple of Doom** (*Temple du Péril* in French), for which you have to be 1.4m (4ft 3in) tall or at least eight years old, and **Big Thunder Mountain** (1.02m/3ft 1in tall, or at least three years old).

Other star rides include **Pirates of the Caribbean** and **Haunted Mansions**, both of which appeal to all age groups. Avoid Main Street USA until you're on the way out; this is where the souvenir shops are, and you don't want to waste time looking round those while other people are heading for the rides.

Getting there: 32km (20 miles) east of Paris. RER train: line A, to Marne-la-Vallée-Chessy. By car: A4 to exit 14, then follow signs to Disneyland.

Marne-la-Vallée. Tel: 0990 030303 in the UK; 01 60 30 60 30 in France; www.disneylandparis.com. Open: July–Sept daily 0900–2300; Oct–June Sun–Fri 1000–1800 and Sat 1000–2000; check first, as exact seasonal opening times may vary.

> " Three castles on a hill,
> three churches in a
> cemetery, three towns in a
> valley – this is Alsace. "

Alsatian proverb

Eguisheim

Tourist information: 22a Grand'Rue. Tel: 03 89 23 40 33.

Bones of Cro-Magnon man have been discovered on the outskirts of Eguisheim, one of the oldest settlements in Alsace. (The bones are now available for inspection at *Homo Egisheimiensis* in Colmar.) In Eguisheim itself, circular streets follow the line of medieval walls from the central point of the château. It is an almost perfect tableau of Renaissance fountains, bulging half-timbered houses and ornate oriel windows. Its artistic highlight is the 12th-century tympanum in the church.

The three ruined castles of **Weckmund**, **Wahlenbourg** and **Dagsbourg** overlook Eguisheim. There are others in the area and the local tourist board has created an itinerary for a circuit around seven of them. The real highlight is the *donjon* (keep) of Wahlenbourg, from which you can contemplate the surrounding hilltop vestiges of the Middle Ages and the fine panorama of the Alsatian plains and vineyards. Eguisheim is a major stop on the *Route des Vins* (wine route) and its *cave coopérative* (cellar) is the largest in Alsace.

Épernay

Tourist information: 7 avenue de Champagne. Tel: 03 26 53 33 00.

Épernay is at the very heart of the Champagne region. Surrounded by low hills with vines angled to catch the sun, its 28,000 citizens live almost entirely from the production of the world's favourite fizzy drink. Work up a thirst for the stuff at the **Musée du Vin de Champagne** (*13 avenue de Champagne; open: Mar–Nov Wed–Sun 1000–1200 and 1400–1800; ££*), where the viticultural story is told in bone-dry detail.

Visiting the **grand maisons de Champagne** is another matter. They all offer tours, with a *dégustation* (tasting) included in the price of admission. **Moët et Chandon** (*18 avenue de Champagne; tel: 03 26 51 20 00; open: daily mid-Mar–Nov 0930–1130, 1200 and 1400–1600; ££*) is the most famous *cave* of them all but others are more fun.

Mercier (*70 avenue de Champagne; tel: 03 26 51 22 22; open: Mon–Sat 0930–1130 and 1400–1630, Sun until 1750, closed Tue–Wed during winter; ££*) allows visitors to cruise the cellars by electric train, while at **Castellane** (*57 rue de Verdun; tel: 03 26 51 19 11; open: daily May–Oct 1000–1200 and 1400–1800, shorter hours in winter; ££*) you can climb to the top of the neo-classical tower that is one of Épernay's main landmarks.

> " *Tiny bubbles in the wine make me happy, make me feel fine.* "
>
> **Don Ho, Hawaiian singer (1970)**

Fontainebleau

*65km (40 miles) southeast of Paris. Tourist information: 31 place N-Bonaparte.
Tel: 01 64 22 25 68; fax: 01 64 22 43 31.*

The château

The Capetian kings had a hunting lodge here as early as the
12th century, but the present **Palace of Fontainebleau**
(*open: daily except Tue, May–Oct 0930–1700, Nov–Apr
0930–1230 and 1400–1700; ring for details of tours: 01 60
71 50 70; ££*) dates from the remodelling by François I,
which began in 1528. French architecture made a sudden
leap here, from the early Renaissance style of the châteaux
of the Loire Valley to Mannerism, a late Renaissance
style that anticipated the baroque. The Italian artists who
worked on transforming the vast medieval château included
Benvenuto Cellini and Francesco Primaticcio. Rosso obliged
with the Galerie de François I, completed in 1545 and
combining for the first time
painted frescos and stucco
relief sculpture.

Henri II (1547–59), Catherine
de Médicis (1529–89) and
Henri IV (1589–1610) expanded
the palace. The 18th-century
French-style gardens were
created under Louis XIV by
landscape architect André
Le Nôtre, who was also
responsible for the virtuoso
shrubwork at Versailles.
Fontainebleau is famous as
the venue for many important
signings: the Revocation of the
Edict of Nantes by Louis XIV
(1685), the concordat between
France and Rome (1814) and
Napoleon's act of abdication,
also in 1814.

Fontainebleau Forest

The 25,000-hectare (61,755-acre)
Forêt de Fontainebleau, popular
with Parisians since the 19th
century, is one of the most scenic
woods in France. It's enjoyed
by groups of birdwatchers or
mushroom-pickers, depending
on the season, as well as walkers,
cyclists, picnickers and horse-
riders. Unusual rock formations
draw rock-climbers here. There are miles of marked trails –
a map is available from the tourist office – and cycles are
available for hire too. Michelin map number 196 (*Environs
de Paris*) also shows the trails.

Langres

Tourist information: square Olivier Lahalle. Tel: 03 25 87 67 67; fax: 03 25 88 99 07.

Forgotten in its hilltop time warp, Langres still rejoices in strategic advantages that have served it well for 15 centuries. The Romans built one of the **gates** in the 2nd century AD, while other gates and towers in the 4-km (2.5-mile) **ramparts** date from the 15th to 16th centuries. The **Cathédral St-Mammès** is a tale of two styles – Burgundy Romanesque and Gothic. Enlightenment philosopher Denis Diderot was born here.

The **Musée de Langres**, on place du Centenaire, is devoted to local archaeology. Langres has a strong craft tradition, having been known for glazed terracotta and the production of dining knives since the late Middle Ages.

Laon

Tourist information: Hôtel Dieu, place du Parvis de la Cathédrale. Tel: 03 23 20 28 62; fax: 03 23 20 68 11; www.ville-laon.fr/. The upper and lower towns are linked by the Poma automatic monorail service.

Few towns in Champagne can rival Laon for first impressions. It offers a striking panorama of the surrounding region, particularly from the ramparts in the *ville haute* ('upper town'). Laon was actually the capital of France, or at least that part of it ruled by the Carolingian kings, from 840 to 987. Its **Cathédrale de Notre-Dame** ranks as one of the greatest achievements of the early Gothic style. The amazing west front was a model for Chartres, Reims and Notre-Dame in Paris. Although it has a rare and powerful sense of unity, it is also a truly eccentric work of art; some of its seven towers are adorned with life-sized sculptures of oxen and sheep.

" *It is as if Noah's Ark sailed by here as the floods were receding. Some of the animals just jumped off.* "

Marcel Proust on the cathedral of Laon

Lille

Tourist information: Palais Rihour. Tel: 03 20 21 94 21.

Lille is the largest city in northern France and the most important along the route from Paris to the Channel Tunnel. It is a major industrial city, the textile centre of France and a communications hub.

Vauban

Sébastien le Prestre (the Marquis de Vauban) was one of the highest-achieving figures of 17th-century France. He was a soldier, an engineer and an architect, who built 33 fortresses and an aqueduct from scratch, and refurbished hundreds of other citadels. He travelled all over France, particularly to the farthest reaches of the country's ever-expanding borders.

Lille also has some fine museums and a historic quarter (*Vieux Lille*) that blends French and Flemish traditions. The **place du Général de Gaulle**, more popularly known as the **Grand' Place**, honours the great general, who was a native of Lille; his birthplace (*Maison Natale de Charles de Gaulle, 9 rue Princess*) is open to visitors. On the *place*, indulge in window-shopping, or regale yourself in one of the many excellent fish restaurants.

Lille's **Musée des Beaux-Arts** (*place de la République; tel: 03 20 06 78 00; open: Mon 1400–1800, Wed–Thu, Sat–Sun 1000–1800, Fri until 1900; £*), established by decree of Napoleon Bonaparte in 1801, has one of the finest art collections in France. It started with 46 paintings from the Louvre, as well as a share of the art seized by revolutionary French armies, including a famous Rubens altarpiece.

On the edge of town lies the impressive **citadel** built for Louis XIV (1667–70) by the great military engineer Vauban. In the War of the Spanish Succession, Lille resisted for over three months. The fortress is still in use by the army but parts of the star-shaped complex are open to the public, including the ramparts.

Metz

Tourist information: place d'Armes. Tel: 03 87 55 53 76; fax: 03 87 36 59 43.

Metz is located at a highly strategic point where a limestone cliff overlooks the junction of the Moselle and Seille rivers in the otherwise flat Lorraine plateau. The Moselle divides into multiple arms as it flows through the city, where it passes beneath 22 bridges.

In 1871, French troops were besieged at strongly fortified Metz by the Prussian army. The 100,000 Frenchmen surrendered after 54 days, and the town was annexed by the new German empire. Later, it became the focal point of the Schlieffen Plan, a First World War strategy to invade France to the north of the town (via neutral Belgium). After the peace of Versailles, Metz became a lynchpin in the Maginot Line fortifications, built to prevent future offensives.

The glorious Gothic **cathedral of St-Étienne** was constructed by the joining of two 12th-century churches. Its nave is one of the tallest in France. The cathedral is nicknamed the *Lanterne du Bon Dieu* ('God's Lantern') because of its vast expanses of stained glass, mostly created between the 14th and 16th centuries. There is a modern window by Chagall in the north transept. Metz's **black Madonna** (there are many in France, although no one knows exactly why), Notre Dame de Bon Secours, is the fairest in the country. She wears lacy cuffs and a gown with a canopy of lilies over her black head.

The **Musée d'Art et d'Histoire** (*2 rue du Haut-Poirier; tel: 03 87 75 10 18; open: daily except Tue 1000–1200 and 1400–1800, until 1700 in winter; ££*) displays a major collection of Gallo-Roman archaeological exhibits. The chancel of **St-Pierre-aux-Nonnains** is one of the most important works of medieval sculpture in France.

Nancy

Tourist information:
14 place Stanislas.
Tel: 03 83 35 22 41;
fax: 03 83 37 63 07.

Once the capital of the dukes of Lorraine, Nancy is a mix of 18th-century neo-classical elegance and 19th-century art-nouveau fantasy. Although it has monuments from its Roman and medieval past, the atmosphere today is dominated by the memory of Stanislas Leczinski, the last of the dukes, who joined the old quarter and the 'new town' in the space of just three years, from 1752 to 1755.

Stanislas was the father-in-law of Louis XV and, briefly, the king of Poland. After his death, the province of Lorraine became French. He is honoured in the **place Stanislas** (formerly the place Royale), where five imposing palaces look down on his statue. The long history and traditions of Lorraine province are on display at the **Musée Historique Lorrain** (*Palais Ducal, 64 Grande-Rue; tel: 03 83 32 18 74; open: daily, except Tue, May–Sept 1000–1800, Oct–Apr 1000–1200 and 1400–1700; £*).

Famous for its crystal (baccarat), ceramics and metalworking, Nancy played a prominent role in the art-nouveau movement, creating the style known as 'School of Nancy'. *Objets d'art* from that era are on view at the **Musée de l'École de Nancy** (*36 rue Sergent-Blandan; tel: 03 83 40 14 86; open: daily except Tue, 1000–1200 and 1400–1800, until 1700 in winter; £*), particularly glass pieces by Emile Gallé and Antonin Daum. Art-nouveau façades and windows are found all over the city and in the architecture of the **passage Pommeraye**, a turn-of-the-(19th)-century shopping mall. The baccarat glass factory is outside the city but it is possible to visit the **Cristallerie Daum** workshop in the rue des Cristalleries.

Reims

Visitors normally come to Reims for two reasons: its champagne and its cathedral. The prestigious wine was first given its fizz by Dom Pérignon at Hautvillers Abbey in the 17th century; he found that double fermentation did the trick. Reims's huge Gothic cathedral has played a major part in the history of France, for many centuries the venue for the coronation of French kings.

Clovis, the first king of the Franks, was the first to be crowned at Reims. An illiterate warrior, he had himself and 3 000 companions baptised before his coronation and then became the only Christian king in Europe after the crown was set on his head in 498. The most memorable coronation took place almost a millennium later, in 1429, when Charles VII, attended by Joan of Arc, was crowned king of France during the Hundred Years War with England.

> " *The cathedral expresses the intimate bond between interior and exterior that western Christendom had been trying for a century ... a faith in which truth lay in the openness of a man's heart to God ... these find more perfect embodiment in Reims than anywhere else.* "

Jacques Le Goff, *Realms of Memory, The Construction of the French Past. Volume III: Symbols* (1998)

The exterior of the **Cathédrale de Notre-Dame** (*place du Cardinal Luçon; tel: 03 26 47 55 34; open: daily 0730–1930; free*) is famous for its soaring lines and the smiling angel (the *Sourire de Reims*) on its west front. The interior is even more impressive for its ineffable fusion of space and light, achieved by a subtle transition from nave to transept and spectacular stained-glass windows. It was in this cathedral that bar tracery was perfected – a pattern in which radiating

and intermediate bars connect to form pointed arches at the outer edge. You can see it in action in the façade's vast Gothic rose window. The modern stained-glass window by Chagall in the east chapel is a strikingly harmonious addition.

By the end of the First World War, following repeated artillery bombardment, Reims' magnificent cathedral was in ruins. Most of its old stained glass was lost. Much of the war damage has been repaired (with generous funding from the Rockefeller Foundation) but, although the famous angel is smiling again on the western front, many of the sculptures remain weatherworn; the restoration programme is ongoing. Incidentally, the rest of the city suffered terribly; in 1918, only 60 of its original 14,000 houses remained habitable.

Reims sits on top of hundreds of kilometres of tunnels filled with millions of bottles of champagne. Many of the big *maisons de champagne* (champagne houses) are located in town near the place Droits-de-l'Homme and place St-Nicaise. Three of the most famous can be toured without an appointment: **Mumm** (*34 rue de Champ de Mars; tel: 03 26 49 59 70, fax: 03 26 49 59 01; open: daily Mar–Oct 0900–1100 and 1400–1700, shorter hours in winter; ££*), **Taittinger** (*9 place St-Nicaise; tel: 03 26 85 84 33, fax: 03 26 85 84 05, www.taittinger.fr; open: Mon–Fri 0930–1200 and 1400–1630, Sat–Sun 0900–1100 and 1400–1700, weekdays only in winter; ££*) and **Piper Heidsieck** (*51 boulevard Henry Vasnier; tel: 03 26 84 43 44, fax: 03 26 84 43 49; open: daily Mar–Nov 0900–1145 and 1400–1715, shorter hours in winter; ££*).

Tourist information: 12 boulevard Général Leclerc. Tel: 03 26 77 45 00; fax: 03 26 77 45 19; e-mail: TourismReims@netvia.com; www.tourisme.fr/reims; www.ville-reims.com.

Ribeauvillé

Tourist information: 1 Grand'Rue. Tel: 03 89 73 62 22; fax: 03 89 73 36 61.

Located at the foot of the Vosges mountains and encircled by three ruined castles, Ribeauvillé (Rappoltstein, or Rappschwihr, in Alsatian) is surrounded by vineyards producing the famous Riesling and Traminer wines. Enter the town through its hoary medieval gate, the **Porte des Bouchers**, and wander down cobbled streets where few of the houses date from later than the 14th century. There are two Gothic churches – **St Gregory** and **St Augustine** – a storybook town hall, Renaissance fountains and the ruined 13th- to 15th-century **château of Haut-Ribeaupierre**. Ribeauvillé also has a saline spring known as the **Carolabad**.

Day of the Pipers

Traditionally, the lords of Rappoltstein were the protectors of wandering minstrels, and the minstrels had their own pilgrimage chapel near by. The Pfifferdi, or 'Day of the Pipers', is a colourful celebration of this tradition that takes place on the first three Sundays of September.

Riquewihr

Tourist information: 2 rue de 1ère Armée. Tel: 03 89 49 08 40; fax: 03 89 49 04 40.

Riquewihr, synonymous with fine Riesling wines, is a strong candidate for the title of 'most charming village in Alsace'. Inside a ring of medieval walls, it has a perfect assortment of half-timbered homes, most of them built for vintners. In summer, many are bedecked with flowers. Riquewihr's **Thieves' Tower** is complete with torture chamber and a wine shop – **Hugel et Fils** – that was founded in 1494. The steep and cobbled **Grand'Rue** is quaint but also unabashedly touristy. In summer, you can hop aboard a tourist choo-choo train but, for visitors who don't mind walking, the side streets are a better place to step back in time.

Vallée de la Somme

Tourist information: Comité Départemental du Tourisme de la Somme, 21 rue Ernest Cauvin, 80000 Amiens. Tel: 03 22 71 22 71; fax: 03 22 71 22 69. Maps and guided tours available from this office. Guided tours also available by reservation.

The first Battle of the Somme, in 1916, was the most notorious disaster in British military history, dreamed up by arguably the worst British general ever. The plan was to smash the German lines and put an end to the stalemate of trench warfare that had existed since the end of 1914.

The battle was preceded by an artillery barrage lasting seven days and seven nights. General Haig was so confident that he ordered his men to walk – not run – at the German trenches; furthermore, he insisted that they do it in parade formation, each carrying 60lb of equipment. The result was the heaviest loss of life ever suffered by the British Army in a single day, with almost 20,000 men killed and 40,000 wounded. Eventually, the Battle of the Somme would cost the lives of nearly a million men.

" *What passing-bells for these who die as cattle? Only the monstrous anger of the guns.* "

Wilfred Owen, *Anthem for Doomed Youth* (published posthumously, 1921)

The 60-km (37-mile) **Circuit du Souvenir** ('Remembrance Circuit') evokes the invasion of August 1914, the 'race to the sea', the Battle of the Somme and the great offensives of 1918. The route goes around the main battlefields, memorials, cemeteries and reconstructed villages in the Somme.

A new visitor centre will be built on the river in the near future close to the **Memorial for the Missing of the Somme** at **Thiepval**. Plans have also been drawn up for the creation of a permanent 'frontline' of blood-red poppies, 19km (12 miles) long and 100m (328ft) wide, following the trench lines of the Battle of the Somme.

Strasbourg

The cultural and economic capital of Alsace, Strasbourg stands on the Rhine at the gates of central Europe. The city is also the Seat of the Council of Europe and, more controversially, the headquarters of a European Parliament that still spends most of its productive time in Brussels. The region's people are proud of being French and suffered greatly under German occupation for 52 of the past 142 years, but they are also proud of their local heritage and language, Elsässisch, *a German dialect.*

Strasbourg has long formed a junction between some of the oldest highways on the continent, routes linking London to Milan, and central to eastern Europe. It was a free city within the Holy Roman Empire for much of its history, only becoming French at the end of the Thirty Years War in 1648. For all its impressive past and pan-European ambition, Strasbourg is delightfully compact and 'liveable', with a wealth of gracious architecture and formidable gastronomy. Treat yourself to *foie gras*, *choucroute*, onion tart and fine chocolates, accompanied by the wines of Alsace or the local *eaux de vie*.

As a monument of Gothic art, Strasbourg's **Cathédrale Notre-Dame** has few rivals; as a harmony of German and French influences, it has none. The cathedral spire was the highest in the world when it went up in 1439 and would remain so until the 19th century. Climb up the tower, and look down to see Strasbourg lying at your feet. It seems that artisans and craftsmen from every century have collaborated here to perfect the whole: there are glass windows from the 13th, 14th and 15th centuries, a cycle of 14th-century tapestries depicting the life of the Virgin, a 16th-century astronomical clock and an 18th-century organ.

> " *The Rhine is as swift as the Rhône, wide as the Loire, deeply embanked like the Meuse, winding as the Seine, limpid and green as the Somme, historic as the Tiber, royal as the Danube, mysterious as the Nile, spangled with gold like a river of America, covered with fables and phantoms like a river of Asia.* "
>
> **Victor Hugo, *Le Rhin* (*The Rhine*) (1838)**

83

The **Château des Rohan**, south of the cathedral, has a trio of noteworthy museums: the **Musée des Arts Décoratifs** (Decorative Arts Museum), the **Musée des Beaux-Arts** (Fine Arts Museum) and the **Musée Archéologique** (Archaeological Museum) (*2 place du Château; tel: 03 88 52 50 00; all open: daily except Tue, 1000–1200 and 1330–1800, Sun until 1700; ££*). The quaint **Musée Alsacien** (*23 quai St-Nicholas; tel: 03 88 35 55 36; open: daily except Tue, 1000–1200 and 1330–1800, Sun until 1700; ££*) gives an intimate look at the region's crafts and folklore.

One of the best ways to see the watery quarter of **La Petite France** ('Little France') is by boat. Take a commented *bateau-mouche* trip through this beautifully restored district, where medieval fishermen, tanners and millers plied their trades. Locks allowed boats from the Rhine to come right into the city around here, facilitating trade. Strasbourg is also a cycling city and the tourist office will be more than happy to help you hire a bike.

Tourist information: 17 place de la Cathédrale. Tel: 03 88 52 28 28. Information also available in the train station. The Strasbourg Pass *includes admission to one museum (and a second for half price), the cathedral platform and astronomical clock, a daytime boat tour and use of a bicycle for one day.*

Troyes

Tourist information: 16 boulevard Carnot. Tel: 03 25 82 62 70; fax: 03 25 73 06 81; e-mail: troyes@club-internet.fr.

The ancient capital of Champagne, Troyes likes to call itself the *bouchon de champagne* ('champagne cork'), referring to the shape of its old city. Narrow alleys such as the **rue Champeaux** are full of bulging, half-timbered mansions from the 14th century and the town's skyline is still interrupted by ancient belfries and medieval steeples.

Troyes has no less than three watery medieval districts. The **Quartier de la Cité** is wedged between the Seine and a canal. On the island stands the huge **cathedral of St Peter and St Paul**. It has more medieval stained glass, in terms of surface area, than any church in France. The two other ancient districts – the **Quartier St-Jean** and the **Quartier de Vauluisant** – contain 13 Gothic churches, including the **St-Jean au Marche** where, in 1420, Henry V married Catherine of France. As a result, Troyes was English for nine years, until Joan of Arc took it back for the French.

Troyes has strong links to Arthurian romance and the cult of **knighthood and courtly love**. Local 12th-century poet Chrétien de Troyes was the first to publish a narrative on the knights Lancelot and Percival. In 1128, the Synod of Troyes officially recognised the order of the Knights Templar, the keepers of the Holy Grail. It is said that the order still has its headquarters in a forest near by.

Among the numerous museums, the **Musée d'Art Moderne** (*Palais Episcopal, place St-Pierre; tel: 03 25 76 26 80; open: daily except Tue, 1100–1800; ££*), housed in a Renaissance mansion, stands out for its canvases by Matisse, Modigliani, Picasso and Cezanne.

Tip

Troyes' andouillettes *(sausages) are famous all over France. Local butchers' shops proudly display the original recipe on their walls.*

Verdun

Tourist information: place de la Nation. Tel: 03 29 86 14 18; fax: 03 29 84 22 42.

The First World War battle of Verdun was the most terrible in European history. It began in 1916 with a German barrage of almost two million shells, lasted almost two years and killed three-quarters of a million men. Today, Verdun is still a potent symbol in the Franco-German relationship that dominates the European Union. French President François Mitterrand and Chancellor Helmut Kohl of Germany made the most of it when they walked hand in hand among the graves in 1984.

The town of Verdun is contained in an oxbow bend of the River Meuse, and encircled by the Ardennes mountains. It does not look all that battle-scarred today but the Rodin memorial (at the corner of St-Paul and avenue Garibaldi) – a horrifying version of *Winged Victory* – will remind you of what you came to see.

Outside Verdun, there are three places that sum up what happened. The village at the **Musée-Memorial de Fleury** (*open: daily mid-Mar–Sept 0900–1800, Sept–mid-Mar 0900–1200 and 1400–1700, closed 19 Dec–22 Jan; free*) has been returned to the way it was at the end of the battle. The **Fort de Vaux** (*for information, tel: 03 29 86 14 18; open: daily 0900–1830; £*) is a complex of underground bunkers, and the **Ossuaire de Douaumont** (*Douaumont; tel: 03 29 84 54 81, fax: 03 29 86 56 54; open: daily Apr–Sept 0900–1730, Mar, Oct and Nov 0900–1200 and 1400–1700; free (charge for audio-visual)*) is a vault containing the bones of several hundred thousand corpses, French and German, that have never been identified.

Eating and drinking

Le Doyen
11 rue Doyen, off place Dalton, Boulogne. Tel: 03 21 30 13 08. £. Best value for money among Boulogne's fish restaurants.

Bar Jazz
55 rue Basse, Lille. ££. One of several trendy bars along the rue Basse in Lille's old quarter. Cool jazz entertains *branché* Lillois.

La Huitrière
3 rue des Chats-Boussus, Lille. Tel: 03 20 55 43 41. ££. A candidate for France's most beautiful fish shop, with lots of art-deco blue and gold tiles and a dining room at the back where you can eat all sorts of marine delicacies including oysters and fresh braised sardines.

Château d'Adomenil
Rehainviller, Lunéville, near Nancy. Tel: 03 83 74 04 81; fax: 03 83 74 21 78; e-mail: adomenil@relaischateaux.fr. £££. The duke of Lorraine's 'petit Versailles' in all its 18th-century glory, complete with moat, swans and a vast, romantic park.

L'Excelsior
50 rue Henri-Poincaré, Nancy. Tel: 03 83 35 24 57. ££. Art-nouveau brasserie.

Au Petit Comptoir
17 rue de Mars, Reims. Tel: 03 26 40 58 58. ££. An annexe to the famous restaurant of star chef Gérard Boyer that serves imaginative dishes at down-to-earth prices. All of it goes well with champagne.

La Vigneraie
14 rue de Thillois, Reims. Tel: 03 26 88 67 27. ££. Superb for regional specialities at fair prices.

Christian
18 rue Mercière. £. The best place in Strasbourg – perhaps in all Alsace – to eat the Alsatian cake, *kougelhopf*. Another speciality is the *tarte aux pommes amandes* (with apples, cinnamon and almonds), or try its luscious sorbet.

D'Choucrouterie
20 rue St-Louis, Strasbourg. Tel: 03 88 26 52 87. £. Popular for *choucroute* in the front room and cabaret acts in the back room.

Auberge la Touraine Champenoise
51150 Tours-sur-Marne. Tel: 03 26 58 91 93; fax: 03 26 58 95 47. ££. One of the top addresses for food in the Champagne region, beginning with the 'mosaic' of *foie gras*. There are nine rooms where you can sleep over.

Cheese

Nothing sums up the originality and diversity of French culture more succinctly or delectably than cheese. Most of the French cheese now sold in supermarkets is mass-produced, so go to the source whenever possible: Meaux and Melun for earthy brie; Chavignol in the Loire Valley for its famous crottin of goat cheese; blue-veined fourme d'Ambert in the province of Auvergne; and pungent Munster cheese in Alsace. If time is short, just go to a serious cheese shop.

> " *How can anyone govern a nation that has 246 different kinds of cheese?* "
>
> **Charles de Gaulle, in an interview for** *Newsweek* **(New York, 1 Oct 1962)**

Shopping

Espace Belgrand
rue Belgrand and corner of boulevard du 14 Juillet, Troyes. The garment business is a major industry in Troyes. This is a factory outlet where you can buy designer clothes at a discount.

Still or sparkling?
La Route du Champagne

The region where champagne is produced is not quite the party capital of France that you might expect. First, there is the climate. It is the furthest north of any French wine region and its average annual temperature is only 10°C (50°F). Second, it is haunted by memories of war and invasions. Its best-known town, Reims, for example, was completely destroyed in the First World War. Last but not least, the people of Champagne (the Champenois*) have a work ethic that is not automatically associated with living it up. However, they are uncommonly hospitable, despite having to work long hours in the vineyards and the 250km (155 miles) of underground cellars to create the world's most elegant drink. They don't get to enjoy much of it – 80 per cent of all champagne is exported.*

The *Route du Champagne* (Champagne Trail) is marked by bright blue-and-yellow signs with bubbles on them. It

inevitably takes you through the towns of Reims and Épernay, via the big champagne houses, but for many travellers the real highlight will be a stop in one of the small villages (Rilly, Ludes, Mailly, Verzenay, Verzy, Bouzy …). They are all home to independent winemakers who make their own champagnes, and most of them

Tip

Alsace is the only region in France where the wines are named by grape – Riesling, Gewürztraminer, Pinot Blanc – rather than according to location.

will happily offer a *dégustation*, either in the family cellar or, sometimes, in their own living room.

The village of Hautvillers is where it all started. People have been cultivating vines and making wine in the Champagne region for 2 000 years but it wasn't until the 17th century that a monk and cellarmaster named Dom Pérignon (1638–1715) developed the *méthode Champenoise*. Using the monk's method, black grapes are vinified as if they were white (without skins) and fermented a second time in the bottle to give the wine a sparkle.

La Route du Vin

The Route du Vin (Wine Trail) strings together almost one hundred villages in Alsace, covering nearly 100km (62 miles) between the River Rhine and the heavily wooded slopes of the Vosges, where many castles – some of them ruined and overgrown – overlook the vineyards. Picturesque villages such as Riquewihr, Ribeauvillé and Turckheim are worth a visit for their half-timbered houses, Renaissance town halls, carved stone fountains and historic gateways.

The atmospheric villages of the Alsace are justly famous for the quality of their white wines, too – the top vineyards receive the appellation *Grand Cru*. The region is blessed with exceptional soils and wine-friendly microclimates; Colmar, for example, is one of the driest and sunniest towns in France – which is quite a surprise! The vines ripen quite late, which gives Alsatian wines their intense aroma. In striking contrast to the German wines just across the Rhine, they tend to be dry and contain slightly more alcohol. Using winespeak, you could say they have a floral nose, much fruit and spice, and a rich finish.

Burgundy and the Rhône Valley

Most people know nothing of Burgundy other than its rich, red wines. In fact, this green, prosperous region is one of the most thoroughly civilised places in the world. The Dukes of Burgundy, whose empire was vast, established a norm of excellence and a love of fine things, from architecture to food. That sophistication remains today, in Lyon, the gastronomic capital of France, as in the rural towns and villages, where a perfect Beaujolais often graces the most ordinary of tables.

BURGUNDY AND THE RHÔNE VALLEY

Burgundy and the Rhône Valley

Getting there: *The region's major airports are Lyon-Satolas and Dijon-Bourgogne. Geneva and Paris are useful alternatives, with rail connections to Lyon and Dijon, or Valence. The road route from the Channel ferries is the A26 direct from Calais to Troyes.*

Sens

Montargis

①

⑥

Abbaye de
Fontenay

Semur-
en-Auxois

③

②

Vesoul

Ronchamp

Belfort

Besançon

Dole

Pontarlier

Nevers

Autun

Chalon-sur-
Saône

Lons

Tournus

Moulins

Cluny

Mâcon

Bourg-en-Bresse

Lac Léman

Roanne

⑤

④

⑦

Aix-les-
Bains

Annecy

Chamonix

Albertville

Chambéry

St Jean

St-Étienne

Grenoble

Briançon

Privas

Valence

North
↑

0   100 km
0   50 miles

① Auxerre

Wander round the atmospheric old quarter of a thoroughly Burgundian town, stroll alongside the river, then go to see France's oldest church frescos. **Page 97**

② Beaune

One of the highlights of the area, the choice of the Dukes of Burgundy and now the centre of the Burgundy wine region, with exquisite tiled roofs, and ample opportunity to taste red wine of all ages and vintages. **Pages 96–7**

③ Dijon

Enjoy classic Burgundian meals in this gastronomic capital – bring a hearty appetite for *coq au vin*, *boeuf bourguignonne* and *pauchouse* – then walk it off up and down the staircases of the vast Palace of the Dukes. **Pages 102–3**

④ Lyon

Don't drive on by on the Autoroute du Soleil. France's second largest city is worth a few days of anyone's time. Linger in a *bouchon* or a *mère* (tiny traditional restaurants), explore its curious *traboule* corridors and climb the hill (or take the funicular) for panoramic views. **Pages 106–7**

⑤ Pérouges

Imagine yourself on the film set of *The Three Musketeers* in this perfectly preserved flint village, prosperous in the Middle Ages and revived in the early 20th century. **Page 108**

⑥ Vézelay

The relics in Vézelay's marvellous Romanesque basilica have been proved not to be the bones of Mary Magdalene, but they still attract thousands of pilgrims every year. If you don't come for the bones, come for the restored hilltop village, with its chic restaurants and appealing little shops. **Page 112**

⑦ Vienne

Walk in the footsteps of the Romans, and see Vienne's impressive and remarkable Gallo-Roman remains, then splash out at the town's temple to gastronomy – where *nouvelle cuisine* had its roots. **Page 113**

Abbaye de Fontenay

5km (3 miles) from Montbard, and 3km (2 miles) from Marmagne on D32.
Tel: 03 80 92 15 00; fax: 03 80 92 16 88; www.abbayedefontenay.com/. Open:
daily for 45-min guided visits every hour (except 1300) from 0900–1700. ££.

The approach to this famous Cistercian abbey, along a lane through the village of Marmagne and alongside the quiet green and wooded valley of a little stream, is itself a joy. The abbey, elegant and pale, is arranged around neat gardens and fountains. It was founded in 1118 by the Bishop of Norwich, who came here as abbot. Much damaged during the French Revolution and then turned into a paper factory, the building was purchased in 1906 by a member of the family of the factory owners. He stopped production and extensively restored the abbey, carefully removing all traces of the factory.

Aix-les-Bains

Tourist information: place Jean Mollard. Tel: 04 79 35 05 92.

Aix-les Bains owes its fame to its huge spa complex, which caters for more water-cure enthusiasts annually than any other spa in France. The Romans discovered the site and the remains of their baths can still be seen beneath today's complex, the 19th-century **Thermes Nationaux**. As all spa visitors know, it is the overall ambience that contributes to the cure, and Aix lacks nothing in soul-inspiring beauty, a fact that has attracted poets and painters to rhapsodise over the blue waters of the mountain lake on which the town sits, and the distinctive shape of the Cat's Tooth mountain on the opposite shore. You can see pictures and sculpture by some of the Impressionist artists who came here at the **Musée Faure** (*Ville des Chimères, 10 boulevard des Côtes; tel: 04 79 61 06 57; open: Wed–Mon; £*) where the exhibits include works by Rodin and Degas. Taking to the lake, you can hop on a boat and enjoy an excursion to the lovely Benedictine **Abbaye d'Hautecombe**, with its exhibitions on monastic life, its 12th-century barn, and the graves of 40 members of the royal House of Savoy, including that of Umberto II, the last king of Italy.

Autun

Tourist information: 2 avenue Charles de Gaulle. Tel: 03 85 86 80 38; fax: 03 85 86 80 49; e-mail: office.du.tourisme.autun@wanadoo.fr; www.autun.com/. Open: weekends in May; daily June–Sept 0900–1900; Oct–Apr Mon–Sat 0900–1200 and 1400–1800.

Autun has a long and illustrious history. Before Roman colonisation in 15 BC it was the principal settlement of the powerful *Aedui* tribe of Gauls. The town of *Augustodunum* – 'Rome's sister', as Caesar called it – was built partly to subdue the Gauls and partly to honour them and bring them into Roman life. It was to become a great centre of education, art, entertainment and commerce.

Today, this thriving country town centres on its huge main square, the Champs de Mars. The highlight of Autun is its superb Romanesque **Cathédrale St-Lazare** (*5 place du Terreau; open: daily; £*), constructed to welcome the thousands of pilgrims who flocked here to see the supposed tomb of Mary Magdalene's brother, Lazarus.

Just north of the main square there's a small medieval district, Quartier Marchaux, enclosed by 15th-century fortifications. Walk the **ramparts** for part of the way. Beside the ramparts lie the scant remains of what was once Gaul's largest **Roman theatre** – with more than 12,000 seats, and standing room for thousands more! Two of the four Roman city gates survive: Porte St-André and the smaller Porte d'Arroux. In Roman times, the main road ran through this gate to the *Via Agrippa*, the great north–south highway of eastern Gaul.

Beaune

Glorious Beaune is set amid rich vineyards, enclosed by ancient ramparts and ornamented with fine medieval buildings. The town's central area is a maze of narrow cobbled streets and attractive busy squares. Beaune is the centre of the Burgundy wine trade, and set into the walls of its tree-covered ramparts are the caves of wine producers.

Superb traditional Flemish-Burgundian coloured roof tiles hide inside the lovely cobbled courtyard of the famous **Hôtel Dieu** (*rue de l'Hôtel Dieu; tel: 03 80 24 45 00, fax: 03 80 24 45 99, www.hospices-de-beaune.tm.fr/htgb/home; open: daily all year; ££*). The glazed and patterned roof descends steeply over a timbered first-floor gallery resting on slender pillars. This hospice for the poor, founded in 1443 by Nicolas Rolin, the fantastically wealthy chancellor of the Dukes of Burgundy, served as a general hospital right up to 1948.

The grand 14th- to 16th-century former residence of the Dukes of Burgundy, the **Hôtel des Ducs de Bourgogne** (*rue d'Enfer; tel: 03 80 24 56 92; open: daily 0930–1800, Dec–Mar, closed Tue; ££*) is now given over entirely to Beaune's prestigious wine museum. In the cellars, there are huge wine-presses and a curious collection of implements. At the atmospheric **Marché aux Vins** (wine market) (*2 rue Nicolas Rolin; tel: 03 80 25 08 20, fax: 03 80 25 08 21, e-mail marcheauxvins@axnet.fr; open: daily 0930–1200 and 1400–1800; ££*), buy a *tastevin* – a shallow drinking cup for wine-tasting – and sample some of the finest Côte d'Or wines.

Three in a bed ...

When Louis XIV visited the main ward of Beaune's hospice, he was amazed to find up to four patients in each bed, and immediately had to order that women and men patients should not be placed in beds together!

Beaune's 13th- to 16th-century **ramparts** are fortified with a succession of sturdy 'bastions' and towers, and draped with greenery in places. The ancient moat, now largely filled in, and much of the ramparts have become a shady, pleasant walk.

Tourist information: 1 rue de l'Hôtel Dieu. Tel: 03 80 26 21 30; fax: 03 80 26 21 39; e-mail: ot.beaune@wanadoo.fr. Open: daily 0930–1800.

Auxerre

Tourist information: 1–2 quai de la République. Tel: 03 86 52 06 19; fax: 03 86 51 23 27; www.webhdo.com/bourgogne/89/auxerre/tourisme and www.auxerre.com/. Open: Mon–Sat 0900–1230 and 1400–1830; Sun 1000–1300.

Auxerre (pronounced 'Ossaire') is a thoroughly Burgundian town, beside a thoroughly Burgundian river. Its old quarter is wonderfully picturesque, with narrow, winding, cobbled lanes climbing between tall, timbered houses with steep tiled roofs. At the foot of the hill are the *quais* beside the River Yonne, and an attractive part of the old town, called 'Quartier de la Marine'. Beside the river, the 12th-century belfry of the **Ancien Abbaye St-Germain** (*2 place St-Germain; tel: 03 86 51 09 74; open: daily except Tue, June–Sept 1000–1200 and 1400–1800, Oct–May 1000–1830; ££*) is a beautiful landmark. Beneath the abbey-church, in an atmospheric crypt, are frescos that are nearly 1 200 years old – the oldest in France.

The heart of the old quarter is around the place de Hôtel de Ville, with pedestrianised streets and several well-preserved old houses in and around place Robillard, place des Cordeliers and place Surugue. On rue de l'Horloge, the former town gate, the 15th-century Tour de l'Horloge, has a flamboyant astronomical clock showing the movements of the sun and moon, as well as the time of day.

Besançon

Tourist information: 2 place de la 1ère Armée Française. Tel: 03 81 80 92 55.

The Swiss would have you believe that they are the world's supreme clockmakers, but the watchmakers of Besançon were once renowned as Europe's finest. Their legacy can be seen in the extraordinarily complex **Horloge Astronomique**, with its multiple dials and its automata that pop out on the hour, gracing the bell tower of the city's 12th-century cathedral. Many elegant buildings with wrought-iron balconies grace the city centre, including the majestic 16th-century **Palais Grenvelle** in Grande Rue. The old Cornmarket has been transformed into a rewarding **Musée des Beaux Arts et d'Archéologie** (*1 place de la Révolution, tel: 03 81 81 44 47; open Wed–Mon*), covering European art from the Renaissance (Bellini and Cranach) to the 20th century (Matisse and Picasso).

Bourg-en-Bresse

Tourist information: Centre Albert Camus, 6 avenue Alsace Lorraine. Tel: 04 74 22 49 40; fax: 04 74 23 06 28; www.bourg-en-bresse.org. Open: 0900–1230 and 1400–1830 (to 1800 Sat).

To gourmets everywhere, the name of Bresse means just one thing: poultry. The only chicken to have its own *appellation contrôlée*, it is judged to be the most delicious in the world. All around the region, you'll see its famous free-range hens, pullets and capons out in all weathers (sheltering inside hedges on rainy days), in and around the traditional, broad, low farmhouses. Made of timbers and narrow bricks under wide, shallow roofs, each house stands comfortably in its own space among fields and copses. The gently rolling, lush countryside has the most rustic, old-fashioned feel. Many villages and small farms have kept their old arcaded pavements, and the village markets are full of old-world character.

Tip

The town of Bourg is pronounced 'Bourk', and its people are called 'Bourgeois'.

Bresse poultry – beware of imitations!

The famed poultry of Bresse has many imitators. That's why it has its own wine-style appellation d'origine contrôlée, *and it is an offence to describe chicken as Bresse poultry unless it meets several strict requirements, laid down in the Bresse Chicken laws of 1957 and 1989.*

Bresse poultry is recognisable by its colours: pure white plumage, skin and flesh; ears white or lightly reddened; pure, sleek blue feet; bright red crest and 'beard'. Among other things, all Bresse poultry must be: pure Bresse breed; raised in Bresse; completely free-range, living on lush grass until the last two to four weeks of life; given only unadulterated sweetcorn, cereals and dairy products to eat; certified after slaughter by the merchant's tricolour seal at the base of its neck, in addition to the Volaille de Bresse appellation d'origine contrôlée *label.*

Briançon

Tourist information: place du Temple. Tel: 04 92 21 08 50.

Briançon's great claim to fame is that it is Europe's highest town, located at an altitude of 1 320m. Naturally enough, that makes it an excellent centre for skiing in the winter months and for a whole range of madcap sports in summer, from cycling up near vertical slopes to jumping off high rocks with a hang-glider attached. Because the town straddled one of the most important mountain routes linking France and Italy, it has always been well defended, and the present town looks like a fortification, with its stout 18th-century gates and walls, all designed by the European master of 18th-century defences, Sébastien Vauban. Interestingly, Vauban also designed the **cathedral** at the heart of the maze of narrow streets in the old town – it, too, looks as if defence, rather than worship, was its primary purpose. Fans of military architecture can join tours of Vauban's works, organised by the tourist office.

Two important national parks lie on Briançon's doorstep: the **Parc National des Ecrins** and the **Parc Régional du Queyras**. Both offer sheer peaks, glaciers and a profusion of alpine flowers during the summer months.

Vauban – military architect to Louis XIV

Vauban (1633–1707) is one of a handful of military architects whose ideas changed the face of Europe – from Sicily and Malta to Maastricht and Leiden (and even as far away as America) his ideas were quickly adopted by military engineers, keen to protect their cities from attack and siege. His innovations included multiple projecting bastions – like the points of a star – to serve as gun platforms and to ensure that there were no blind spots in the defences, where the enemy could launch a surprise attack. Master of the large-scale city defence, he also invented the socket bayonet.

Cluny

Tourist information: Tour des Fromages, 6 rue Mercière. Tel: 03 85 59 05 34; fax: 03 85 59 06 95; e-mail: cluny@wanadoo.fr; www.perso.wanadoo.fr/otcluny. Open: daily, except Sun in winter. Frequent one-hr, themed tours of the town.

Little is left of the Benedictines' **Abbaye de Cluny** (Cluny Abbey) (*tel: 03 85 59 12 79, fax: 05 85 59 02 65; open: summer 0900–1800, out of season 1000–1200 and 1400–1600; visits inside on half-hour guided tours only; ££*), but it still dominates the village. The abbey at Cluny reached the height of its power in the 12th century. Only the Pope had greater influence than the Abbot of Cluny – but even he would not have risked a split with the abbey. The abbey-church was the largest in the world until St Peter's in Rome was built. The minute fraction that remains is not disappointing. Pillars, doorways, corridors and vaults of such celestial proportions all speak volumes about the grandeur of the place as it was. Surviving towers mark the edges of the abbey, and the **Tour des Fromages** (*open: 1000–1230 and 1430–1900; closes 1800 Nov–Mar; no midday closing July and Aug*) offers an ideal vantage point from which to imagine how it once looked, in its green, rolling countryside.

To visit the abbey, apply at the **Musée Ochier** (*rue K. Comantl; tel: 03 85 59 23 97; open same hours as abbey*), the museum of art and archaeology housed in the 15th-century former abbot's palace. Several Romanesque houses in the village date from as far back as the 12th century.

Dijon

This ancient seat of the Dukes of Burgundy is today Burgundy's lively modern capital, and a centre of haute cuisine. Dijon's central quarter has a welcoming and walkable feel, with great atmosphere and scores of fine old buildings, including the imposing ducal palace. Place de la Libération is a magnificent semicircle of grand old honey-tinted stone houses, and handsome Renaissance back streets with museums, galleries and boutiques.

The most notable of all Dijon's grand historic buildings is the **Palais des Ducs** or 'Palace of the Dukes' (*place de la Sainte-Chapelle; tel: 03 80 74 53 59; open: daily except Tue, 1000–1800; ££*), where the ghosts of the Dukes of Burgundy walk the splendid corridors, staircases and courtyards. This vast edifice in pale stone is now Dijon's town hall, and also houses the impressive collections of the city's outstanding Fine Arts Museum. Its other rooms are sumptuously decorated in 17th-century style.

Dinner in Dijon

Dijon is the gastronomic capital of a gastronomic region. Its name is synonymous with the best of French mustard – moutarde de Dijon *– the highest-quality* crème de cassis *(blackcurrant liqueur used in the classic aperitif* kir *), as well as* pains d'épices *(cakey gingerbread),* jambon persillé *(ham with parsley), and* escargots *(snails). Many of the town's excellent restaurants serve the great Burgundian classics, such as* coq au vin *(chicken, onions, mushrooms and wine),* boeuf bourgignonne *(Charolais beef in onions, mushrooms and wine) and* pauchouse *(fish and wine stew).*

The palace fell into disrepair when the French took over Burgundy. Two hundred years later, it was restored and enlarged by the Estates of Burgundy from 1682 onwards, a time when French control over the duchy was being consolidated. Much was added, and the **Palais des Beaux-Arts**, on the east side, is only 150 years old.

Dijon's **Cathédrale St-Bénigne** (*place St-Bénigne; tel: tourist office on 03 80 44 11 44; open: daily (crypt open: Easter–Oct only, 0900–1900); pilgrimage to the cathedral every 20 Nov*), a former abbey-church of the 11th, 13th and 14th centuries, is an excellent example of the Burgundian Gothic style, with survivals of its Romanesque predecessor. Its external buttresses, towers and coloured tiles are in contrast to the plain, austere interior.

The most famous family in Dijon lives in one of the two bell towers of the distinctive 13th-century **Notre-Dame** church.

The father, Jacquemart, sounds the hours by striking a bell with a hammer; he's been performing this duty (in various incarnations) since the year 1382. A century later, he found a wife, and after another hundred years, the couple produced a son, Jacquelinet, who strikes the half-hours. It was almost another 170 years before their daughter, Jacquelinette, appeared, to strike the quarter-hours.

There are several impressive 16th- and 17th-century mansions in the streets around the **Palais de Justice** (law courts) (*rue du Palais; no tel; open: 0900–1200 and 1400–1700*). This area, once rather aristocratic, was the central point of the Romans' fortified colony *Divio*, the original Dijon. The Law Courts themselves were once Burgundy's parliament building and have kept a Renaissance façade. Inside, the lobby – once a grand meeting place for wealthy people – has an exquisite vaulted panelled ceiling.

Tourist information: Head office: Hôtel Chambellan, 34 rue des Forges. Tel: 03 80 44 11 44; fax: 03 80 30 90 02; e-mail: infotourisme@ot-dijon.fr. Open: May–mid-Oct Mon–Sat 0930–1300 and 1400–1800; out of season Mon–Fri; closed national holidays. Main office (personal callers only): Pavillon du Tourisme, place Darcy; open: all year round.

Grenoble

Grenoble, host to the Winter Olympics in 1968, is a busy commercial and industrial city – one of the most important in the Alps.

It continues to be the pace-setter in French high-tech industry, a fact helped by the thriving university in the city's midst, and the enjoyable lifestyle that attracts some of the country's best minds to come and live here (newcomers from Paris and elsewhere make up around 80 per cent of the city's population). Encircled by high alpine peaks, the call of the ski slopes is an ever-present temptation.

The city owes its rapid growth to hydro-electric power, and that in turn led to the development of companies specialising in turbines, hydraulics and electro-metallurgy. Now the city thrives on nuclear research (it is the location of one of Europe's most important particle accelerators), as well as computers and data processing.

To the visitor, this business prowess manifests itself in the high-rise buildings that ring the city's 18th-century inner core. Grenoble looks, at first sight, more like an American city than a French one. But there is a French heart in the form of the pedestrianised **place Grenette** area, on the left bank of the River Isère. Here the boutiques and open-air cafés are patronised by smart business executives and young professionals. Slightly more cutting edge are the trendier and cheaper student haunts of the **place St-André** area, which sits at the centre of the medieval city, where the **Église St-André** and the 15th-century **Maison de Justice** are to be found.

To get a full sense of how big the city is, you can take the **cable car** up to the **Fort de la Bastille**, the rocky 16th-century citadel rebuilt by Vauban. The cable car gondolas (*daily from 2100 to midnight in summer, to 1930 in winter*) take you from the old town across the River Isère to the fortress site from where there are panoramic views.

The city's museums include the **Musée Dauphinois** (*30 rue Maurice Gignoux; tel 04 76 85 19 01; open: Wed–Mon; £*), covering regional history, life and crafts, and the **Musée de Grenoble** (*5 place de Lavalette; tel: 04 76 63 44 44; open: Wed–Mon; £*), with works by Picasso and Matisse.

To the south and west of Grenoble, the Vercors is a mountain wilderness of gorges, waterfalls and caves set amidst pine forest. Highlights include the limestone **Gorge de la Bournes** and the narrow sheer-sided gorge at **Grands Goulets**.

Tourist information: 14 rue de la République. Tel: 04 76 42 41 41.

Lyon

Built on silk and socialism, modern Lyon – now a World Heritage City – combines luxury with earthy directness.

Originally Greek, then Roman, Lyon's setting on two large rivers is striking. On the Saône's right bank rises the city's atmospheric old quarter. On the narrow peninsula (*presqu'île*) between the two rivers lies the **town centre**, a tangle of narrow old streets and tinier squares, edged with high old buildings and small restaurants. In the middle is the broad pedestrianised **rue de la République**, lined with chic boutiques and grandiose 19th-century façades in pale golden stone. The **place des Terreaux** ('Earthwaters') has a wildly ornate lead fountain; its pavement is pierced with a multitude of small waterspouts that often catch pedestrians unawares.

Lyon's *traboules*

These curious passageways are rights of way running beneath or through private buildings – often via a central courtyard. Hundreds of them make a secretive maze. They date from the 16th century, when they started as short cuts for silk carriers. Over the centuries they have served as escape routes during times of unrest, rebellion and persecution, and helped to make Lyon a centre of resistance during the Second World War.

Six bridges cross from the peninsula to **Vieux Lyon** ('Old Town'), below the **Fourvière** hill (which can be climbed – for a magnificent view of the city – by funicular from Gare St-Jean). Many of this quarter's 300 or so magnificent Renaissance houses stand on Roman foundations. The main street is **rue St-Jean**. Other picturesque streets and lanes are cut across by steep stairways called *montées*, and vaulted old *traboules*.

Vieux Lyon grew up around two important churches. The oldest, **Cathédrale St-Jean** (*place St-Jean; tel: 04 78 42 25 75; variable hours; £*), built from the 12th century, has an unusual façade, with 320 medallions and ornate carvings. Built not long after, **Église St-Paul** (*rue St-Paul; tel: 04 78 28 34 45; open: 1200–1800; £*) has an attractive octagonal bell tower.

Lyon's wealth was built on the silk industry, and the **Musée des Tissus** (Fabrics Museum) (*34 rue de la Charité; tel: 04 78 38 42 00, fax: 04 72 40 25 12; open: 1000–1200 and 1400–1730, closed Mon; ££*) displays dazzling collections of beautiful fabrics.

Once the run-down proletarian neighbourhood of the *canuts*, Lyon's badly paid silk-workers, the characterful hillside **La Croix-Rousse** district has become rather trendy. In 1831, protesting silk-workers marched down the steep Montée de la Grande Côte, with their black flags and their slogan 'Live working or die fighting', into gunfire – 600 of them died. Also don't miss the **Amphithéâtre des Trois Gaules** (*free access*), dating from about 19 BC. The *traboules* (*see opposite*) of this district are especially intriguing.

Lyon was a focal point for the Resistance in the Second World War. Across the river from the Perrache area, the harrowing **Centre d'Histoire de la Résistance et de la Déportation** (Centre for the History of the Resistance and Deportation) is housed in the former Gestapo headquarters (*14 avenue Berthelot; open: Wed–Sun 0900–1730; £*).

On the menu

Lyon has over 1 000 restaurants in its central districts. Lyon favourites include gras-double *(ox tripe) and* cervelas *(garlic-rich pork sausage). A hundred years ago, female chefs serving robust set meals at a modest price gave rise to the traditional Lyonnais bistros, which became known as* mères *('mothers'). Another Lyon tradition is the* bouchon, *the down-to-earth traditional restaurant specialising in local dishes.*

Tourist information: Pavillon du Tourisme, place Bellecour. Tel: 04 72 77 69 69; fax: 04 78 42 04 32; e-mail: lyoncvb@lyon-france.co; www.lyon-france.com. Open: daily all year.

Pérouges

Tourist information: at the town entrance. Tel: 04 74 61 01 14. One-hour guided tours all year.

In this perfectly preserved hilltop town, a number of French films have been shot among the houses with overhanging eaves, narrow steps, twisting lanes and a fortified church from the Middle Ages. Almost everything is constructed of the local flint, and dates from the 13th to the 16th century. In that period (apart from the siege of 1468), the town prospered from its cloth-making and weaving. After the Industrial Revolution and the start of the railway age, rustic, isolated Pérouges began to decline. By the first decade of the 20th century, many houses had fallen into ruin and were demolished. In 1909, journalist Anthelme Thibault wrote a moving article about the death of the medieval village. Immediately taken up by artists and historians from Lyon, it began a dramatic revival.

Rue des Rondes, encircling the old heart of the town, has managed to keep most of its medieval character. The main street, rue du Prince, leads round the **Grand Maison des Princes de Savoy** (now a museum of regional folk culture), to place de la Halle, the delightful old market square dominated by its lime tree, planted at the Revolution. A marked walking tour meanders through the town, and another path (promenade des Terreaux) follows the former moat from Porte d'en Haut (the Upper Gateway) round to the Porte d'en Bas (the Lower Gateway).

Ronchamp

Tourist information: place du 14 juillet. Tel: 03 84 63 50 82. Open: Apr–Nov.

Few visitors would set foot in the somewhat anonymous former mining town of Ronchamp were it not for one remarkable building: Le Corbusier's innovative chapel of **Notre-Dame-du-Haut**, built in 1955 as a memorial to all the soldiers who lost their lives here towards the end of the Second World War. The chapel is far from typical of Le Corbusier's work. Its organic form anticipates late 20th-century buildings, such as the Guggenheim Museum in Bilbao. Though built of concrete, the walls look like adobe and the billowing pillow-like roof like thatch – its appearance has been compared to that of an African mud-and-reed hut. Standing at the top of the town, the chapel is visible for miles around and serves its purpose well as a constant reminder of the sacrifice made by so many brave soldiers. Inside, the simple chapel is lit by sunlit filtered through stained-glass windows of red, yellow and blue, and no extraneous furnishings detract from the impact of the simple crucifix.

Semur-en-Auxois

Tourist information: beside the fortified gateway at 2 Place Gaveau. Tel: 03 80 97 05 96; fax: 03 80 97 08 85; e-mail: tourisme.pays.auxois@wanadoo.fr; www.parisgifts.com/semur. Open: daily 1000–1200 and 1500–1800. Summer 'tourist train' trips at 1700 and 2200.

Cobbled lanes, four mighty towers, a massive stone gateway into the fortified old quarter: many remnants of the Middle Ages survive at this appealing little country town. Walk through the 15th-century barbican in rue Buffon and beneath the double gateway of Guillier (13th century) and Sauvigny (15th century). To either side, old houses of stone and timber line the way. **Église Notre-Dame** is a good example of Burgundian architecture of the 13th and 14th centuries. Continue past the massive Tour de l'Orle d'Or, split from top to bottom, via rue des Remparts, to the small park on top of the 15th-century **ramparts**. From here, the town's extraordinary position can be fully appreciated: perched on a high spur, it rises from a bizarre loop in the River Armançon. Pause on the **Pont Joly**, the bridge over the river, to get the full picturesque effect of the towers and houses clustered on the pink granite.

Sens

Tourist information: place Jean-Jaurès. Tel: 03 86 65 19 49; fax: 03 86 64 24 18; www.mairie-sens.fr/.

Tree-lined boulevards in this tranquil country town run along the line of daunting ramparts that stood here for 2 000 years. Sens was a powerful archbishopric, with authority over Paris, and in 1130 the construction of the first Gothic cathedral in France – **Cathédrale St-Étienne** – was begun here. (The architect, William of Sens, used it as a model for his work at Canterbury Cathedral.) In 1234 it served as the setting for the marriage of Louis IX of France to Margaret of Provence.

Today, the cathedral (*place de la République; tel: 03 86 65 19 49; open: daily; £*) stands at the heart of the oval-shaped old centre. Despite evident damage, it is magnificent. The high, light interior contains beautiful stained glass. The oldest example, dating from the 12th century, includes images of Thomas à Becket with Henry II. Becket's vestments can be seen in the **Cathedral Treasury**.

Facing the cathedral across place de la République, there's a fine wood-and-iron **19th-century covered market**. Among several historic houses, the 16th-century **Maison d'Abraham** and **Maison du Pilier** on the corner of rue de la République and rue Jean Cousin have astonishing carved timberwork. Many half-timbered houses stand along Grande Rue.

Tournus

Tourist information: 2 place Carnot. Tel: 03 85 51 13 10; fax: 03 85 32 18 21; www.perso.wanadoo.fr/tournus/. Open: Mon–Sat 0900–1200 and 1400–1800.

Walled Tournus (the 's' is silent) is a small, quiet and old-fashioned town, once a Roman fort, where riverside *quais* follow the curving Saône. Arcaded sidewalks and shopfronts – hiding delicious *pâtisseries* and *épiceries* – and some imposing mansions, make the town centre an attractive place to stroll or shop. Close to quai du Midi, modest little 12th- to 15th-century **Église Madeleine** has a superbly simple whitewashed interior. The 17th-century **Hôtel Dieu** (charity hospital) (*21 rue de l'Hôpital; tel: 03 85 51 23 50; open: Apr–Oct 1100–1800 (closed Tue); ££*) preserves its original apothecary, and served as a hospital right up to 1982.

At the other end of town stands the huge **Ancienne Abbaye** (former abbey) (*rue Thibaudet; tel: 03 85 51 13 10; open: daily; guided tours in summer; £*). Its **Église St-Philibert** is unusual: three churches built on top of each other over the course of a couple of centuries – 9th to 11th – creating a single curious and original building in pure Romanesque style, with castellations. Standing on top of the vestibule is another church, St-Michel, reached by an outdoor staircase. Extraordinarily, this part of the abbey was built before the nave of the main church. Don't miss the cloisters and other abbey buildings.

Vézelay

Tourist information: rue Saint-Pierre. Tel: 03 86 33 23 69; fax: 03 86 33 34 00; www.morvan.com/vezelay/vezelay and www.cef.fr/sens-auxerre/vezelay/. Open: daily 1000–1300 and 1400–1800 (closed Thu out of season).

Picturesque, ancient, with steep lanes of perfectly restored stone cottages, lovely ramparts and medieval gates, it's hard to believe that this hilltop village was completely abandoned just a hundred years ago. Since then, it has been transformed into a chic haven of tourism. Fortunately, the reason for it all, the **Basilique Ste-Madeleine** (Basilica of Mary Magdalene) (*information: Fraternité Monastique de Jérusalem, Service des Visites, Vézelay; tel: 03 86 33 26 73, fax: 03 86 33 36 93; very busy July and Aug – come soon after breakfast to beat the tour buses*), has remained unscathed by the commercialism.

The basilica, originally the abbey-church of Vézelay Abbey, founded here in the 9th century, is considered to be one of the greatest masterpieces of Romanesque architecture. From outside it appears deceptively plain. However, the interior is immense, light and overwhelming, making visitors look tiny. There is almost no decoration although dim traces of old frescos round the choir show that it was not always so bare. In the dark crypt a little shrine contains relics, once thought to be the bones of Mary Magdalene. After centuries of inspiring pilgrimage and intense devotion, it has been acknowledged that these are not her bones at all.

Vienne

Tourist information: Cours Brillier (at Rhône end). Tel: 04 74 53 80 30; fax: 04 74 53 80 31; www.culture.fr/culture/arcnat/vienne/fr/. Open: Mon–Sat, Sun am. Town tours July and Aug.

This quiet, civilised town has a hint of the South, plus abundant treasures left by the passing centuries, particularly its illustrious period as capital of Roman Gaul.

The 1st-century rectangular Roman **Temple d'Auguste et de Livie** (Temple of Augustus and Livia) (*place Charles-de-Gaulle; admission free*) stands elegantly in a square. The **Théâtre Antique** or **Théâtre Romain** (Ancient or Roman Theatre) (*7 rue du Cirque (colline de Pipet); tel: 04 74 85 39 23; open: daily Apr–Aug, Tue–Sun, closed public holidays*), a semicircle of seat-terraces, would have held as many as 13,500 people.

The **Musée des Beaux-Arts et d'Archéologie** (Museum of Fine Arts and Archaeology) (*place de Miremont; tel: 04 74 85 50 42, fax: 04 74 53 34 59; open: Tue–Sun, closed public holidays*) displays Vienne's impressive collection of prehistoric and Gallo-Roman objects found all over the town.

113

Across the river, **St-Romain-en-Gal** was a large commercial area of Roman villas, bath-houses, workshops and warehouses. Hundreds of valuable finds have been excavated here, including exquisite mosaics. (*D502, by the west end of Pont de Lattre de Tassigny; open: 0930–1830, closed Mon; ££.*)

Vienne's history

100 BC: main settlement of the Gaulish Allobroges tribe.
0 AD: Roman Vienne founded as Vienna Senatoria.
177: Vienne is a wealthy and cosmopolitan town, with a large Christian and Jewish presence.
413–534: capital of the Burgundian territories in the Rhône Valley.
687–1032: capital of the Provençal kingdom of Arles.
12th to 14th centuries: an important ecclesiastical centre.
15th century: now part of Dauphiné, becomes French.
16th/17th centuries on: Lyon grows in importance, Vienne declines.

Eating and drinking

Brasserie Le Quai
place St-Nicolas, Auxerre. £–££. This large well-placed brasserie beside the river in the Quartier de la Marine is a cheerful and inexpensive place for a drink or a meal.

La Ciboulette
69 rue de Lorraine, Beaune. Tel: 03 80 24 70 72; fax: 03 80 22 79 71. £. Unpretentious but stylish little town-centre restaurant with excellent food at affordable prices.

Jardin des Remparts
19 rue de l'Hôtel Dieu, Beaune. Tel: 03 80 24 79 41; fax: 03 80 24 92 79. £££. Congenial, welcoming and stylish – perhaps the best restaurant in Beaune. *Foie gras*, fresh fish, delicious sauces: try the asparagus and haddock *gelée* with asparagus *coulis*. Good value set menu on weekdays.

Bistrot des Halles
10 rue Bannelier, Dijon. Tel: 03 80 49 94 15; fax: 03 80 38 16 16. £. For a good meal at a modest price, head for this excellent wine bar and restaurant.

Pré aux Clercs
13 place de la Libération, Dijon. Tel: 03 80 38 05 05; fax: 03 80 38 16 16. Closed Mon, and Sun pm. ££. In handsome historic premises opposite the Palais des Ducs, imaginative dishes are based on classic local specialities.

Simpatico
30 rue Berbisey, Dijon. Tel: 03 80 30 53 33. Closed Mon. £. Among the eateries of this popular area, this convivial Italian is one of the very best, with authentic dishes at modest prices.

Brasserie Georges
30 cours de Verdun, Lyon. Tel: 04 72 56 54 54. £–££. Alongside Perrache station, this huge, popular art-deco bar-restaurant has been in business since 1836.

Léon de Lyon
1 rue Pleney, Lyon. Tel: 04 72 10 11 12; fax: 04 72 10 11 13. £££. One of the most famous names in France, this gastronomic haven offers refined, accomplished cooking of classic Lyonnais dishes. Next door is *Le Petit Léon* (*£*), the much less expensive lunchtime bistro.

La Tour Rose and
Maison de la Tour
*22 rue du Boeuf, Lyon. Tel: 04 78 37
25 90; fax: 04 78 42 26 02. £££.*
This glorious 17th-century Renaissance
mansion in the old quarter is the setting
for creative Lyonnais gastronomy.
In the open courtyard is the more
informal **Terrasses de la Tour** (*££*),
covered and heated in winter, open air
in summer.

Restaurant Le Soleil Levant
*51 rue Émile Zola, Sens. Tel: 03 86 65
71 82. £.* Excellent seafood and fish
dishes at an inexpensive, traditional
provincial restaurant near the station.

Le Bec Fin
*7 place St-Maurice, Vienne. Tel: 04 74
85 76 72; fax: 04 74 85 15 30. Closed
Sun pm and Mon. ££.* Best of the town-
centre restaurants, by the cathedral,
this locals' favourite serves classic,
well-prepared dishes.

L'Estancot
*4 rue Table Ronde, Vienne. Tel: 04 74
85 12 09. Closed Sun and Mon. £.*
Tucked away in a town-centre back
street, a good place to come for a
variety of ambitious, tasty dishes at
low prices. If it's full, there are several
similar near by.

La Pyramide
*14 boulevard Fernand Point, Vienne.
Tel: 04 74 53 01 96; fax: 04 74
85 69 73. Closed Tue and Wed.
£££.* Vienne's must-visit site for
gastronomes, where Fernand Point
taught the chefs who pioneered
nouvelle cuisine – notably Bocuse and
the Troisgros brothers. An excellent,
imaginative restaurant serving pricey,
lavish dishes.

BURGUNDY AND THE RHÔNE VALLEY

Burgundy's vineyards

*The **Côte d'Or** is the most famous part of Burgundy. The name means 'Golden Slope', and this 60-km hillside is certainly gold-tinted in morning sunlight. From its earth come the celebrated wines that have made the name of Burgundy famous throughout the world. Each village along its length is charming, surrounded by immaculate fields of vines. Many a label bears the name of a particular* clos, *sometimes known locally as a* climat, *being a tiny area of grapevines, often a walled field.*

The Côte d'Or is divided broadly into two large regions: the **Côte de Nuits** and the **Côte de Beaune**. Côte de Nuits red wines are rich, long lasting and much sought after, while the Côte de Beaune excels for whites. On both Côtes, the best wine comes from the oldest vines and from those nearest the top of the hill.

Despite a spartan regime, it was Cistercian monks who developed the cultivation of the grapevine on the Côte d'Or. The Cistercian Order was founded at **Cîteaux** in 1098, with the aim of elevating unostentatious simplicity to something of an art form. Most of the wine produced was consumed by the monks themselves, though any surplus was given away to influential and useful friends.

Famous names of the Côte d'Or

Just outside the village of Vougeot, the **Château du Clos de Vougeot** stands splendidly amid its vineyards. It was constructed in the 12th century, then largely rebuilt in the 16th century, by the Cistercians at Cîteaux. The château is now the base of the international **Confrèrie des Chevaliers du Tastevin**, the 'Brotherhood of the Knights of Winetasting',

a Burgundian growers,
association dedicated to
Confrèrie gathers here at
the year for its ritualised
banquets, with up to 600

At **Gevrey-Chambertin**,
encircle the village, which
appellations. Chambertin and ... de Bèze are the
pick of the crop. A nicely aged bottle of a good
vintage Chambertin was, it is claimed, Napoleon's
favourite tipple.

Slightly off the beaten track, **Meursault**, with its beautiful
Gothic church spire, is where the *Trois Glorieuses* celebrations
(*see below*) come to an end. The village is considered to be
the 'capital' of white Burgundy, and several wine producers
and sellers give tours of their magnificent old premises.

Nuits-St-Georges is the small commercial hub of the Côte
de Nuits. The wines of Nuits became fashionable among
Europe's aristocracy after 1680 when they were prescribed
for Louis XIV by his physician 'to restore his strength'. The
town's own vineyards are 1 000 years old.

The pretty village of **Aloxe-Corton** (pronounced 'Alosse'),
one of the world's oldest and greatest wine names, marks
the start of the Côte de Beaune. The ancient charity of the
Hospices de Beaune owns extensive high-quality vineyards,
especially in the distinguished area between Aloxe and
Meursault. On the third Saturday, Sunday and Monday in
November – *Les Trois Glorieuses* – *viticulteurs* and their
merchants get together in Beaune to feast and do business.
The weekend starts with a big banquet. On the Sunday, the
annual wine auction, timed by a burning candle, takes place
in the cellars of Beaune's Hôtel Dieu. The day concludes with
another banquet. On the third night, growers bring their
own wine to the Paulée, a huge party and banquet at
Meursault. *(For information, tel: 03 80 26 21 30.)*

All profits from the Hospices auction of its 39 vintages go
to charity. In addition, the auction plays an important role
in establishing prices for each year's new vintage, with a
knock-on effect for prices of wines from other regions of
France and all around the world.

Provence
and the
South

An invisible frontier somewhere in the Rhône Valley separates two utterly different countries – France and Provence. South of that frontier, the people enjoy a warmer climate and a way of life that is both more enthusiastic and more leisurely. During the long summer months, millions of people come here, yet the deep heart of the region is little visited. Provence, at peace after a long and turbulent past, today celebrates light, art and life – it's la vie en plein air, *life in the open air.*

Getting there: *Nice Côte d'Azur and Marseille Marignane are the principal airports. Overnight Motorail allows you to travel by train, with your car, direct from Calais to Avignon (12¹/₂ hours) or Nice (14¹/₂ hours). The main access roads for the region are the A7 and N7, which follow the Rhône from Lyon to Orange. The N7 continues into Provence via Aix-en-Provence to Cannes and Nice. The A7 terminates at Marseille and connects with the A8 and other autoroutes for the Riviera. The 1 200-km (745-mile) drive from the Channel ports to the Riviera takes around 12 hours.*

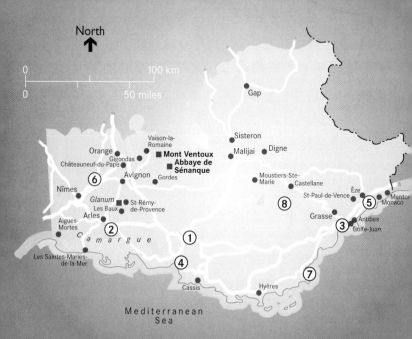

North

0 — 100 km
0 — 50 miles

Gap

Sisteron
Malijai   Digne

Vaison-la-Romaine
Orange   Gigondas   ■ Mont Ventoux
Châteauneuf-du-Pape   Abbaye de
             Avignon   Sénanque
⑥   Gordes   Moustiers-Ste-Marie
Nîmes   Castellane
        Glanum ■ St-Rémy-   St-Paul-de-Vence   Èze
       Les Baux ■ de-Provence   ⑧   ⑤ Menton
    Arles   Monaco
Aigues-   Grasse
Mortes   ③ Antibes
       C a m a r g u e   ①   Golfe-Juan
Les Saintes-Maries-
de-la-Mer   ②

                               ④   ⑦
                           Cassis   Hyères

        M e d i t e r r a n e a n
              S e a

① Aix-en-Provence

Watch the world go by at a café on the elegant and lively Cours Mirabeau, in this quintessential southern town, the birthplace of the painter Cézanne.
Page 123

② The Camargue

See white horses and black bulls, as well as many and varied species of birds, within the national park of the largest wetland in Europe. Step back in time in the Crusaders' fortified town of Aigues-Mortes, or immerse yourself in gypsy culture at Les Saintes-Maries-de-la-Mer. Page 126

③ Cannes

First popular with British aristocrats in the 19th century, Cannes' Riviera seafront promenade is lined with palm trees and mimosa and lavish hotels, while its back streets teem with first-class shops and restaurants. Pop into the Hotel Carlton for a coffee on the terrace. Page 127

④ Marseille

Eat the best bouillabaisse fish stew in France in this ancient, teeming, multi-cultural port city, France's second; its architects range from the ancient Greeks to Le Corbusier. Page 131

⑤ Nice

Don't dismiss this classic Riviera resort – 'Queen of the Riviera' – with its melting pot of cultures, and its extremes of wealth and squalor. Enjoy world-class art museums and galleries and lose yourself in the colour and exuberance of the indoor and outdoor markets. Page 134

⑥ Pont du Gard

Walk along the top level, or drive across the middle level of this spectacular three-tiered Roman aqueduct, or paddle a canoe underneath it, then lie on the riverbank and contemplate an extraordinary feat of engineering.
Page 137

⑦ St-Tropez

Sex kitten 'BB' and husband Roger Vadim made this fishing port into the sophisticated, bohemian, glamorous place it became in the 1950s. Taste St-Trop's high life today, with a stroll along the harbour front, and then dance into the small hours in one of its many clubs. Page 138

⑧ Grand Canyon du Verdon

Drive along the winding road at the top of France's very own Grand Canyon – carved by the Verdon river – to see almost 1 000m of rock rising up sheer from the ribbon of water below.
Page 141

Festivals in Provence

The climate of the South lends itself well to outdoor celebration, and almost every village has its festival day in the sun, while the bigger towns attract top international names to their world-renowned arts events.

Aigues-Mortes

Tourist information: Porte de la Gardette. Tel: 04 66 53 73 00; fax: 04 66 53 65 94.

No Camargue town is more perfectly preserved than the Crusaders' fortified seaport of Aigues-Mortes. The name means 'dead waters' – the town, within an imposing square of medieval ramparts, stands among salt flats where nothing can live. The town was constructed as a seaport in the 13th century, but silting-up eventually rendered the harbour and waterways unusable. Within the town walls, enticing but touristy old streets – in the grid pattern typical of the many fortified 'new towns' or *bastides* of the Middle Ages – lead to a central main square, now full of restaurant tables. The principal landmark is the **Tour de Constance**. Starting from this tower, a walk around the ramparts takes about 30 minutes.

Antibes

Tourist information: 11 place Général de Gaulle. Tel: 04 92 90 53 00; fax: 04 92 90 53 01.

Antibes is a characterful ancient town of Greek origin, with a lively working centre. Historic 17th-century ramparts, with a daunting fortress wall plunging into the sea, edge its authentic old quarter, **Vieil Antibes**, where the streets are lined with attractive, Italianate old houses. Place Nationale is encircled by trees and filled with café tables, and place des Martyrs de la Résistance has shops, more cafés and a carousel.

A heavily fortified possession of the Grimaldi family in the Middle Ages, for centuries Antibes stood on the frontier of France. The 12th- and 16th-century **Château Grimaldi** now contains the Riviera's leading **Picasso Museum**, with an extraordinary collection of ceramics and pottery.

" *The great classical landscapes, our Provence, and Greece, and Italy, are those where light is spiritualised.* **"**

Paul Cézanne

Aix-en-Provence

Tourist information: 2 place Général de Gaulle. Tel: 04 42 16 11 61. Open:
Mon–Sat 0830–1900 (2000 Apr–Sept); Sun 1000–1300 and 1400–1800.

No wonder it's the capital of Provence. Aix exudes joy, yet has an air of dignity. It revels in the simple pleasures of life, yet epitomises civilisation and refinement. Good King René built it up as a place of elegance, festivities, art and culture, and it has remained as such. Later, streets of Renaissance mansions were built. Today, their lavish architecture adds to the appeal of the town.

Paul Cézanne (1839–1906), now one of the world's most popular artists, was born in Aix, at 28 rue de l'Opéra. He was largely unappreciated locally until later in life, but now Aix makes much of him, with hotels, restaurants, even garages named after him.

Cours Mirabeau

Much of Aix's mood centres on its wonderful central avenue, Cours Mirabeau, the perfect southern street. Its pavement tables, shaded by leafy plane trees, are the ideal place to watch the passing crowd, strolling on surely one of the grandest, most beautiful avenues ever built. On the north side, cafés, bookstores and other shops face grandiose 17th- and 18th-century private mansions on the south side. Four fountains along the middle of the avenue include the moss-covered Fontaine d'Eau Thermale, a natural hot spring with water pouring out at 34°C. Cours Mirabeau marks the southern edge of the old quarter of Aix, a peaceful tangle of narrow, traffic-free streets and lanes opening suddenly into elegant little squares enclosed by fine mansions.

Arles

Tourist information: Esplanade Charles de Gaulle, boulevard des Lices. Tel: 04 90 18 41 20; fax: 04 90 18 41 29. Open: Mon–Sat 0900–1900; Sun and holidays 0900–1300.

Arles is an attractive, pleasing, rather arty provincial market town on the Rhône's left bank. The Roman *arènes* (arena or amphitheatre) (*Rond Point des Arènes; no tel; open: daily; ££*) are still used for bullfights, both *mise-à-mort* (Spanish-style, to the death) and *course à la cocarde* (Provençal-style, in which the bull generally survives the 'race', only to be slaughtered afterwards). The incongruous towers at each end of the structure date from the 12th century, when the arena became a fortified village. At that time, there were 200 houses, and even a church, within its walls.

Van Gogh

Vincent van Gogh lived in Arles during his most prolific and disturbed period. He was happy when he first arrived in the town, writing to a friend: 'In the Midi, all the senses are enhanced, the hand is swifter, the eye livelier, the mind clearer.'

Next to it, the **Roman theatre**, less well preserved, is a grand setting for open-air plays. The medieval **Cathédrale et Cloître St-Trophime** (*place de la République; no tel; open: daily; ££*) is on the site of one of the first Romanesque churches to be constructed in France (6th century), though the present building is largely 12th century. It's a good example of what became the Provençal style, though the highly decorative west front is untypical. Through the Bishop's Palace, the lovely, airy cloisters mix Gothic and Romanesque styles.

In later centuries, Arles became the greatest city of Provence. It is proud of its Provençal ancestry, and was the base for 19th-century poet **Frédéric Mistral**'s struggles to revive the Provençal language.

The Félibrige

In 1854, Frédéric Mistral (1830–1914), acclaimed Provençal-language author, brought concerned writers together to reinvigorate Provençal, which had been undermined. Called the Félibrige (from felibre, 'doctor'), they published Armana Provençau *magazine, and Mistral compiled the Provençal grammar and dictionary.*

Avignon

Tourist information: 41 cours Jean-Jaurès. Tel 04 90 82 65 11. Open: Mon–Sat 0900–1300 and 1400–1800 (1700 Sat).

Within Avignon's walls, the town seems quintessentially southern; it bursts with energy, yet echoes with history. It calls itself the Cité des Papes, city of the popes, because in the Middle Ages a line of breakaway popes made it their capital, from 1309 to 1403. The city and its surrounding countryside remained papal property, and did not become part of France again until 1791.

Tip

*The **Festival d'Avignon** (Avignon International Arts Festival of Theatre) (* early July to early August; tel: 04 90 86 24 43 *) features programmed events with top names, plus countless fringe shows, and a party atmosphere.*

The **Palais des Papes** (Popes' Palace) (*place du Palais; tel: 04 90 27 50 74; open: Apr–Oct 0900–1900 (2000 21 Aug–30 Sept), rest of year 0900–1245 and 1400–1800; ££*) is more like a fortress than a palace. Its imposing walls are etched with arches, and topped with castellations and pointy towers. Inside, there are massive halls, gorgeously frescoed walls and decorated timber ceilings.

The **place de l'Horloge**, a square lined with leafy plane trees, is still Avignon's focal point. Even in winter, it's a delight to linger here, watching people pass by.

The picturesque **Pont St-Bénézet** (*tel: 04 90 85 60 16; open: daily Apr–Sept 0900–1830, rest of year Tue–Sun 0900–1300 and 1400–1700, closed public holidays; ££*) is the famous

bridge of the nursery rhyme – 'Sur le Pont/ d'Avignon/on y danse'. Begun in 1177, the bridge originally had 22 arches, but most of it was swept away during the catastrophic Rhône floods of 1668.

125

The Camargue

Where river and sea water merge, the Rhône fans into a huge delta, creating the largest wetland in Europe, most of which falls within the **Parc Naturel Régional de Camargue**. Within the National Park, look-outs have been erected for visitors. A multitude of water channels and shallow salty lakes provide refuge for vast numbers of birds. Black bulls have long been bred here, for use in bullfights, and they may be spotted in the distance, roaming freely. They are herded by Camargue herdsmen, who ride like Wild West cowboys astride the famous white horses.

Les Saintes-Maries-de-la-Mer

Tourist information: avenue van Gogh. Tel: 04 90 97 82 55. Open: summer daily 0900–1200 and 1400–1900; winter Mon–Sat 0900–1200 and 1400–1700, Sun 0900–1200.

This small, picturesque town, with its medieval fortified harbour on the Mediterranean, has become a busy focal point for visitors to the Camargue. The massive walls and strange open bell tower of the fortified Romanesque **church** are the most attractive feature. Known as Les Saintes-Maries ('The Holy Marys') for short, the town takes its name from an improbable Catholic legend. It claims that a boat carrying Mary Magdalene, a sister of the Virgin Mary who was also called Mary, Mary, the mother of the Apostles John and James, their Ethiopian maidservant Sarah, Martha, Lazarus, Maximinus and Sidonius put to sea after Christ's crucifixion and landed at this spot. Two of the Marys and their servant stayed at Les Saintes-Maries. They are remembered every year in the dramatic gypsy **Festival of St Sarah and St Mary**.

Gypsy festival

Gitans, *or gypsies, have strong connections with the Camargue. Sarah, the maidservant of 'The Holy Marys', was adopted a long time ago by the* gitans *as La Vièrge Noire, 'the Black Virgin'. Every year, on 24 and 25 May, gypsies gather here in their thousands to honour her. After a service in the old fortress church, Sarah's statue is carried at the head of a huge procession, right into the sea.*

Cannes

Tourist information: Palais des Festivals, 1 boulevard de la Croisette. Tel 04 93 39 24 53; fax: 04 93 99 37 06.

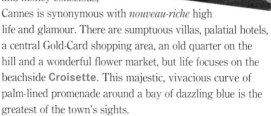

Slick, stylish and money-conscious, Cannes is synonymous with *nouveau-riche* high life and glamour. There are sumptuous villas, palatial hotels, a central Gold-Card shopping area, an old quarter on the hill and a wonderful flower market, but life focuses on the beachside **Croisette**. This majestic, vivacious curve of palm-lined promenade around a bay of dazzling blue is the greatest of the town's sights.

Lord Brougham of Cannes

Cannes' days as a fishing community ended abruptly in 1834. In that year, charismatic English politician Lord Brougham, accompanied by his sick daughter Eleonore, was denied access to Nice because of a cholera outbreak. Pausing at Cannes, Brougham was so taken with the place that he bought land west of the village and had a luxurious villa built. Scores of leading figures followed his example, rapidly transforming the village into a high-class resort.

In a magnificent setting, the lavish *belle-époque* waterfront hotels range from the domed, richly stuccoed **Carlton** hotel, the film stars' favourite, via the **Majestic**, to the art-deco **Martinez**. The central stretch of sand is mostly out of bounds, except for guests of the grand hotels, who pay to sit under themed coloured parasols. Alternatively, there are public areas of beach at both ends.

127

Le Suquet and the Port

At the western end of the Croisette is the appealing marina and old port area, where a more homely, laid-back mood prevails. On the busy road behind, there are shops and good restaurants. A delightful flower market in allées de la Liberté is adorned with a statue of Cannes' 'discoverer', Lord Brougham. The historic quarter of Cannes is little Le Suquet, rising west of the port, where narrow medieval lanes and stairways wind around the hill. The lovely tree-lined terrace from the 16th-century Provençal Gothic church to the **Tour du Suquet** gives a wonderful view over the city, port and bay.

Cassis

Tourist information: place Baragnon. Tel: 04 42 01 71 17; fax: 04 42 01 28 31.

This jaunty little town backed by pale cliffs is known throughout France for its wines; it is one of the oldest vineyard regions in the country. Its white is the most famous, though local growers also make reds and *rosés*. Cassis also made a name for itself in the 1900s as the regular summer meeting place of the artists Matisse, Dufy, Derain and Vlaminck. It's easy to see what drew them here. The attractive port is busy with yachts, there's a little museum of local history, an old castle, a small, crowded sand-and-pebble beach, and woods of fragrant *garrigue* and parasol pines rise up behind the town.

Châteauneuf-du-Pape

Tourist information: place Portail. Tel: 04 90 83 71 08; fax: 04 90 83 50 34.

North and south from Avignon, the Rhône passes a succession of feudal fortresses, and on its banks are famous vineyards. None is more acclaimed than this exquisitely pretty, if somewhat touristy, village, with its pristine, restored medieval buildings, lovely riverside views and heady rich red wine. All around are the well-kept vineyards, and in a historic wine cellar there is a museum of winemaking, the **Musée des Outils de Vignerons**. Only ruins survive of the popes' fortress where they came for summer outings from Avignon.

Èze

Tourist information: place Général de Gaulle. Tel: 04 93 41 26 00; fax: 04 93 41 04 80.

A classic *village perché*, tiny fortified Èze stands atop an extraordinary pinnacle hundreds of metres above the sea. Today, thousands of visitors wander its picturesque narrow lanes, alleys and stairways. The old houses have become arty little shops, and the village has been lovingly painted and adorned with flowers. Through a fine 14th-century gateway, a tangle of lanes leads to the **Chapelle des**

Pénitents Blancs of the same period. The remains of the village's castle are encircled by the **Jardin Exotique** cactus garden. The views from the site are breathtaking – sometimes taking in Corsica.

Gigondas

On the quiet slopes of the Dentelles de Montmirail, Gigondas produces one of the best of the local red wines. With its old houses and lovely shaded main square, it is also one of the prettiest villages in the area.

Gordes

Tourist information: place du Château. Tel: 04 90 72 02 75.

The atmospheric old village of Gordes is built in a curious manner – one house almost on top of another – on the sides of a steep hill with a **château** at the summit.

The village streets are narrow – sometimes arcaded, sometimes in steps. All around Gordes are settlements of *bories* – ancient and primitive stone huts, lived in seasonally by peasants and labourers up until the 19th century.

Abbaye de Sénanque

Tel: 04 90 72 05 72. Open: Mar–Oct 1000–1200 and 1400–1700; rest of year 1400–1700. Closed Sun and all Christian holidays. ££.

The tranquil 12th-century Sénanque Abbey is hidden in the deep Sénancole valley close to **Gordes**. In summer, its simple beauty is enhanced by lines of thick purple lavender growing right up to the building. The monks make and sell oils and other products from their lavender.

Grasse

Tourist information: Palais de Congrès, 22 cours Honoré Cresp. Tel: 04 93 36 66 66; fax: 04 92 83 76 89.

The rather industrial town of Grasse is acknowledged to be the world's 'Capital of Perfume', with 75 per cent of all the world's bottles of perfume using Grasse essences. In the 16th century, Grasse quickly became acclaimed as having the most exquisitely scented perfumes, and spent the next century building up its industry. The town's three great *parfumeries* are **Molinard**, **Galimard** and **Fragonard**. All three combine factories with an elegant house and gardens, and offer enjoyable guided visits. The **Musée de la Parfumerie** deals with perfume's 3 000-year history. The appealing **Old Town** is a medieval district of narrow alleys, steep stairways and tall, thin houses.

Hyères

Tourist information: Rotonde J Salusse, avenue Belgique. Tel: 04 94 65 18 55; fax: 04 94 35 85 05.

This sedate, pleasant coastal town is the most southerly of the Riviera resorts, and also one of the oldest. A Greek town established well over 2 000 years ago, by the 18th century, it was already being discovered as a resort. Today's Hyères has a resolutely modern look, with broad, light, palm-lined boulevards. **Avenue Godillot** is one of the most beautiful streets; its Anglican church is a reminder that the place found favour with English visitors, including Queen Victoria. At the heart of the modern districts is the **Vieille Ville** (Old Town), enclosed by a defensive wall of dwellings. Tall Italianate buildings line steep paved streets and lanes, and triangular place Massillon is filled either with market stalls or restaurant tables.

On the menu

The classic Provençal fish stew bouillabaisse originated in Marseille and – so gastronomes claim – can only be made correctly here. Marseille fish restaurants generally offer several versions of the dish, and the most dedicated sign up to a deadly serious bouillabaisse charter.

Marseille

Tourist information: 4 La Canebière. Tel: 04 91 13 89 00; fax: 04 91 13 89 20.
Open: Mon–Sat 0900–1900; Sun 1000–1700. Longer hours in peak season.

France's second city is a sprawling, squalid, teeming, energetic and visually stunning Mediterranean metropolis, which encloses a major industrial harbour. Sightseeing in Marseille spans the centuries, from museums of its ancient Greek beginnings and remnants of medieval defences, to the concrete tower block – la Cité Radieuse – designed by Le Corbusier.

Marseille's new port

The Port Autonome de Marseille (Marseille Port Authority) is today's governing body for the city's shipping and sea-trading, carried on here continuously for over 26 centuries. Today it is Europe's third-largest port. The Vieux Port has been abandoned to pleasure craft; the city's maritime activities now occupy the 30km (18¹/₂ miles) of quays and warehouses from La Joliette (next to Vieux Port) to Fos-sur-Mer.

Vieux Port

The lively Vieux Port area, with its boat-filled harbour and narrow streets, is *the* place to stroll, relax and enjoy a meal of classic Marseille fish dishes. The historic port is the best (and best known) of all the sights in this ancient maritime city. The original harbour was constructed here in 600 BC. Today's rectilinear fortified harbour, with its handsome Italianate quays, is mainly 17th century. Facing west, under Marseille's typically clear blue skies, it is full of space and light. Overlooking one end of Vieux Port rises the daunting **Fort St-Nicolas** citadel. Behind it, **Basilique St-Victor** is a remarkably heavily fortified Romanesque church with an interesting 5th-century crypt. On the other side of the port entrance, the **Fort St-Jean** stands guard. To the south rises **Notre-Dame-de-la-Garde**, standing high and alone with its vast gilded statue.

Monaco

Tourist information: 2A boulevard des Moulins. Tel: (00-377) 92 16 61 16; fax: (00-377) 92 16 90 00. Open: Mon–Sat 0900–1900; Sun 1000–1200.

On a precipitous mountain slope plunging into a rocky sea, the mini-state of Monaco is a curious, privileged anomaly. There's little to do here but stroll, shop, people-watch and enjoy life, but it is beautiful and the setting is awe-inspiring.

Monaco-Ville

In the 13th century, the Genoese Grimaldi family acquired a medieval fortress, and have held it ever since as the capital of their tiny independent state. Dominating the rock today is the small 13th- to 17th-century **Palais du Prince** (Prince's Palace) (*tel: 93 25 18 31; open: June–Oct 0930–1830, closed if royal family present; ££*) within its robust fortifications. The entertaining **Changing of the Guard** takes place (*daily at 1155*) in the courtyard outside. Behind the palace, the **Vieille Ville** (Old Quarter) has attractive shaded streets.

Monaco's best attraction is the **Musée Océanographique** (*avenue St-Martin; tel: 93 15 36 00, fax: 92 16 77 93; open: Mar–Oct 0930–1900, Nov–Feb 1000–1800, closed on Sun pm of Grand Prix; £££*), one of Europe's leading marine science and sea-life museums. Its magnificent **aquarium** has around 350 different species.

Monte-Carlo

This zone, created in 1866, is the Monaco of glamour and glitz, with grand hotels and the opulent **Casino** (*place du Casino; tel: 92 16 23 00; open: daily all year from 1200; £££; over-21s only – passport required; no casual dress in* Salons Privés). Outside, there are immaculate palm and flower gardens. Inside, the extravagant Pink Saloon bar has ceiling frescos depicting nudes smoking cigars.

Menton

Tourist information: Palais de l'Europe, 8 avenue Boyer. Tel: 04 93 57 57 00; fax: 04 93 57 51 00.

Once one of the most prestigious Riviera resorts, sedate Menton was a winter haunt of many aristocratic and well-to-do Victorians, including Queen Victoria herself, who visited in 1882. It still has some charm, with lemon and orange trees growing on steep terraces behind the town, and interesting connections with the artist Jean Cocteau.

Tip

Thanks to its sheltered position, Menton has the warmest winters on the Riviera, and is the only place in France where oranges and lemons are cultivated. At the Maria Serena exotic garden, the temperature has never been below 5°C, even though in 1990 snow fell during the Lemon Festival – for the first time on record.

Rising steeply behind the Les Sablettes beach is the Italianate **Vieille Ville**, the mainly 17th-century old quarter of steps, alleys and mansions. Rue St-Michel, pedestrianised and lined with citrus trees, and place aux Herbes, are focal points. In Menton's 17th-century Italianate town hall, the **Salle des Mariages** (Wedding Room) is decorated with an allegorical mural by Cocteau.

Mont Ventoux

In the northwest corner of Vaucluse rises a great Provençal landmark, the pale conical mass of Mont Ventoux (1 909m, or 6 263ft), listed as a World Biosphere Reserve by Unesco. The name means 'windy mountain', and it certainly is, with temperatures substantially lower at the summit than at the foot (usually the drop is about 11°C/20°F). The view from the top is quite amazing on a clear day, taking in the Alps, the Rhône Valley and the Vaucluse Plateau. Although it's a popular excursion, the drive to the summit should not be undertaken lightly; on cold winter days, the temperature at the top can fall to –25°C. From Christmas to Easter, the summit is usually snow-capped. In early summer, it becomes green and flower-covered.

Nice

Tourist information: Gare SNCF, avenue Thiers. Tel: 04 93 87 07 07; fax: 04 93 16 85 16. Open: summer Mon–Sat 0800–2000, Sun 0800–1200; winter Mon–Sun 0800–1900.

The majestic azure sweep of Nice's Baie des Anges and its immense sidewalk, with its mimosas and palm trees, still take the breath away. For 200 years Nice has been the dynamic and sophisticated 'Queen of the Riviera'.

In the northeast of the town, **Cimiez**, once very grand, has two exceptional art museums and the Roman **Parc des Antiquités** (*avenue Monte Croce; open: Apr–Sept 1000–1200 and 1400–1800, Oct–Mar 1000–1300 and 1400–1700; £*). In the park, the **Musée Henri Matisse** (*164 avenue des Arènes de Cimiez; tel: 04 93 81 08 08, fax: 04 93 53 00 22; open: Apr–Sept 1000–1800, Oct–Mar 1000–1700, closed Tue and holidays; ££*) is housed in a beautifully adapted 17th-century mansion.

Nice's majestic, elegant seafront **Promenade des Anglais** was built by the British gentry in the 1820s. Among the glorious buildings lining it is the world-famous pink-domed **Hôtel Negresco**.

Le Vieux Nice – Old Nice – is a haven for strolling, shopping, exploring or lingering over a coffee. The old quarter is bordered on the north and west by the wide green **Promenade du Paillon**, which is the site for the world-famous **Musée d'Art Moderne et d'Art Contemporain** (Museum of Modern and Contemporary Art) (*promenade des Arts; tel: 04 93 62 61 62, fax: 04 93 13 09 01; open: 1000–1800, closed Tue and some holidays*).

Villefranche

On the outskirts of Nice. Tourist information: square François Binon. Tel: 04 93 01 73 68; fax: 04 93 76 63 65.

This fascinating little harbour town is on a hill so steep that some streets tunnel beneath houses in other streets! Its appeal lies in its Italianate buildings in ochre, pastel pinks and yellows and its picturesque quayside.

Nîmes

Tourist information: 6 rue Auguste. Tel: 04 66 67 29 11; fax: 04 66 21 81 04. Opening times for all Roman monuments: daily June–Sept 0830–1930; Oct–May 0900–1200 and 1400–1700 (closed Sun mornings, Tue, 1–2 Jan, 1 and 11 Nov, 25–26 Dec). Entry to Roman monuments is cheaper with a combined ticket. ££.

This city west of the Rhône has an impressive collection of Roman monuments, but its vibrant, up-to-date character dates from the 19th century, when it was a leading textile-processing town. Here, Levi Strauss found the cloth he needed to manufacture the first jeans – *de Nîmes* became 'denim'.

Gladiator!

Judging by the height of its podium wall, the 20,000-seat Nîmes arena was almost certainly primarily given over to contests between human beings rather than animals. The most spectacular and popular of entertainments were the gladiatorial combats – fights to the death between trained men. Today, the arena is in frequent use for traditional Spanish-style bullfights.

The most remarkable remnant of Roman *Nemausus* is its astonishingly intact, oval amphitheatre (*Les Arènes, place des Arènes; tel: 04 66 67 29 11; open: summer 0900–1830, winter 0900–1200 and 1400–1700; ££*), constructed early in the 1st century. The interior retains its rows of seats, and beneath the seating are fascinating vaulted corridors. During the medieval period the arena was entirely filled with squalid dwellings. Clearance began in the late 18th century, and the arena was used again in about 1850.

135

The Maison Carrée (*place de la Comédie, off rue Perrier; tel: 04 66 67 29 11; open: summer 0900–1900, winter 0900–1200 and 1400–1800, closed holidays; ££*), a 'squared-off (*carrée*), neatly beautiful building, is a temple standing by itself in a little square. It has survived since AD 5 astonishingly well, yet the extreme praise it has inspired is somewhat puzzling. Irascible author Smollett described it as 'ravishingly beautiful', and the well-travelled writer Arthur Young called it 'beyond all comparison the most pleasing building I ever beheld'.

Orange

Main tourist information: Cours A Briand. Tel: 04 90 34 70 88; fax: 04 90 34 99 62. Summer office: place Frères Mounet. Guided tours available.

The busy town of Orange, the Catholic principality that came into Dutch hands, formally became part of France as recently as 1713. It possesses some striking antiquities, including an immense wall that Louis XIV described as 'the finest in my kingdom'.

The other side of the wall was the original backdrop for the **Théâtre Antique** (Roman Theatre) (*tel: 04 90 34 70 88; open: Apr–Sept 0900–1830, rest of year 0900–1200 and 1330–1700, closed 1 Jan and 25 Dec; ££*), which still provides the setting for concerts and plays today. It's the best-preserved Roman theatre surviving anywhere. From the adjacent hill, a viewing platform gives an excellent overview of the Roman district. Across the road, the **Musée Municipal** displays the Romans' Land Survey of Orange, inscribed on marble.

The lively and attractive medieval central district, called **Vieil Orange**, has little squares, narrow streets and cafés. On the north side of town, standing incongruously on an island encircled by the N7, the **Arc de Triomphe** is a majestic three-arched monument covered in carvings, dating from about 20 BC. The north side has survived in remarkably good condition.

Pont du Gard

3km (2 miles) from Remoulins. Tourist information: tel: 04 66 37 00 02. Out of season: tel: 04 66 21 02 51. To drive across the bridge (strictly out of season only), approach from the north bank.

This amazing honey-coloured stone bridge was essential to the existence of Roman Nîmes. High and narrow, it strides across the broad, shallow Gard in its deep green valley. It has three tiers of elegant arches, and is a triumph not just of engineering but of design and aesthetics. It is awesome to think of all the (slave) labour and mathematical skill that the Romans expended on carrying a water pipe across a river.

The lower arches now carry a roadway, which provides the main access to the bridge. Along the top runs a small covered water channel, the original purpose of the edifice – the rest was built just to hold this channel at the right height and angle. Through it 20,000 cubic metres (706,714 cubic ft) of water flowed daily.

Part of a 50-km (31-mile) aqueduct built in 19 BC to bring fresh stream water from Uzès to Nîmes, the Pont du Gard was in use for a thousand years, 500 without any maintenance, yet it survives today in nearly intact condition. The lofty water channel can be walked through, and daredevils even walk along the unprotected top of the bridge, which is 3.5m (11 1/2 ft) wide and has a 50m (164ft) drop. The riverbanks at the foot of the bridge are beach-like and popular for sunbathing.

St-Paul-de-Vence

Tourist information: Maison Tour, rue Grande (part of the fortifications at the village entrance). Tel: 04 93 32 86 95; fax: 04 93 32 60 27.

This ancient hilltop fortress-village remains beautifully preserved, with imposing **ramparts** that are spectacular from afar. Despite the touristy shops, the village is stunningly picturesque. Its early Gothic **church** contains extraordinary art treasures, including a Tintoretto. St-Paul was a great favourite of Picasso, Braque, Chagall (who died here), Modigliani and other artists. Millions of francs' worth of their work hangs on the walls of the **Auberge de la Colombe d'Or**, where art pieces were once accepted as payment for meals and drinks.

St-Tropez

Tourist information: quai Jean-Jaurès. Tel: 04 94 97 79 08; fax: 04 94 97 45 21. Bus station. Tel: 04 94 97 41 21; www.nova.fr/saint-tropez

True, St-Tropez has long traffic queues, palatial yachts, a pounding nightlife, chic boutiques and thousands of self-conscious visitors, including the rich and famous, but it's still a nice, pretty, friendly little town with a busy port and attractive houses. The **harbour** is lined with boutiques and bars.

Along the shore, **La Ponche** is the former fishermen's quarter. On a hilltop at the east end of town, the imposing **Citadelle** gives wonderful views over St-Trop' and the sea. Explore away from the harbour, too, in the little squares and narrow paved streets of the **Vieille Ville** (Old Town), and watch boule being played under the leafy plane trees of the **place des Lices**.

St-Rémy-de-Provence

Tourist information: place Jean-Jaurès. Tel: 04 90 92 05 22; fax: 04 90 92 38 52. Guided tours.

St-Rémy is a delightful, historic yet modest Provençal country town and market-gardening centre. At its heart it has a picturesque old quarter of lanes and squares with fine old 16th- to 18th-century mansions and fountains, and avenues shaded by plane trees. Cult astrologer Nostradamus (1503–66) was born here.

Les Antiques and *Glanum*

Beside the D5, 1km (¹/₂ mile) outside St-Rémy. Free unsupervised access.

Les Antiques were the last structures left standing after the destruction of the Roman town of *Glanum* by barbarians in the 3rd century. The dramatic **Roman mausoleum**, 18m tall, is the best surviving example anywhere. Next to it, the handsome **Roman arch** is also decorated with carvings, probably by Greek craftsmen. The more serious *Glanum* **archaeological site** (*beside the D5; tel: 04 90 92 23 79; open: Apr–Sept 0900–1900, rest of year 0900–1200 and 1400–1700, closed holidays; £££*) has a huge number of relics.

Les Baux-de-Provence

Tourist information: 30 Grande Rue. Tel: 04 90 54 34 39; fax: 04 90 54 51 15.

On a dramatic cliff edge at the heart of the Alpilles, Les Baux was an important seigneurial fortress of the Middle Ages. Today, the village has hardly any permanent residents, but many craftspeople thrive on the day visitors who come to see the narrow, picturesque streets of restored buildings. The town now consists of a 'modern', mainly 16th-century village, and the ruins of its spectacular rock-carved medieval stronghold. There is plenty to see, including views over the surrounding hills.

Vaison-la-Romaine

Tourist information: place Sautel (between the two Roman sites). Tel: 04 90 36 02 11; fax: 04 90 28 76 04.

The agreeable small town of Vaison, with its big, colourful weekly market, is a place for strolling and relaxing at open-air tables, and a good base for exploring the region. In fact, Vaison is three towns, all of them interesting, the newest lying partly on top of the oldest. On the north bank of the Ouvèze was the Gallo-Roman city *Vasio Vocantiorum*. In the Middle Ages the town moved over to the better defended hill south of the river. During more recent times, life extended back on to the north bank, and many of the Roman ruins were built over. The original **Pont Romain**, an elegant 2 000-year-old single-arch cobbled bridge crossing the Ouvèze, still links the medieval **Ville Haute** with the north bank.

Since 1907, in a succession of excavations, the Roman town has been partly uncovered again in two large sites (covering over 15 hectares, or 37 acres). The huge upper site, **Quartier du Puymin**, has paved streets, walls, frescos, mosaics, statuary and a complete restored theatre. The best features of the smaller lower site, **Quartier de la Villasse**, are the street of little shops and the mosaic floors of the villas. The **Musée Archéologique** has an impressive collection of Roman sculpture.

The Vaison flood

On 22 September 1992, a violent storm over the Dentelles increased in intensity. Between Beaumes and Vaison, already saturated, 256 litres per square metre fell in three hours. The Ouvèze rose 20m (65¹/₂ ft) in one hour and flowed right over the top of Vaison's Roman bridge. The river destroyed a riverbank campsite and 104 new waterside houses. The Roman bridge survived almost intact, but 43 people around the Dentelles lost their lives, including 22 at Vaison.

Grand Canyon du Verdon

Moustiers-Ste-Marie tourist information: Hôtel-Dieu. Tel: 04 92 74 67 84; fax: 04 92 74 60 65.

On both sides of France's Grand Canyon, sheer rock faces (up to 700m (2 297ft) high) plunge down to the twisting ribbon of the Verdon river. On the clifftop road, a succession of *Points Sublimes* offer amazing views into and across the precipitous ravine, the deepest and most impressive river gorge in Europe. On the north side of the canyon, a circular drive of 23km (14 miles) gives a succession of breathtaking vistas. The south side – the Corniche Sublime, a longer drive – is even more grandiose. A tortuous 75-km (47-mile) round trip views the gorge from both the north and the south. The Verdon canyon ends at **Moustiers-Ste-Marie**.

Moustiers-Ste-Marie

Tourist information: Hôtel-Dieu. Tel: 04 92 74 67 84; fax: 04 92 74 60 65.

Moustiers is a marvellously picturesque medieval village of narrow streets and stairways, and attractive old houses, built precariously on the slopes of a spectacular ravine. Curiously, a gilded star hangs on a chain right across the ravine; it's said to be a votive offering made by a Crusader who was freed from captivity. The town's **church** is a fine Romanesque building with a curious Gothic choir. The name of Moustiers is synonymous with a certain style of fine earthenware, made here from the 17th to the 19th centuries. The craft was revived in the 1920s, and modern examples are on sale in many shops in the town.

Eating and drinking

L'Amphytron
2–4 rue Paul Doumer, Aix-en-Provence. Tel: 04 42 26 54 10; fax: 04 42 38 36 15. Closed Sun, Mon midday. ££. Picture-book Provence where you can eat out of doors, with high-quality fresh-from-the-market menus of regional dishes and local wines.

Le Bistro Latin
18 rue de la Couronne, Aix-en-Provence. Tel: 04 42 38 22 88; fax: 04 42 38 22 88. Closed Sun, Mon midday. £. In a narrow Vieil Aix street, simple, excellent Provençal menus in an intimate art-deco setting.

Café des Deux Garçons
Cours Mirabeau, Aix-en-Provence. £. One of the most famous bars in France with a convivial atmosphere, traditional service and an original late 18th-century interior.

In **Arles**, scores of town-centre restaurants and brasseries offer value-for-money set menus, particularly along boulevard des Lices and in place Forum.

Belle Arti
19 rue des Lices, Avignon. Tel: 04 90 27 30 24. £. First-class authentic Italian cooking using fresh seasonal produce, served in a warm, convivial atmosphere at very modest prices.

Les Domaines
28 place de l'Horloge, Avignon. Tel: 04 90 82 58 86. ££. The place de l'Horloge has many eating places, but most offer predictable tourist menus. At this one, the cooking is a cut above the rest.

Hiely Lucullus
5 rue de la République, Avignon. Tel: 04 90 86 17 07. ££. Long-established Avignon favourite offering acclaimed and inspired cooking, with excellent fish dishes and exquisite sauces, in a relaxed setting. Prices represent an amazing bargain.

You'll find hundreds of pricey places to eat on and off **Cannes'** boulevard de la Croisette. For lower priced places look along rue Meynadier, quai St-Pierre on the west side of the port, and along rue Suquet and rue St-Antoine which climb into Le Suquet.

Restaurant La Magnanerie
Avenue Georges Pompidou, Le Cannet. Tel: 04 93 46 44 22; fax: 04 93 45 38 93. ££. Enjoy good cooking with local wines, served either indoors at this atmospheric 18th-century house or on the flowery terrace.

Restaurant Montagnard
6 rue du Marcéchal Joffre, Cannes. Tel: 04 93 39 98 38. ££. This vegetarian restaurant just off la Croisette offers creative and skilful cooking of the highest standard. Imaginative dishes (including some fish) reflect what is fresh, organic and in season.

Restaurant Pacific
8 rue du Suquet, Cannes. Tel: 04 93 39 43 43. £. Robust cooking using whatever is available from the fishing boats, served in a convivial setting popular with locals.

Oustalet

place Portail, Gigondas. Tel: 04 90 65 85 30. £. A delightful spot – tables out of doors in the main square of this tiny village, tasty dishes made from local ingredients, and local wines at modest prices.

In **Marseille, rue St-Saens** is lined with restaurants serving *fruits de mer, marmite du pêcheur* and other fish specialities. For bouillabaisse alongside the Vieux Port, **Miramar ££** (*12 quai du Port; tel: 04 91 91 10 40, fax: 04 91 56 64 31*) is the place. Michelin-rosetted, it's more than a cut above most of the other quayside eateries.

Café de Paris

place du Casino, Monaco. Tel: 92 16 20 20; fax: 92 16 38 58. ££. Good Italian food at a huge, historic *belle-époque* brasserie beside the Casino.

Restaurant Polpetta

2 rue du Paradis, Monaco. Tel: 93 50 67 84. ££. Italian is one way to eat well at modest prices in Monaco. This convivial, likeable, home-from-home restaurant has found favour with visiting Italian stars.

Restaurant Fleur de Sel

10 boulevard Dubouchage, Nice. Tel: 04 93 13 45 45. £. Nice's waterfront and Vieille Ville are packed with good little eateries. Here, away from the tourist trail, you can enjoy exceptional Provençal cooking, an attractive setting and good service at remarkably low prices.

Restaurant Zucca Magica

4 bis quai Papacino (port), Nice. Tel: 04 93 56 25 27. £–££. Idiosyncratic harbourside vegetarian restaurant serving imaginative, delicious dishes of fresh, seasonal produce straight from the market.

Le Colombier

Beside Pont du Gard on the right bank. Tel: 04 66 37 05 28. £. An unpretentious, traditional little hotel with an inexpensive terrace restaurant – the best spot from which to view the aqueduct, and the best place to be if you'd like to see the bridge after the crowds have gone home.

Touristy restaurants and brasseries cluster around the port of **St-Tropez**. Famous but overpriced brasseries include **Bar Tea Room Senequier** (*tel: 04 94 97 00 90; £££*); Pâtissier-Chocolatier Senequier, next door, is one of the best in town. In La Ponche, there are places with more local character. Place des Lices is the 'ordinary' end of St-Tropez, with some less expensive restaurants.

143

PROFILE

The *Route Napoléon*

In 1815, **Napoleon Bonaparte** *escaped from exile on the island of Elba and made his way to the French coast, landing on 1 March at Golfe-Juan. With a band of a thousand armed supporters, he made his way*

inland, meeting no resistance from local authorities and inspiring enthusiasm in the population. Today, the route he followed, mainly the N85, is marked by the sign of an eagle, and is a glorious drive through the mountainous backcountry of Provence.

For many French people, their national glory reached its height under the Corsican 'Little Emperor'. Born to militant Corsican separatists in 1769, Napoleon went on to make France the most powerful country in Europe, and to crown himself emperor. Along the way, he eliminated the old French regions, imposed a new legal system and invented the kilometre.

It took the combined might of Prussia, England, Austria and Russia to check the growing power of France under the emperor's leadership. By 1814, these ill-assorted allies had banished Napoleon to 'house arrest' on the island of Elba, close to Corsica. Although he escaped from Elba, Napoleon was destined to meet his Waterloo a matter of weeks later.

Compellingly attractive and in a superb location, **Castellane** is probably the most popular point on the *Route Napoléon*. (On 3 March 1815, at the invitation of the local authorities, Napoleon rested here at what is now the tourist office.) This modest mountain town has become terribly overcrowded, although local men still play boule in the main square.

Digne is another significant place on the *Route Napoléon* (the emperor stopped here for lunch). It is a bright, clean, prosperous and appealing town, refreshing and airy, dominated by the surrounding green hills, and is a great centre for lavender.

Napoleon's route – March 1815

1 March – 0500: Napoleon and around a thousand supporters land at **Golfe-Juan**. The men set up camp but later march to **Cannes** and rest briefly on the beach. They turn inland and walk through the night.

2 March – 0500: rest stop at **Grasse**. Lunch break at St-Vallier-de-Thiey. 1700: rest stop at **Escragnolles**. Night stop at **Séranon**. Napoleon is invited by the mayor of Grasse to spend the night in the **Château de Brondet**.

3 March – 0700: the men move off again. At the small town of **Logis du Pin**, refreshments are offered. 1200: lunch at **Castellane**. 2000: stop for the night at **Barrême**.

4 March – after an early start the group marches along a difficult mountain trail through the barren Pré-Alpes de Digne (now mainly the D20). The men pause in **Digne**. 1500: the group moves off again. Overnight stop beside the River Bléone at **Malijai**, where Napoleon spends the night at the château.

5 March – 0600: the group continues on the left bank of the Durance. At Volonne: a rest stop. Braced for resistance, the men enter **Sisteron**, but are not challenged. They take a break there. Napoleon lunches at the Hôtel du Bras d'Or. 1500: the men continue the journey and march until 2200, when they arrive at **Gap** and set up camp.

Languedoc and the Massif

This varied region remains predominantly rural and off the beaten track. It's less well known – and less crowded – than its neighbour, Provence, yet it offers glossy coastal resorts, wild remote plateaux, towering mountains, deep gorges, forests and caves, and charming, low-key cities and towns – and a rich and fascinating history. Today, vineyards cover the flat Languedoc plain and stretch up the sunny slopes of the Corbières hills, transforming the landscape as their leaves change colour.

LANGUEDOC AND THE MASSIF

Languedoc
and the Massif

Getting there: *The main airports are Montpellier, Toulouse and Carcassonne. The main stations are Montpellier and Toulouse. From Paris, the A71 is the most direct road to the Languedoc. The journey from Calais is 1 000km, or 621 miles. The shortest route across France is from the port of St-Malo.*

① *Albi*

The 'red town' at the centre of the bloody anti-Cathar Albigensian Crusades, and the birthplace of world-famous artist Toulouse-Lautrec. **Page 150**

② *Carcassonne*

Walk the ramparts of this perfect reconstruction of a fortified medieval town and take yourself back in time. It's actually two cities – the citadel and the lower town – one a place of fantasy and one that brings you back to reality. **Page 151**

③ *The* Causses

In the four great limestone plateaux of the Cévennes, sheep graze and birds of prey wheel above a wild landscape. Rivers have cut their way between the *causses*, and now flow in deep wooded ravines that twist below towering 500m cliffs. The roads cut into the cliff sides offer views of some of the most dramatic scenery in France. **Page 152**

④ *Conques*

Difficult to get to in its mountain fastness, Conques is well worth the journey if you are a fan of Romanesque architecture. This is one of the finest of the churches built along the pilgrimage route that linked southwestern France to the Pyrenees and the road to Santiago de Compostela in northwestern Spain. **Page 153**

⑤ *Gorges du Tarn*

One of the most famous stretches of river in France, cutting through limestone to create a deep canyon. Driving on the twisting and steep roads around here is not for the faint-hearted. **Page 155**

⑥ *Perpignan*

Enjoy the Franco-Spanish atmosphere of this lively, sunny southern city. Sit at a pavement café, witness the traditional Catalan dance, the *sardana*, or pop down the coast to the delightful port of Collioure for a seafood supper. **Pages 160-1**

⑦ *Toulouse*

The 'pink city' that grew rich on the production of blue dye, or woad, Toulouse is today the centre of France's aerospace industry. Find an outside table at one of its excellent restaurants, and enjoy the sight of the setting sun lighting up its elegant red-brick mansions. **Pages 164-5**

149

Albi

Tourist information: Palais de la Berbie, place Ste-Cécile. Tel: 05 63 49 48 80; e-mail: mairie.albi@ilink.fr; www.mairie.albi.fr.

Built in brick, this vivacious little city has two major features – its fortress-like cathedral and its associations with the artist Toulouse-Lautrec. In the 13th century the city lent its name to the bloody Albigensian Crusade, when Catholics wiped out the local Cathars. In the 16th century, it grew rich from woad, and in 1896, Jean-Jaurès founded France's first trade union at a local factory.

Fact

Albi's cathedral has a unique treasure in its organ, which is France's biggest, and has 3 500 pipes.

The forbidding **Cathédrale Ste-Cécile** was built at the end of the Crusade, to emphasise the power of Catholicism. Constructed in long thin pink bricks, it is a masterpiece of southern Gothic style. Inside, surprisingly, the huge vaulted roof is covered in beautiful, mainly royal blue and pale yellow frescos.

Place du Vigan, a large bustling 18th-century square, separates the medieval and modern quarters of the town. On summer evenings, crowds congregate in its cafés and bars. The 900-year-old **Pont Vieux**, with six uneven arches, is one of France's oldest bridges. It had houses on it until 1766, when floods swept them away.

Toulouse-Lautrec

The artist Henri de Toulouse-Lautrec was born in Albi in 1864. His birthplace, the **Hôtel de Bosc** mansion (*14 rue Toulouse-Lautrec; not open to the public*), has been in his family for over 300 years. He suffered a couple of awkward falls in this house and these, compounded by genetic problems (his parents were cousins), ultimately caused his disablement. The world's largest collection of his work is housed in the **Musée Toulouse-Lautrec** (*Palais de la Berbie, next to cathedral; tel: 05 63 49 48 70; open: daily (variable hours) Apr–Sept, Wed–Mon Oct–Mar; ££*), where formal gardens blaze with colour in summer.

Carcassonne

Tourist information: 15 boulevard Camille-Pelletan, Ville Basse. Tel: 04 68 10 24 30; www.tourisme.fr/carcassonne/. Open: Mon–Sat (Sat morning only). Guided tours. Or Porte Narbonnaise, la Cité. Tel: 04 68 10 24 36. Open: daily. Guided visits June–Sept.

Carcassonne has two distinct faces – **la Cité** and the **Ville Basse** – separated by the River Aude. The former is a formidable medieval citadel on a high crag, completely restored at the end of the 19th century. The Ville Basse is the 'New Town', which King Louis IX had built in 1260, on a grid layout typical of a bastide (fortified town).

The citadel is a very convincing 19th-century restoration of a 12th-century fortified town. Only 130 people actually live there, but Carcassonne attracts over a quarter of a million visitors each year. It has high double walls stretching for over 1km (1/2 mile), and 52 towers. Its highlights are the castle – the **Château Comtal** (*guided visits only, daily; ££*) – and the **Basilique St-Nazaire**, which has outstanding 14th- to 15th-century stained glass. A 3-km (2-mile) broad grassy ditch – *les lices* – runs round la Cité. It was used for jousting tournaments and arrow-shooting practice.

The 'New Town' was built following the destruction of the area during the Albigensian Crusade. Wide boulevards shaded by plane trees have replaced the ramparts. The **Cathédrale St-Michel**, in rue Voltaire, is typically southern Gothic in style, with a single large nave. The town's oldest mansion is the 13th-century **Maison du Sénéchal** (*rue du Dr Albert Tomey*), where the king's representative lived.

The *Causses*

The *Grands Causses* are the four massive limestone plateaux lying to the west of the Cévennes – Sauveterre, Larzac, Noir and Lévézou. Topped by poor dry soil, because water drains easily away through the rock, they are impressively bleak and barren, though grazed by sheep in summer. The coarse tufty grass is dotted with hardy plants such as thistles, lavender and juniper. In winter, cold winds whistle relentlessly across the *causses*.

La Couvertoirade

Tourist information: Mairie (town hall). Tel: 05 65 58 55 59. Entrance including 20-minute video about the village £ Easter–Nov (then free but the rest of the village is closed up in winter). Guided visits in English available July–Aug.

La Couvertoirade is a mini-Carcassonne, completely surrounded by high ramparts. It was built by the Knights Templars in 1158 as a staging post for pilgrims on the old Roman road across the *causse*. A few of the buildings have been restored, and there are a handful of shops and cafés. Walk round the ramparts and look down on the main street, which is lined by little 17th-century houses.

Roquefort-sur-Soulzon

Tourist information: avenue de Lauras. Tel: 05 65 58 56 00.

This unprepossessing town at the foot of the Combalou plateau – home of the world-famous cheese – enjoys splendid views over the *Grands Causses*. As early as 1407, Charles VI granted the cheese its own brand name. Two cheese producers, **Caves de Roquefort Société** (*avenue François Galtier; open: daily; £*) and **Le Papillon** (*rue de la Fontaine; open: daily Apr–Sept, Oct–Mar Mon–Fri; free*), offer guided visits to their chilly caves.

Roquefort cheese

Made from unpasteurised ewes' milk, this ancient, world-famous cheese is injected with penicillium roquefortii *mould to produce its characteristic and tasty blue veins. The limestone caves under the Combalou plateau at the side of the town play a crucial role in its production; their temperature and humidity remain constant all year.*

Conques

153

Tourist information: Abbaye de Ste-Foy, Conques. Tel: 05 65 69 85 12.

Conques is a real treat for lovers of Romanesque architecture. Not only is the **Abbaye de Ste-Foy** a remarkable church, it is enhanced by a wildly romantic setting, against a background of wooded hills in the wild and lonely heart of the Massif Central. Highlights of the abbey-church are the tympanum carved with a vividly imagined tableau of the Last Judgement, and the Treasury, which contains one of Europe's finest and most important collections of medieval reliquaries, some dating from as early as the 5th century.

Corbières hills

Tourist information: 5 promenade du Tivoli, Limoux. Tel: 04 68 31 11 82.

The lively little town of **Limoux** is one of the highlights of the Corbières hills. Around it is Blanquette country, where, nearly 500 years ago, the world's first sparkling white wine was produced in the monastery at St-Hilaire. To the east, around **Lagrasse**, the vineyards that produce Corbières wines stretch up the hillsides, dotted with *domaines* (estates) where you can sample and buy. The scenery consists of limestone crags peeping through wooded hillsides, and long views to the distant Pyrenees. Ruined castles and the remains of ancient monasteries are forlorn reminders of the area's turbulent past.

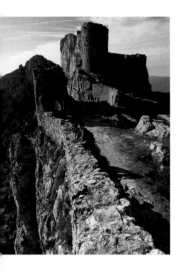

Château de Peyreperteuse

Access from Duilhac, up a winding 3.5km road to car park. Open: daily. ££.

This medieval fortress is the least ruined of the area's castles and one of the marvels of the Corbières. Dramatically sited on top of a rocky crest, on a site first used by the Romans, the ruins of two castles are spread along a 300-m (984-foot) ridge. The upper castle is only accessible on foot, which makes the feat of building the courtyards, towers and arches with the simple tools of the 12th century all the more remarkable.

Lagrasse

Tourist information: 6 boulevard de la Promenade. Tel: 04 68 43 11 56.

The capital of the Corbières, set beside the River Orbieu, surrounded by hills, is classified as one of the most beautiful little towns in France. The quaint medieval centre has a maze of narrow streets with several fine houses dating from around the 14th century, when the inhabitants made a good living from tanning leather and making cloth.

An 11th-century hump-backed bridge across the river leads to a splendid Benedictine abbey, **Ste-Marie d'Orbie**, founded in 799. Its buildings include a simple Romanesque church, the abbot's chapel with its decorative tiled floor, and a bell tower, worth climbing for the views.

Gorges du Tarn

From its source on Mont Lozère, the River Tarn flows west towards the *Grands Causses* where it cuts its way through the limestone plateaux. The Gorges du Tarn, one of the most spectacular in France, starts past Quézac and continues for 50km (31 miles) to le Rozier, running between orange cliffs and steep wooded hillsides below the *Causse Sauveterre* (to the north) and *Causse Méjean*. The river is fed by 40 springs, which burst from under ground and tumble into it as waterfalls. Villages are few and far between, as the water level can vary dramatically and unpredictably. Canoeing, pot-holing and rock-climbing are popular pursuits here.

In hiding

During the French Revolution, many nobles are known to have hidden in caves in the Tarn gorge.

Limoux Carnival

Every weekend from January to April the centre of Limoux is filled with carnival crowds, and costumed revellers dancing solemnly around the arcades accompanied by brass bands, pausing for refreshment at the bars. Some wave wands decorated with coloured strips of paper, while others carry sacks of coloured confetti to throw over the spectators. On the final evening a bonfire is lit in the centre of the square. Limoux's carnival tradition dates back to the Middle Ages when the local millers celebrated by throwing sugared almonds and flour.

Le Puy-en-Velay

Tourist information: place de Breuil. Tel: 04 71 09 38 41.

Woad

In the 16th century the 'golden triangle' between Toulouse, Albi and Carcassonne was famous throughout Europe for its woad (pastel in French), used for dyeing cloth to a fashionable blue. At the height of the trade, 500 mills were in operation, drying and preparing the yellow-flowered plant to create the dye. Eventually, woad was superseded by indigo, imported from India, but a few local people still grow it.

Le Puy is a remarkable town, not easy to get to but worth the effort for its theatrical setting and the drama of its chapel-topped volcanic peaks. The local bishop, Godescalk, made what is claimed to be the first pilgrimage to the shrine of St James at Santiago de Compostela in northwestern Spain in AD 962. He returned to build the **Chapelle St-Michel d'Aiguilhe**, which sits on top of one of the town's basalt peaks and is reached by climbing 265 steps. Other pilgrims followed, and the town's **Cathédral de Notre-Dame** was built to provide them with a suitably splendid building to mark the start of their 1 600-km (994-mile) walk. This extraordinary domed building was one of the first in Europe to incorporate Muslim elements, the architectural influence coming via Spain's trade links with the Arab world. The highlights of the church include the so-called Fever Stone, a prehistoric standing stone incorporated into the building and said to have curative powers, the statue of the Black Virgin (a copy of one destroyed in the Revolution) and the magnificent cloister, with its Romanesque carvings.

Limoges

Tourist information: boulevard de Fleurus. Tel: 05 55 34 46 87.

Limoges was renowned in the medieval period for the quality of its religious enamels, which can be seen incorporated into reliquaries throughout France and Europe – one 12th-century Limoges enamel depicting the martyrdom of Thomas à Becket recently fetched record prices at auction. Examples can be seen in the town's **Musée Municipal de l'Évêché** (*place de la Cathédrale; tel: 05 55 45 61 75; open: daily July–Aug, Wed–Mon rest of year; £*). In the 18th century Limoges enjoyed another craft renaissance when fine kaolin clay deposits were found close to the town, and the name of Limoges became synonymous with fine hand-painted porcelain: the **Musée National Adrien-Dubouché** contains enough examples to satisfy even the most devoted fan (*place Winston Churchill; tel: 05 55 33 08 50; open: Wed–Mon; £*).

Minerve

Tourist information: rue des Martyrs. Tel: 04 68 91 81 43. Guided tours include Église St-Étienne, which is closed otherwise.

For its dramatic setting and poignant history, this small village is the jewel of the Minervois. Its sandy coloured old houses with red roofs cluster along a rocky ledge with deep river gorges on either side. The main access is over a triple-arched bridge from which narrow streets lead up to the chimney-like tower of its ruined castle, past the 900-year-old Église St-Étienne. A handful of shops, cafés and *caves* offer tastings of Minervois wines.

A Cathar stronghold, the village held out for five weeks in 1210, besieged by Simon de Montfort and 7 000 men, finally giving in when de Montfort destroyed the only well. About 180 stood by their faith and were burned alive. Their courage is commemorated by a memorial stone on place de la Marie.

Tip

*Mirepoix's speciality is a **sauce** made from onions, carrots and celery. The recipe was first concocted for the Duke of Lévis-Mirepoix in the 18th century.*

Mirepoix

Tourist information: place Maréchal Leclerc. Tel: 05 61 68 83 76.

This attractive little town is a typical *bastide*, built in the shape of a grid around a central square, which has a covered market hall with a splendid 19th-century cast-iron roof. Many of the other buildings, 500 to 600 years old, are half-timbered

with sturdy carved beams jutting over ground-floor arcades. The square is a pleasant spot to pass the time of day. The **Cathédrale St-Maurice** has the widest nave in France.

Montpellier

Tourist information: le Triangle, allée du Tourisme. Tel: 04 67 58 67 58. Open: daily. Guided visits. Information kiosks: at the railway station, tel: 04 67 92 90 03; at the Rond Point des Prés d'Arènes (Sortie Sud autoroute exit), tel: 04 67 22 08 80 (June–Sept); www.cr-languedocroussillon.fr/tourisme/.

The citizens of Montpellier have a reputation for being sociable and good-natured. Much of this temperament is on view in the enormous **place de la Comédie**, laid out in the 18th century, and now surrounded by cafés and restaurants. At the heart of the city, it's a popular spot for chatting over Languedoc wine. The city used to be focused on the handsome **place de la Canourgue**, surrounded by grand mansions.

Montpellier has a student population of nearly 50,000. The city first made its mark on the world through its **medical school**, founded in 1220 (one of the oldest in the world) and still the most prestigious in France. It occupies former abbey buildings, much enlarged and renovated. Rabelais, the 16th-century French satirist, was one of its most famous graduates. In 1593, France's oldest botanical garden was planted, to enable the medical school students to study medicinal plants. The **Jardin des Plantes** (*163 rue Auguste Broussonnet; tel: 04 67 63 43 22; closed Sun; free*) has a 400-year-old *phillyrea latifolia* tree among its treasures.

Today, the city prides itself on being forward-looking – **Antigone**, constructed during the 1980s, is a daring post-Modern housing development in pseudo-classical style. Tall beige buildings, with columns, arches and pediments, face wide circular symmetrically tiled piazzas.

Narbonne

Tourist information: place Salengro. Tel: 04 68 65 15 60. Guided tours 15 June–30 Sept at 1000, 1400 and 1600. Information also at the Town Hall, place de l'Hôtel de Ville; www.Mairie-Narbonne.fr.

This small, vibrant city, surrounded by vineyards, inspires every visitor with a sense of history – in the centre, you can walk on the flat grey stones of a real Roman road. Founded by the Romans in 118 BC, the city became the capital of Gaul, their largest province. In the 12th century it was a thriving port; its cathedral – never completed – remains a remarkable symbol of that time.

Narbonne's massive **Cathédrale St-Just-et-St-Pasteur** (*rue A Gauthier*) was intended to be the biggest in Christendom. Sixty years after the first stone was laid, work was stopped, when the municipal authorities refused to allow the destruction of part of the city wall. By the time the wall was no longer needed for defence, the Narbonnais could not afford to extend the building.

Now what should have been the transept is a courtyard with delicately vaulted cloisters leading into the opulent **Palais des Archévêques** (Archbishops' Palace) (*place de l'Hôtel de Ville; open: daily; guided tours 15 June–15 Sept; ££*), a grand complex of halls, passages, towers and courtyards.

L'Horreum (*7 rue Rouget-de-l'Isle; tel: 04 68 32 45 30; open: daily Apr–Sept, closed Mon rest of year; ££*) is an extraordinarily well-preserved underground Roman storehouse. Because of its location, Narbonne traded extensively with other parts of the Roman empire, exporting meat and cheese from the Cévennes as well as oil, woad and hemp.

Perpignan

Basking almost continuously in Mediterranean sunshine, Perpignan has an attractive Franco-Spanish ambience – it used to be capital of French Catalonia – and always seems to buzz with activity. In the old town, paved with glistening red marble, the narrow streets are crammed with shops and pavement cafés. An aroma of spices wafts from the Arab quarter. By contrast, the avenues around the area are wide and lined with plane trees and palms. On Sundays and holidays, local people dance the traditional Catalan sardana *in the streets.*

The grand Gothic **Cathédrale de St-Jean** (*place de Gambetta; open: 0730–1200 and 1500–1900*) is topped by a bell encased in an intricate wrought-iron cage. The attractive façade is made of thin red bricks and river pebbles – frequently used in Roussillon because of the scarcity of stone. Next to the cathedral, the **Campo Santo** (*rue Amiral Ribeil; open: daily except Tue*), the former cemetery, is completely surrounded by cloisters. One of only two like it in Europe, it is now used for exhibitions and concerts.

Perpignan's **Hôtel de Ville** (*rue de la Loge*) also has a typical Roussillon façade of pebbles. Peep through the gates to see Maillol's famous bronze nude, *La Méditerranée*, on its patio.

The 15th-century red-brick **Le Castillet** gatehouse (*place de Verdun; tel: 04 68 35 42 05; open: daily except Tue; free*), with crenellations and a pink dome, is the only surviving part of the town's fortified walls. Climb the 142 steps to the top for a splendid panorama.

The **Palais des Rois de Majorque** (palace of the kings of Majorca) (*rue des Archers; open: daily; ££*) was built in 1276 when Perpignan, part of the kingdom of Majorca, became the mainland capital. It's more a fortress than a residence; flights of steps zigzag up to the ramparts and gardens. The kings of Aragon once kept lions in the moat. From the roof of the entrance tower, **Tour de l'Hommage**, there are splendid views towards the Canigou peak, symbol of Catalan unity.

Tourist information: Palais des Congrès, place Armand Lanoux. Tel: 04 68 66 30 30; www.little-france.com/perpignan. Guided walking tours. J'Informe *is a free monthly list of events.*

Collioure

Tourist information: place du 18 Juin. Tel: 04 68 82 15 47.

On the coast south of Perpignan, charming Collioure has been a magnet for artists since Matisse settled there in 1905. Narrow cobbled streets lead back from its much-painted harbour and small church, with its pink-domed tower. Along the quay, fishing boats tie up to deposit the anchovies for which the town is renowned. Unsurprisingly, Collioure's quayside restaurants are noted for their seafood.

St-Martin-du-Canigou

3km (2 miles) south of Vernet-les-Bains. Tel: 04 68 05 62 28. Walk up from the village of Casteil (45 minutes) or go by guided 4x4 vehicle from Vernet or Villefranche-de-Conflent. £.

Perched on a rocky outcrop at 1 055m (3 461ft), this monastery's red rooftops and square bell tower provide a landmark for miles around. The monks had to abandon it during the French Revolution, but in 1902 the ruins were bought by the Bishop of Perpignan, and the monks were finally able to move back in 1972.

The Little Yellow Train

The unique fortified medieval town of Villefranche-de-Conflent is the starting point of the Petit Train Jaune (Little Yellow Train), one of Europe's most scenic railway lines. Constructed between 1910 and 1927, to connect the remote villages in the foothills of the Pyrénées, the bright yellow electric trains are now mainly used by tourists. Walk around Villefranche's ramparts (open: daily) to be transported back in time.

St-Guilhem-le-Désert

Tourist information: 2 rue de la Font du Portal. Tel: 04 67 57 44 33. Guided walks.

This medieval village is spread up the narrow Verdus gorge between green hillsides. Small houses in beige stone line the two narrow lanes leading up to its 11th-century monastery church, the massive, rather plain and austere **Abbaye de Gellone** (*guided visits every afternoon June–Sept; £*). Its main treasure is a fragment of Christ's Cross given to Guilhem by his lifelong friend Charlemagne.

Salers

Tourist information: place Tyssandier d'Escous. Tel: 04 71 40 70 68.

Salers is one of the most attractive towns in the Monts Dore region, renowned for the survival almost intact of its beautiful turreted medieval and Renaissance houses, so that the town centre looks unchanged since the 16th century. Many of the houses are grander than might be expected of such a remote place, but Salers was once the administrative capital of the Auvergne, and its townspeople lavished money on their homes to emphasise their prestige.

Salers can be very busy with visitors in summer, but escape is at hand if you want to head for the highlands. You can drive to the top of **Puy Mary**, a distinctive volcanic peak in the Monts du Cantal, where hairpin roads offer a succession of stunning views and the short flower-studded grass is grazed by the red Salers cattle that produce the local Cantal cheese.

Sète

Tourist information: 60 Grand'Rue Mario Roustan. Tel: 04 67 74 71 71.

Sète, developed 300 years ago as part of the grand Canal du Midi project, is the oldest and most interesting town along this part of the coast. It is also an important fishing and industrial port, and has a lovely sandy beach. Narrow streets spread steeply up the hillside from the Canal Royal, where pastel-coloured Italianate buildings – housing small

shops, and lively restaurants and bars – line the busy quays.

Climb up Mont St-Clair (at least 15 strenuous minutes) for splendid views, sometimes as far as the Cévennes and Pyrenees mountains. Behind the terrace, Chapelle Notre-Dame-de-la-Salette, with its elaborate mosaic decorations, is delightful. Built in 1864 on the site of a medieval hermitage, it is a centre for pilgrimages; most importantly in September and October. On the way, linger in the *pâtisseries*, *épiceries* and other small shops.

Sète was the birthplace for two famous French men of words – poet Paul Valéry, and the singer Georges Brassens. They are both remembered in the local history museum, the Musée Paul Valéry.

163

Joutes nautiques

Jousting tournaments provide colourful entertainment during summer, particularly at Sète and Agde. Two splendidly costumed jousters stand facing each other on tintaines – small platforms – in rowing boats, one red, one blue, propelled by teams of ten oarsmen. The one who dislodges the other with his 3-m (10-ft) three-pronged lance is the winner.

Toulouse

Thanks largely to its highly successful aircraft industry, Toulouse is a thriving modern city. In the 17th century, after 200 years of skirmishing, the plague and a disastrous fire, the production of woad (used to make blue dye) made it rich. The magnificent residences that remain from that time give the city its nickname – la ville rose *(the pink city). The colourful skyline – at its most vivid in the setting sun – is best seen from the left bank of the broad River Garonne. Months of sunshine enable Toulousains and visitors to make the most of terrace restaurants serving the city's renowned cuisine.*

The massive Romanesque **Basilique St-Sernin** (*place Sernin; open: daily*) is all that remains of an 11th-century monastery on the pilgrimage route to Santiago de Compostela. Built in pink brick and yellow stone, it is one of the most beautiful cathedrals in France. Its 65m (213ft) octagonal bell tower has five elegant tiers of arched windows topped by a spire. Inside, honey-coloured stone sets off a high barrel-vaulted nave and prettily vaulted galleries.

The only decorative feature of the huge fortress-like church of the **Couvent des Jacobins** (*21 rue de Metz; tel: 05 61 22 21 82; open: daily except Tue; £*), built in countless thin bricks, is its five-tier hexagonal belfry. Founded in 1230, it has a massive nave with two beautiful rose windows – a southern Gothic masterpiece. The huge grey columns rising along each side are known as the *palmiers* (palm trees) *des Jacobins*. The church and its convent buildings were once home to the soldiers and 300 horses of

Tip

Toulouse's *Musée d'Histoire Naturelle (Natural History Museum)* (35 allée Jules Guesde) *in the formal Jardin des Plantes (Botanic Gardens) is renowned for its collection of stuffed monkeys.*

one of Napoleon's artillery regiments; they used the beautiful arcaded cloisters as a paddock and the chapter house as a smithy. The church was reconsecrated only in 1974.

Toulouse has about 80 grand mansions built by wealthy merchants and lawyers during the boom times of the 16th and 17th century. **Hôtel d'Assézat** (*place d'Assézat; tel: 05 61 12 06 89; closed Tue; ££*) is one of the most impressive. It now houses the Fondation Bemberg art collection, which includes works by great masters such as Tintoretto, Canaletto, Gauguin and Bonnard.

The town hall, **Le Capitole** (*place du Capitole; interior rooms open: Mon–Fri 0830–1700 and Sat morning*), named after the *capitouls* – consuls – who ran the city on behalf of the often absent Count of Toulouse, is an impressive symmetrical 18th-century building in pink brick and white stone. Inside, several appropriately grand rooms are hung with paintings depicting the city's history.

Twenty minutes (*by No 19 bus east*) from the city centre, the **Cité de l'Espace** (*avenue Jean Gonord; tel: 05 62 71 64 80, fax: 05 61 80 74 70; open: Tue–Sun 0930–1800, weekdays, and 0900–1900, weekends and hols; ££*) is an interactive space park. Its highlights are full-scale models of the Ariane 5 rocket on its launch pad and of the Mir Space Station. There are plenty of buttons and computer screens to entertain budding young scientists – and their parents.

165

Tourist information: Donjon du Capitole. Tel: 05 61 21 92 32.

La vie en rose

Toulouse, la ville rose, 'the pink city', gets its nickname from the colour of its many brick buildings – which range, in fact, from beige to red. The Romans made the characteristic long thin bricks out of the local clay, originally by hand, as in Italy, in wooden moulds. As a result, Toulouse is the most Italian-looking city in France. Brick is light enough to allow masons to construct churches with wide vaults that can span a single nave, which became the main feature of the southern Gothic style of architecture.

Eating and drinking

Le Goulu
1 place Stalingrad (in the Grand Hôtel d'Orléans), Albi. Tel: 05 63 54 16 56. £. Classic restaurant featuring local dishes at moderate prices.

Brasserie le Donjon
4 rue Porte d'Aude, la Cité, Carcassonne. Tel: 04 68 25 95 72. ££. Local classics in bright surroundings.

La Rotonde
13 boulevard Omer Sarraut, Basse Ville, Carcassonne. Tel: 04 68 25 02 37. £. A lively brasserie near the station which is popular with students, not least because its inexpensive menu includes a cinema ticket.

Les Templiers
quai de l'Amirauté, Collioure. Tel: 04 68 98 31 10. £. Restaurant overlooking the harbour, famous for the paintings that almost cover its walls. Notable for its fish.

As a university town, **Montpellier** abounds in inexpensive good-quality eating places, as well as smart establishments.

Les Bains
6 rue Richelieu, Montpellier. Tel: 04 67 60 70 87. ££. Small arcaded rooms that functioned for 200 years as public baths. A fashionable restaurant serving local specialities at moderate prices.

Café du Théâtre
3 place de la Comédie, Montpellier. Tel: 04 67 66 06 55. £. Offers an inexpensive dish of the day as well as snacks, and a prime position for watching the world go by.

Le César Antigone
place du Nombre d'Or, Antigone, Montpellier. Tel: 04 67 64 87 87. ££. Classic French brasserie.

L'Alsace
2 avenue Carnot, Narbonne. Tel: 04 68 65 10 24. £££. Opposite the railway station, one of the best restaurants in town for seafood.

Le Gone du Littéraire
75 rue Droite, Narbonne. Tel: 04 68 32 47 22. £. Inexpensive menu devoted to Lyonnaise cooking, including treats such as onion tart, *pommes dauphinoises* and *crème brûlée.*

Le Petit Comptoir
4 bis avenue M Joffre, Narbonne. Tel: 04 68 42 30 35. ££. An attractive little restaurant serving local specialities, particularly fish and duck.

Eat outdoors on balmy evenings along **Perpignan**'s palm-lined avenues and narrow streets in the old quarter, from a wide choice of French and Catalan places. **Place F Arago** is a square with brasseries and cafés under magnolia trees. **Rue Fabriques-Nadal** is given over almost completely to small restaurants.

Al Très
3 rue de la Poissonnerie, Perpignan. Tel: 04 68 34 88 39. ££. Small bar-restaurant specialising in Catalan-style seafood.

Casa Sansa
2 rue Fabriques Nadal, Perpignan. Tel: 04 68 34 21 84. £. Gypsy musicians serenade diners late into the night.

Opéra Bouffe
impasse de la Division, Perpignan. Tel: 04 68 34 83 83. ££. Catalan dishes served at outside tables in a very narrow and atmospheric alleyway.

La Calangue
17 quai Gal Durand, Sète. Tel: 04 67 74 28 37. £. Quayside restaurant where you can eat such Sète specialities as *tieles* (fish and tomato pies) and stuffed mussels.

The **Toulousains** have a reputation for being both gourmands and gourmets. Two hundred years ago they formed the first gastronomic association in France. Brasserie restaurants spill out on to most of the squares. Some, particularly around **place du Capitole**, are ideal for watching the world go by. Others, such as those around **place Wilson** and **place St-Georges**, are more intimate.

Le Bon Vivre
15 place Wilson, Toulouse. Tel: 05 61 23 07 17. £. Small friendly restaurant serving local specialities, popular with Toulousains.

Brasserie des Beaux Arts Flo
1 quai de la Dorade, Toulouse. Tel: 05 61 21 12 12. ££. Bustling Parisian-style brasserie with efficient service, plush bench seats and gilded mirrors. Strong on oysters and seafood, as well as local dishes.

Le Van Gogh
21 place St-Georges, Toulouse. Tel: 05 61 21 03 15. £. Small brasserie in shaded square. Enormous salads.

Shopping

The old streets in **Montpellier**'s Centre Historique are delightful for shopping, with many small boutiques in the ground floors of the ancient buildings. Those in rue de l'Ancien Courrier have vaulted ceilings. **Droguerie J Estoul** is an old-fashioned pharmacy on place Castellane, and **Pomme de Reinette**, 33 rue de l'Aiguillerie, is crammed with toys old and new. There's a daily covered food market at place Castellane and an open-air market on the Plan Cabannes along boulevard Gambetta.

Narbonne's recently restored late 19th/early 20th-century market hall **Les Halles**, at cours Mirabeau, is an iron-framed glass building with elaborate stuccoed columns and a grand stone doorway crowned by a huge clock. Inside, 80 stalls sell local produce and wine.

The narrow streets in **Perpignan**'s old quarter are crowded with specialist shops. Look out for traditional Catalan fabrics, and jewellery made using the local red stone, *grenat*. The citizens love their markets, particularly the daily fruit and vegetable one on place de la République.

Toulouse has some memorable markets – food and wine are sold in **Victor Hugo market hall** and fruit and vegetables at the open-air **Marché des Boulevards** along the boulevard de Strasbourg. Place du Parlements is the scene of a seasonal garlic market from the end of August to mid-September.

Castles and *bastides*

Many towns in the Languedoc region have evolved from bastides, *fortified medieval villages. The layout, still to be seen in places such as* **Carcassonne** *(the Ville Basse),* **Mirepoix, Réalmont** *and* **Revel***, was always similar – a grid of straight narrow streets and alleys with*

a square in the centre surrounded by covered arcades. Designed to enable the inhabitants to live safely from attack, they were surrounded by sturdy ramparts and gateways. Most date back to the height of the Franco-English wars in the 12th to 14th centuries.

Rivalry between France and England was not the only cause of conflict in the region. Religion was a major cause of strife, especially since the Languedoc was a stronghold of Catharism from the 10th to the 15th century. The Cathars, named form the Greek word *katharos* (pure) denied Catholic teaching by rejecting the Eucharist, because they felt that bread and wine could not possibly represent Christ's flesh. For them the means to salvation was baptism, passed on by the laying on of hands from individual to individual in an unbroken line since Christ and the Apostles.

The powerful Counts of Toulouse were among many wealthy landowners who were sympathetic to Cathar beliefs, and

when, in the early 13th century, the Counts seemed likely to unite with Catalonia to form a powerful rival to France, King Philippe Auguste decided to act against them. Making the most of the wholehearted support he got from Pope Innocent III, who was anxious to see an end to Catharism, he embarked in 1209 on a ruthless campaign designed to rid the world of these heretics.

Known as the Albigensian Crusade because **Albi** was the first place to offer refuge to Cathars, the anti-Cathar campaign led to the ravaging of many towns and villages. Hundreds of Cathars were martyred, mostly by being burned. Though run with ruthless efficiency and cruelty, their purge was severely handicapped by the fact that the Cathars had no fear of death as they believed hell was already on earth. Consequently nearly a hundred years passed before the 'heresy' was finally eradicated.

Two famous castles, **Peyrepertuse** and **Quéribus**, both played a crucial part in the Cathar movement. They stand on rocky pinnacles that look startlingly inaccessible, even today.

The Southwest

Some of the best things in life are found in this corner of France: gourmet foods and fine wines, prehistoric cave paintings, fortified medieval towns and villages, miles of exhilarating Atlantic beaches and Europe's largest forest. See the great outdoors from a bike or a canoe, or on horseback, or indulge yourself with a few days in the lively city of Bordeaux – and don't miss a trip around those world-famous vineyards.

THE SOUTHWEST

BEST OF
The Southwest

Getting there: *Toulouse, Bordeaux and Biarritz all have airports served by scheduled and 'no-frills' airlines. Bordeaux, Brive and Toulouse are the major railheads in southwest France, with direct services from Paris. The trip from Paris to Bordeaux is 581km (361 miles), via the A10 (toll).*

North

Poitiers

Niort

Île de Ré

La Rochelle

Rochefort

Saintes

④

Royan

Angoulême

Limoges

ATLANTIC
OCEAN

⑤

Lascaux

Libourne

Les Eyzies

⑦

③

Bergerac

⑥

Cap Ferret

①

La Dune
du Pilat

Villeneuve

Cahors

⑧

Agen

Moissac

Mont-de-Marsan

Montauban

Auch

Toulouse

②

Bayonne

Pau

Tarbes

St-Jean-Pied-de-Port

Lourdes

St-Gaudens

| 0 | | 100 km |
| 0 | 50 miles | |

1 Arcachon

Take part in all sorts of activities at this pine-scented resort on France's wild Atlantic coast. Climb Europe's highest sand dune, and enjoy the sunset from its summit. **Page 174**

2 Biarritz

Gracious *belle-époque* villas, thrilling surf, beautiful golf courses, a wonderful climate and an air of faded grandeur – when you're tired of all this, make for the seafront casino and have a cocktail and a flutter. **Page 176**

3 Bordeaux

Architectural treasures, lively bars and restaurants, a fascinating history – closely connected with the English – and, of course, some of the most famous vineyards in the world. Make your pilgrimage to Château Smith-Haut-Lafite or St-Émilion, then come back to wander Bordeaux's historic streets and pick out an eating place to while away the evening. **Page 177**

4 Cognac

Who has not heard of Cognac? Even in the depths of Mongolia, Cognac's name is known and revered as the source of high-status brandy. Come here to find out what all the fuss is about. **Page 178**

5 Périgueux

If you like medieval and Renaissance architecture, this city of art and history will delight you. There's something to see at every turn. It's a gourmet's delight too – and one of the few places where you can buy the Périgord speciality of a truffle knife. **Page 183**

6 Rocamadour

Ignore the souvenir shops, with their shelves of crudely fashioned pottery figures, and just enjoy the spectacular sight of this pilgrimage town clinging to the side of a cliff. Follow in the steps of devotees, who have been coming here for 700 years, since the discovery of the mummified body of St-Amadour. **Page 185**

7 Sarlat

Medieval Sarlat is at its liveliest on Wednesdays and Saturdays, when a traditional produce market takes place around its 'Goose Square'. At other times, it's a place to wander along atmospheric alleyways, and linger in one of the many bars and restaurants. **Page 186**

8 St-Cirq-Lapopie

Is this the most beautiful village in France? Many people think so. Come and make up your own mind about its merits and charms. **Page 187**

173

Arcachon

Tourist information: esplanade Georges Pompidou. Tel: 05 57 52 97 97. Open: summer Mon–Sat 0900–1900, Sun 0900–1300; rest of year Mon–Sat 0900–1230 and 1400–1800, closed Sun. Guided walking tours of Winter Town.

Developed in the 19th century, Arcachon, with its pine woods, sandy beaches and almost land-locked triangular bay, attracts many thousands of visitors. It offers a huge range of activities, from golf and gambling, to diving and hang-gliding, via aquariums, water parks and bird reserves. The **Bassin d'Arcachon** is one of the most popular yachting centres in Europe, with 2 500 boats in its harbour and dozens of trips afloat. The oyster parks, producing 15,240 tonnes (15,000 tons) a year, can be visited by boat or on foot.

The town has four quarters: the seafront stretch, with its pavement cafés and boating events, is in **La Ville d'Eté** (Summer Town), while **La Ville d'Automne** (Autumn Town) takes in the fishing port, fish market and marina. In **La Ville d'Hiver** (Winter Town), on a higher level, grand houses built in an amazing range of architectural styles in the 19th and early 20th centuries for the rich and famous overlook the ocean.

La Dune du Pilat

Tourist information: Rond Point de Figuier, Pyla-sur-Mer. Tel: 05 56 54 02 22.

A century ago, Europe's largest sand dune was 60m (197ft) high. Today it is almost twice that height, more than 2.5km (1^1/2 miles) long and 1km (^{1}/2 mile) wide. Get there for the sunset view from the top – well worth the tiring climb – or take a narrated boat trip from the Bassin d'Arcachon.

Fast play

Every Basque town and village has its fronton, *or court, where* pelota – *described as the world's fastest ball game – is played. The game, which exists in various forms, involves a wall and a ball, and a wicker 'glove'. The fastest version of* pelota, cesta punta *(or* jai alai *), is played in summer contests in Biarritz.*

Bayonne

Tourist information: place des Basques. Tel: 05 59 46 01 46. Open: all year. Guided tours in July and Aug.

Agence Touristique du Pays Basque (tourist agency for the Basque Country): 1 rue Donzac, Bayonne. Tel: 05 59 46 46 64. Open: all year.

The sprawling capital of the French Basque Country is an important port, known for its cured ham (*jambon de Bayonne*), bullfights, Izarra (the local sweet liqueur), and for its support for Basque independence.

For six days at the beginning of August, bullfights and bull-running take place and there's dancing in the street and general merry-making. Outside festival time, Bayonne is worth a visit for the old quarters of **Grand Bayonne**, with its pedestrianised shopping streets, and **Petit Bayonne**. **Château Neuf** is a great fortification built around 1460 at the end of three centuries of English rule. Bayonne's Gothic **cathedral** (*Cathédrale de Ste-Marie, Grand Bayonne; tel: 05 59 59 17 82; open: Mon–Sat 1000–1145 and 1500–1900; £*), dating from the 13th century, was one of the stopping places on the pilgrimage route to Santiago de Compostela.

Bayonets

The armoury industry in Bayonne prospered from the 18th century. As early as 1703 French infantrymen were armed with bayonets made in Bayonne – hence the name.

Biarritz

Tourist information: Javalquinto, square d'Ixelles, Biarritz. Tel: 05 59 24 20 24. Open: all year.

This great playground of the southwest was a small whaling port until Eugénie, future wife of Napoléon III, launched the fashion for sea bathing in the 19th century. Biarritz – with its fine sandy beaches and its gentle climate – soon developed as a glittering holiday resort. Charlie Chaplin, Ernest Hemingway, Frank Sinatra and the Duke and Duchess of Windsor were all later visitors.

The surf also rises

Surfing in the waves on the Biarritz beaches was popularised by film scriptwriter Peter Viertel during the shooting of The Sun Also Rises *in the 1950s. He introduced some of surfing's pioneers to Biarritz, and they found it an ideal location for the sport. The pounding Atlantic waves have made Biarritz a world-class surfing centre ever since.*

Much of the coast now is lined with smart homes and about a quarter of the population are retired residents. The town's nightlife centres on the seafront **casino**. By day, the town has some of the world's best surfing beaches. Other obsessions are **golf** – the first course in Biarritz was opened in 1888 – and **thalassotherapy** (sea-water treatments), introduced at the Hôtel Miramar in 1979 by a champion cyclist (*Louison Bobet Institute of Sea-Water Therapy, Hôtel Miramar, 13 rue L Bobet; tel: 05 59 41 30 00; £££*).

The **Musée de la Mer** (*esplanade du Rocher de la Vierge, Biarritz; tel: 05 59 22 37 00; open: daily all year, mid-June–mid-Sept 0930–1900, rest of year 0930–1230 and 1400–1800; ££*) is an interesting combined museum, aquarium and scientific research centre, founded in 1835.

The last of the Biarritz watch towers, on the **Plateau de l'Atalaye**, was used centuries ago to sight schools of whales. The plateau can be explored by a series of reefs, causeways and tunnels between rocky islands. A footbridge leads to the Virgin's Rock landmark.

Bordeaux

Tourist information: 12 cours du XXX Juillet. Tel: 05 56 00 66 00; e-mail: otb@bordeaux-tourisme.com; www.bordeaux-tourisme.com. Open: daily all year.

Bordeaux has played a major part in Anglo-French politics and trade for more than a thousand years – Eleanor of Aquitaine and England's Henry II were married here. The city's wine industry has flourished since Roman times and the Plantagenets' penchant for 'claret' cemented a special relationship between the city and English consumers. Bordeaux is an architectural treasure house, with whole streets standing as monuments to a lively past.

Among Bordeaux's fascinating streets and squares are the **Cours du Chapeau-Rouge**, a fashionable residential area in the 1600s, and the **Cours de l'Intendance**, the city's gold-card shopping street. The **Esplanade des Quinconces** is an open space on a grand scale (sometimes filled with fairground attractions and stalls). Its focal point is the massive **Monument aux Girondins**, which honours the Bordeaux *députés* who went to the guillotine during the Revolution. The magnificent **place de la Bourse** was constructed from 1731 to 1755.

The splendid tower of **Porte Cailhau** (*place du Palais; tel: 05 56 00 60 00; open: daily July–Aug 1400–1800; ££*) was completed in 1496 as one of the city's main gates, used by visiting royalty. The 15th-century **Porte du Grosse Cloche** has a huge bell beneath the tower's conical roofs.

Among Bordeaux's many excellent museums, the **Musée d'Aquitaine** (*20 cours Pasteur; tel: 05 56 01 51 00; open: Tue–Sun 1000–1800, closed public holidays; ££, free Wed*) gives a clear insight into the region's history, from humankind's very beginnings.

177

THE SOUTHWEST

Cahors

Tourist information: place François Mitterrand. Tel: 05 65 53 20 65. Guided tours. Departmental Committee of Tourism, 107 quai Cavaignac. Tel: 05 65 35 07 09. Both offices open all year.

Cahors owes its existence to a spring by the Lot, said to have been discovered by Carthusian monks, and the source of the town's drinking water to this day. With its wide squares, its Old Quarter, with its narrow lanes and the **Henry IV House** where the king once stayed, and its riverside gardens, Cahors is a place of charm and character. Most of the city is within a loop of the River Lot, crossed by the **Pont Valentré**, the best-preserved medieval bridge in France. The earliest site is the **Arc de Diane** remains of Gallo-Roman baths.

Following numerous invasions, **Cathédrale St-Étienne** (*place Chapou; open: daily*) was built as a fortress. By the 14th century, ramparts had also been built, turning the city into a virtual island. As prosperity increased, in the 1300s, houses and mansions were built of brick, and stone was used for great arcades. Much of the city dates from this era, and from the Renaissance period that followed.

Every day except Monday is market day in Cahors at the **Market Halls** (*place Galdemer; open: 0800–1230 and 1500–1900, Sun 0900–1200*), where traders offer a vast range of regional food products and wines.

Cognac

Tourist information: 16 rue du 14 Juillet. Tel: 05 45 82 10 71. Open: all year.

Cognac is synonymous with fine brandy, and that is the reason why most people come here – to satisfy their curiosity about a drink that is supposed to be the height of sophistication. It may not come as too much of a surprise to discover that, just like the Madeira and port industries, many of the main players in the Cognac industry were Scottish. Visit **Cognac Otard**, located in the **Château de Cognac** (*boulevard Denfert-Rochereau; tel: 05 45 36 88 86; open: daily in summer, Mon–Fri in winter; ££*) and you can learn the story of one Scottish distiller who turned the town's imposing castle (birthplace of François I) into a barrel-filled shrine to alcohol.

La Rochelle

Tourist information: place de la Petite Siréne, Le Gabut. Tel: 05 46 41 14 68.

If you like your seaside towns quiet and unspoiled, La Rochelle is the perfect summer destination. Its old-world charms include cobbled streets, marine fortifications and a boat-filled harbour, not to mention a museum of seashells and a shark-filled aquarium. There is also a **Musée du Nouveau Monde** (*10 rue Fleuriau; tel: 05 46 41 46 50; open: Wed–Mon; £*), explaining La Rochelle's links with Canada, America and the Caribbean – the city was both an emigration point for settlers who founded French colonies in the New World, and (less creditably) a slaving port.

But La Rochelle's real appeal lies in its proximity to some fine **sandy beaches**, including those of the nearby **Île de Ré**, a 30km (18 1/2 mile)-long barrier island connected to La Rochelle by means of a toll bridge. The island has miles of gently shelving beach, backed by salt marsh and pretty white-washed cottages, and restaurants serving fresh local oysters.

Lascaux

The caves at Lascaux are world-renowned for their stunning prehistoric paintings, dating back some 17,000 years and remarkable both for the naturalistic depiction of horses, mammoth and bison and for the deliberate exploitation of surface irregularities in the cave walls to give the paintings depth and movement. Discovered in 1940 by local boys looking for their lost dog, the caves were opened to the public very briefly until it was realised that the carbon dioxide and humidity introduced by visitors was causing the paintings to deteriorate. Now you can visit a very realistic and convincing reconstruction of the cave at **Lascaux II**

(*Montignac; tel: 05 53 51 95 03; open: daily in July and Aug, Tue–Sun rest of year; £££*), located a short distance from the real cave, and wonder at the artistic genius of our forebears.

Les Eyzies-de-Tayac

Tourist information: place de la Mairie. Tel: 05 53 06 97 05. Open: all year.

Les Eyzies is a long, thin village, totally dominated by a massive, pale limestone cliff, which is riddled with caves and shelters (*abris*), used as homes for thousands of years. There is an extraordinary concentration of other prehistoric sites in the surrounding area. In some, evidence has been uncovered of human activity dating as far back as 35,000 years ago; and, amazingly, some families were still living in caves around here as recently as the 1950s.

For an overview of the area's prehistory, visit the **Musée National de la Préhistoire** (*Les Eyzies; tel: 05 53 06 45 45; open: July–Aug Wed–Mon 0930–1800, mid-Mar–June and Sep–mid-Nov 0930–1200 and 1400–1800, mid-Nov–Mar 0930–1200 and 1400–1700; ££*); for a glimpse into the world of cave exploration, don't miss the **Musée de la Spéléologie** (*Les Eyzies; tel: 05 53 35 43 77; open: daily July–Aug 1100–1800; ££*).

The other cave sites to visit include the **Abri du Cap-Blanc** (*on the D48 in the Beune Valley, 6km (4 miles) east of Les Eyzies*), the **Abri Pataud**, where the oldest evidence has

been found, and the **Abri du Poisson** (*on the D47, 2km (1 mile) northeast of Les Eyzies*), so called because of the figure of a salmon on the roof, dating from around 20,000 years ago.

Delicate carvings and paintings of mammoths and other animals, created about 15,000 years ago, are spread over 100m (328ft) of wall in the **Grotte de Bernifal** (*on the D47 4.5km (3 miles) east of Les Eyzies*). The nearby **Grotte des Combarelles** (*on the D47 3km (2 miles) east of Les Eyzies*), discovered in 1901, has some 300 engravings of bears, bison, horses, reindeer and mammoths.

Grotte de Font-de-Gaume (*on the D47 1km ($1/2$ mile) east of Les Eyzies*) rivals the more famous Lascaux cave in terms of the number and quality of its prehistoric paintings. Among the many remarkable works is a stunning frieze of bison painted on white calcite. The **Grotte du Grand Roc** (*on the D47 2.5km (1$1/2$ miles) northwest of Les Eyzies*) has an amazing display of stalactites, stalagmites and other formations. There is also an excellent view of the Vézère valley from the cave's entrance.

Lourdes

Tourist information: place Peyramale. Tel: 05 62 42 77 40.

Visitors come to Lourdes primarily for religious reasons – indeed, if you are not sympathetic to Catholic rites and beliefs you may find Lourdes an experience to be avoided. The town is single-mindedly given over to succouring the hopes of the many pilgrims who come here every year seeking some sort of divine intervention in their lives, or in the lives of those they hold dear. Many pilgrims are terminally or incurably sick, and having given up hope of a medical cure, they now seek help from the divine – specifically from the Virgin, who is supposed to have appeared to St Bernadette here on 18 separate occasions in 1858. The Virgin led Bernadette to a spring within a cave, whose waters are supposed to possess healing powers. Many people claim to have been cured since that date through contact with the water. Anthropologists would say that this is a Christianisation of pagan water worship; that doesn't stop four million visitors coming here every year for a non-stop round of processions and open-air masses.

Moissac

Tourist information: 6 place Duran de Bredon. Tel: 05 63 04 01 85. Open: daily throughout the year except 25 Dec and 1 Jan. Guided walks with commentary.

Moissac is an attractive little town whose three selling points are **stone**, **water** and **fruit**. The first refers to the wealth of Romanesque art: the exquisite carvings in the cloisters of the Abbaye de St-Pierre – 76 individually carved capitals – and around its south portal have a powerful emotional impact. The water is in the River Tarn, and its port here, which joins the Garonne near by, and in the Canal Latéral à la Garonne. An aqueduct carries the canal over the river. The fruit has been grown in the surrounding countryside since Roman times. Today, 200,000 tonnes (196,850 tons) are produced, as well as 15,000 tonnes (14,764 tons) of the supremely sweet local *Chasselas* table grape.

Moissac is also known for its **arts and crafts shops**. Painters, potters, glass blowers, stained-glass makers and other artists and craftspeople have studios and workshops here, especially in rue Jean Moura.

The **Abbaye de St-Pierre** (*place Durand de Bredon; tel: 05 63 04 01 85; cloisters, tel: 05 63 04 05 73; open: daily 0800–1800, services Mon–Fri 1830, Sat 1930, Sun 1030; ££*), a stopping place for pilgrims on the route of St James, was founded in the 7th century, but was subject to a series of attacks by Normans, Arabs and others. The cloisters, nearly 1 000 years old, cannot fail to impress.

Tip

In September, Moissac celebrates its special grape, the Chasselas*, in a three-day festival, with awards being made for the most beautiful and best-flavoured fruit. The* Chasselas*, with its sweet taste and fine skin, has the rare distinction of being entitled to an* appellation contrôlée*. Its juice can be sampled at the* Uvarium *(closed in winter), a 1930s kiosk decorated in art-deco style (* 2 avenue de l'Uvarium, Moissac, by the River Tarn *).*

Pau

Tourist information: place Royale. Tel: 05 59 27 27 08.

Pau is a lively university town idyllically located in the Pyrénées with views of the snow-capped peaks always on the horizon. The town's main attraction is the **Château de**

Pau, birthplace (in 1589) of Henri IV, the Protestant king who became a Catholic in order to unite his realm (*rue de Château; tel: 05 59 82 38 00; open: daily*). When Wellington's troops occupied Pau in 1814, they liked the place so much that it became a favourite summertime retreat of the English, hence the many tea rooms and parks.

Périgueux

Tourist information: 26 place Fencheville. Tel: 05 53 53 10 63. Open: year-round Mon–Sat; also Sun in peak season. Themed walks.

A 'city of art and history', Périgueux is the compact little capital of the province of Périgord. In the medieval city, the 12th-century cathedral, built in the Roman-Byzantine style, the lingering remnant of the medieval walls and the ancient courtyards and archways, all take visitors back in time. Surrounded by agricultural terrain, Périgueux is also a market town, with truffles and *foie gras*, *charcuterie* and cheeses, pâtés and pies.

Originally the Gallo-Roman city of *Vésune*, with public baths, temples, an amphitheatre accommodating 20,000 people (now the site of a public garden) and smart villas decorated with frescos and mosaics, Périgueux is today rich in medieval and Renaissance architecture. Much of its sightseeing is free. Stroll around, and look out for the narrow medieval alleyways, nail-studded doors, archways, courtyards and corners.

183

The major part of the impressive Gallo-Roman **Tour de Vésune** (Vésune Tower) remains. Its walls were covered in marble plates fastened by iron hooks, which can still be seen. The round **Tour Mataguerre** (*rue de la Bride; discovery visits July and Aug, Mon–Fri 1030; ££*) is the last remaining of the original 28 medieval towers.

The **Musée de Périgord** (*cours de Tourny; tel: 05 53 06 40 70; open: daily except Tue and public holidays; ££*) has an extraordinary array of exhibits, from a 70,000-year-old fossilised Neanderthal skeleton to a Gallo-Roman altar with a sculpture of a bull's head, used for the sacrifice of bulls.

Poitiers

Poitiers is a charming city and the capital of the Poitou region, a land of rich agriculture to the south, and of charming small fields enclosed by hedges to the west. Those fields, called the bocage, *are a legacy of the marriage of Eleanor of Aquitaine to Henry II of England: for 300 years, from 1152, the English ruled this land.*

Today, though, Poitiers is proudly and unmistakably French, with a wealth of attractions that include France's new state-of-the-art theme park, **Futurescope**, located 7km north of the city (*Juanay-Clan; tel: 05 49 49 30 00; open: daily; £££*) and dedicated to developments in film and visual technology. Come here for virtual-reality rides (every bit as vertigo-inducing as the real thing) plus 15 separate cinema pavilions showing 'Special Effects' films and a laser show with dancing fountains to close the day.

Within the city is the ornate church of **Notre-Dame-la-Grande**, a 12th-century masterpiece of Romanesque sculpture and fresco, built as a pilgrimage church on the Santiago de Compostela route. Its elaborate façade eclipses that of the **Cathédral St-Pierre**, whose treasures include France's oldest choir stalls (13th century) and a 12th-century stained-glass east window depicting the Crucifixion, with Eleanor of Aquitaine and Henry II among the worshippers at the foot of the Cross. The **Église Ste-Radegonde** shelters the 6th-century tomb of the founder of the first convent in France, and the 4th-century **Baptistére St-Jean** (one of the oldest religious buildings in France) is now a richly endowed museum of ecclesiastical art dating from the Merovingian, Carolingian and Romanesque eras.

Tourist information: 8 rue de Grandes Ecoles. Tel: 05 49 41 21 24.

Rocamadour

Hanging on the cliff side, all red roofs and pale amber walls, with a castle on top, Rocamadour is an incredible sight. One of the great centres of pilgrimage of the Middle Ages, the town was put on the map by the discovery of the mummified body of St-Amadour in a niche in the limestone in 1166.

Rocamadour's narrow streets are lined with buildings from the 12th to 15th centuries. The long sweep of the Pilgrims' Staircase is dramatic, with some devout visitors making their way towards the **Chapelle de la Vièrge Noire** on their hands and knees. There are seven chapels in all, which can be visited only with a guide.

Just down the road, about 150 monkeys live freely in the 10 hectares (25 acres) of the **Forêt de Singes** (*l'Hospitalet; tel: 05 65 33 62 72; open: Apr–June 1000–1200 and 1300–1800, July–Aug 1000–1900, shorter hours rest of year; ££*). **Le Rocher des Aigles** (*l'Hospitalet; tel: 05 65 33 65 45; open: Palm Sunday–All Saints' Day daily 1000–1200 and 1400–1800; ££*), near the Château de Rocamadour, presents eagles, vultures, owls and other birds of prey flying freely to great heights and returning to their handlers.

Sarlat-la-Canéda

Tourist information: Hôtel de Vienne, place de la Liberté. Tel: 05 53 59 27 67.
Open: all year. Guided tours.

In Sarlat, simply follow your nose along narrow, atmospheric alleyways, into streets and squares lined with ancient houses. The town is, in effect, a museum of architecture. On Wednesdays and Saturdays, Sarlat comes alive, with a massive produce market around place des Oies ('Goose Square').

Sarlat is noted for its medieval *hôtels* – townhouses built mainly during the second half of the 15th century when the town began to prosper again after the Hundred Years War. The two that best exemplify Sarlat's architectural heritage are the **Hôtel de Maleville** (*place de la Liberté*) and the **Hôtel Plamon**. The former was built by a 16th-century 'yuppie', who rose to become Henri IV's financial secretary. It was later combined with two other existing buildings to create a splendid mansion, with stone reliefs of Henri IV and Marie de' Medici at the main entrance. The town's best-known building, both historically and architecturally, is

Maison de la Boëtie (*rue de la Liberté*). Built in 1525, it has two archways at ground level, and the two upper floors have large mullioned windows with carved decorations.

Behind the cathedral is Sarlat's mysterious **Lanterne des Morts**, a cylindrical tower dating from the end of the 12th century. Some say the tower is a 'lantern of the dead' – a tower built to provide light and comfort for souls of the departed at night. The room in the roof, which would have been lit, is sealed.

St-Cirq-Lapopie

Tourist information: place du Sombral. Tel: 05 65 31 29 06. Open: all year.

One of the most beautiful villages in the region – some say in the whole of France – St-Cirq (pronounced 'San-sear') stands dizzyingly on a rocky escarpment that plunges vertically for 80m (262ft) to the left bank of the River Lot. It looks like an illustration in a book of fairy tales, but has had more than its fair share of violence over the centuries. Occupied since Gallo-Roman times, the village is named after St-Cyr who was martyred along with his mother in Asia Minor during the reign of Diocletian. St-Amadour is said to have brought the martyr's relics to the area. The Lapopie part of the name comes from a family of local lords who occupied the castle at the top of the rock in the Middle Ages. The castle attracted the attention of many invaders and was repeatedly besieged. Among those who tried and failed to seize it was Richard the Lionheart in 1198. It was demolished on the orders of Louis XI in 1471, but the ruins were still fought over during the Wars of Religion. Henri de Navarre put an end to the site's importance in 1580 when he had the remaining walls flattened. Today, the village is a delightful jumble of steep, narrow streets of cheerful red-roofed houses.

Eating and drinking

Le Bistrot
3 avenue du Gal de Gaulle, la Teste, Arcachon. Tel: 05 56 66 30 14. £. Traditional bistro fare with modest *prix-fixe* menus and a children's menu.

Chez Yvette
59 boulevard du Gal Leclerc, Arcachon. Tel: 05 56 83 05 11. ££–£££. Open daily all year, the restaurant specialises in oysters, *fruits de mer* and fish and offers a good choice of Bordeaux Blanc wines.

Restaurant de la Tour
5 rue des Faures, Bayonne. Tel: 05 59 59 05 67. £–££. Restaurant in one of the towers in Bayonne's wall, with an innovative menu.

Chez Albert
Port des Pêcheurs, Biarritz. Tel: 05 59 24 43 84. £–££. Locals and visitors come here for the good seafood and value for money.

Le Bistrot des Quinconces
4 place des Quinconces, Bordeaux. Tel: 05 56 52 84 56. Open: daily 0730–0200, closed 1 Jan. ££. Good food served 18½ hours a day, 364 days a year in this centrally located bistro. Musical soirées are a feature.

Café des Arts
138 cours Victor Hugo and 184 rue Ste-Catherine, Bordeaux. Tel: 05 56 91 78 46. Open: daily 0830–0200; closed 25 Dec and 1 Jan. £. Large and lively establishment serving simple but well-cooked dishes. Wine by the glass. Jazz concerts and traditional *chansons françaises* in the evenings.

La Tupiña
6–8 rue Porte-de-la-Monnaie, Bordeaux. Tel: 05 56 91 56 37. ££–£££. Authentic traditional cuisine, with the emphasis on specialities of the Southwest. Owner Jean-Pierre Xiradakis is probably Bordeaux's best-known chef.

Auberge du Vieux
144 rue St-Urcisse, Cahors. Tel: 05 65 35 06 05. Closed Tue evening and Wed except in high season. £–££. Regional cuisine, fish and *fruits de mer* are the specialities of this restaurant in the south of the city.

Le Bistrot de Cahors
46 rue Daurade, Cahors. Tel: 05 65 53 10 55. £. Popular small bistro serving good regional food.

À la Tentation

34 place Chapou, Cahors. Tel: 05 65 35 31 44. Closed Mon and all Jan and Feb. £–££. Traditional and regional fare at a popular spot opposite the cathedral.

La Grande Vigne

Martillac. Tel: 35 57 83 11 26. £££. Run by Didier Banyol and awarded two Michelin stars, this gourmet restaurant is at the hotel on the Château Smith-Haut-Lafite estate. Monsieur Banyol also runs the country-style brasserie **Le Table du Lavoir** *(££)*, where the décor is based on the place where grape-pickers traditionally washed their clothes.

Restaurant de Clos St-Front

5 rue de la Vertu (access through rue St-Front), Périgueux. Tel: 05 53 46 78 58. £. Restaurant with a shady terrace for outdoor eating.

Le Rocher de l'Arsault

15 rue de l'Arsault, Périgueux. Tel: 05 53 53 54 06. ££–£££. The air-conditioned restaurant with Louis XIII décor is run by a mother and daughter, who take pride in serving fresh products from the land and sea.

Le Médiéval

place de la Porte Bouqueyre, St-Émilion. Tel: 05 57 24 72 37. £–££. Typical small-town French bar-restaurant: good food and service and an attractive outdoor setting.

Shopping for food

Look out for local produce all over the gastronomic region of **Périgord**, which is famous throughout France for its highly individualistic cuisine.

You can buy *pâté de foie gras* and other duck and goose products directly from farms throughout Périgord and Quercy. You may not want to know the details. After three months of free-range living, the birds are placed singly in cages and force-fed for two to three weeks on ground meal and whole corn. Their livers expand until they are three or four times the normal weight.

The aromatic gourmet speciality, the **truffle**, is the 'black diamond' of Périgord. Sniffer dogs or specially trained pigs are used to find this rare black fungus, usually underground at the base of an oak tree. The pleasant little market town of **Sorges** is the capital of the truffle, and even has a museum dedicated to it.

In **Bayonne**, in the French Basque Country, cured ham is a speciality. At the **Pierre d'Ibaialde Cannery** in the town (*4 rue des Cordelier; £*), visitors can learn about the curing process and enjoy a sampling.

189

Bordeaux vineyards

Even if your interest in wine has been restricted to its taste and its effect, a visit to Bordeaux, one of the great wine-growing regions of France, is almost sure to kindle a desire to learn more about one of nature's most delectable products.

The Bordeaux region, in which the Garonne and Dordogne rivers flow, has up to 121,410 hectares (300,000 acres) of vineyards, with 57 *appellations* and six main families of Bordeaux wine. There are at least 5 000 wine châteaux, many of which offer highly informative guided tours of their cellars, and a tasting. Villages of pale stone houses with crinkly tiled red roofs punctuate the miles of farmland and the straight rows of vines.

For nearly 1 000 years, the Bordeaux vineyards have been producing fine wines in a variety of landscapes. The region has a steady temperate climate and state of humidity, and Europe's largest forest protects it from the wind. Different soil types and grape varieties result in a range of flavours, each distinctively Bordeaux. Good wine is produced from poor, gravely soil, which encourages the vines to push their roots deep, to reach water and the elements of the subsoil, bringing richness into the grape. Vine roots can penetrate underground for 12m to 15m (39ft to 49ft).

Bordeaux regions

Côtes wines – Côtes de Bourg, Premières Côtes de Bordeaux, Premières Côtes de Blaye, Côtes de Castillon and others – come from a vast area stretching from the edge of the Charentes in the northwest to the Périgord region in the

east. The vines are grown on wide slopes, some on clay soils that absorb sunlight. The Merlot grape is the basis of these wines from the right banks of the Garonne, Dordogne and Gironde rivers.

To the east, **St-Émilion**, heartland of the Merlot grape, is known as 'the hill with a thousand châteaux'. The small but lively town itself has narrow, steep streets and ancient buildings. Its major attraction – apart from its wine cellars and vineyards – is the **Église Monolithe**, the largest troglodyte church in France.

Sweet and semi-sweet white wines, among them **Barsac** and **Sauternes**, are grown in the southern parts of the Bordeaux wine region. These wines spend two or three years in the cellar before bottling.

The **Château Smith-Haut-Lafite** estate (*Martillac; tel: 05 57 83 11 22; open: daily by appointment 0900–1830; visit to cooperage; free tasting; ££*), in the **Graves** wine-growing region southeast of Bordeaux, dates from the time of the Crusades. The property devotes 44 hectares (109 acres) to red wines and 11 hectares (27 acres) to white. The estate also has a unique vinotherapy spa. Treatments include wine and honey wraps, barrel baths using micro-exploded chilled grapes, and Merlot wraps, using crushed grape pips, for anti-ageing.

191

The power of the rose

The yellow roses between the vine rows are not purely for decoration. Highly susceptible to vine diseases, the roses give early warning of any such problems affecting the vines.

The Loire Valley

The Loire is the longest river in France, flowing for 1 020km (634 miles) past orchards, vineyards and game-filled forests. Its tributaries – the Loir, Cher and Indre – may offer better scenery, but no river in Europe has more architectural grandeur than the Loire. There are enough châteaux to satisfy every feudal fantasy, and all have stories to tell. Ironically, the 'heart of France', as the Loire is often called, was once English; Richard the Lionheart is buried at Fontevraud Abbey.

THE LOIRE VALLEY

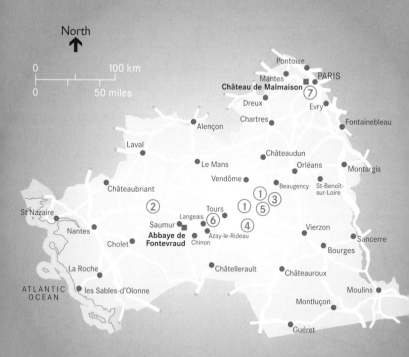

BEST OF
The Loire Valley

*Getting around: Nantes has an international airport, served by **Brit Air** (tel: 020 8742 6600) from London Gatwick. **Brittany Ferries** (tel: 0990 360 360) makes the crossing up to three times daily between Portsmouth and Caen and once daily between Portsmouth and St-Malo. High-speed trains (TGV) link Tours and Nantes with Paris in one and two hours respectively. By car, the fastest road is the A10 autoroute from Paris.*

North

0   100 km
0   50 miles

Pontoise
Mantes   PARIS
Château de Malmaison ⑦
Dreux   Evry
Chartres   Fontainebleau
Alençon
Laval
Le Mans   Châteaudun
Vendôme   Orléans   Montargis
Châteaubriant   Beaugency   St-Benoît-sur-Loire
① ③
St Nazaire   ②   Langeais   ① ⑤
Nantes   Saumur   ⑥ Tours
     Abbaye de   ④   Vierzon
Cholet   **Fontevraud**   Azay-le-Rideau
         Chinon   Sancerre
La Roche   Bourges
ATLANTIC   Châtellerault   Châteauroux
OCEAN   les Sables-d'Olonne   Moulins
           Montluçon
           Guéret

① *Amboise and Blois*

At Amboise, Catholic extremists hanged 1 300 Protestants from the castle ramparts. At Blois, the Duke de Guise (a ladies' man nicknamed 'Scarface') was knifed by order of the French king. **Pages 197 and 199**

② *Angers*

Hell hath no fury like the stitches in the tapestry of the Apocalypse at Angers, which foretells the battle of Armageddon. **Page 199**

③ *Chambord*

Leonardo's double-spiral staircase is to Renaissance architecture what the Mona Lisa is to painting. The roof of Chambord is another Renaissance marvel – a 'city' of towers and chimneys. **Page 201**

④ *Chenonceau*

Strong-willed women created and preserved this château over four centuries. Diane de Poitiers built the bridge across the Cher. Catherine de Médicis added a 60m (200ft) gallery on top of Diane's bridge, and the mother of novelist George Sand saved it from ruin. **Pages 202–3**

⑤ *Ch*

If perfect p[...] centuries i[...] count up t[...] horns or wait for the ritual feeding of the hounds before the aristocrats (still in residence) cut to the chase. **Page 203**

⑥ *Villandry*

The gardens here are the biggest, the most formal and the most famous in the Loire, with 52km (32 miles) of box hedges, many trimmed into geometrical forms symbolising love. **Pages 212–13**

⑦ *Versailles*

This world-famous palace was built by a king who believed himself to be only slightly less important than God. Its décor gives a new meaning to the word 'extravagant', its vast gardens are stupendous, and its role in France's revolutionary history is fascinating. **Pages 214–15**

195

Tip

La Clé des Temps ('The Key to History') *is a one-year pass that allows you to visit ten of the most famous châteaux and monuments at a substantially reduced price. Available at participating national sites and from the National Monuments Information Centre (*Hôtel de Sully, 62 rue St-Antoine, 75186 Paris; tel: 01 44 61 21 50; open: Mon–Fri 0900–1800*).*

Abbaye de Fontevraud

13km (8 miles) southeast of Saumur. Tel: 02 41 51 71 41. Open: June–mid-Sept daily 0900–1900; mid-Sept–May 0930–1230 and 1400–1800. ££.

The prestigious order of Fontevraud was founded around 1101 in a forest near the meeting point of the Anjou, Touraine and Poitou regions. Its founder, Robert d'Arbrissel, was an itinerant preacher whose following was largely female. A year before his death, Robert made the controversial decision to turn the abbey and its brothers over to a woman. The tradition continued, and **36 abbesses**, including 16 of royal blood, ran the order between 1115 and 1792. By the time of the Revolution, Fontevraud was the richest and most powerful abbey in France.

The abbey has a vast **octagonal kitchen** – one of few to have survived from the Romanesque era – built around 1160 with money provided by Henry II, Plantagenet king of England, one of its most important patrons. It fed an enormous number of people.

Fontevraud's abbey church contains the tomb effigies of Henry II and his wife, Eleanor of Aquitaine, who died at the abbey in 1204. Their son, **Richard the Lionheart**, is here as well. The abbesses also had close ties to several kings of France, and the youngest four daughters of Louis XV were raised at the abbey.

Amboise

Tourist information: quai du Général de Gaulle. Tel: 02 47 57 09 28.

Château d'Amboise. Tel: 02 47 57 00 98. Open: daily Apr–June 0900–1630; July–Aug 0900–1930; Sept–Oct 0900–1800; Nov–Mar 0900–1200 and 1400–1700. ££.

The vast **château** at romantic Amboise was an architectural glory of the 15th and 16th centuries. Its Renaissance core has survived, including spiral staircases wide enough for horses, but today the castle has period interiors in several different styles, from Gothic and Renaissance to First Empire and 19th century.

In 1560, judgement was passed in the Assembly Hall on a group of Huguenots (French Protestants) caught in the act of plotting to kidnap François II, the 16-year-old king of France. In a horrific act of revenge, Catholic extremists hanged 1,300 conspirators from the castle ramparts.

The **Chapelle St-Hubert**, built between 1491 and 1496, is a minor Gothic wonder with exquisite sculpture, interior friezes and stained-glass windows. A plaque notes that Leonardo da Vinci was buried here, but local historians now believe this to be inaccurate. However, da Vinci did spend the last years of his life on the outskirts of Amboise, at the manor house of **Clos-Lucé**, dying there in 1519.

Watch your step at the château of Amboise: the original owner, Charles VIII, killed himself by banging his head on a stone lintel here.

197

" *Amboise is certainly supreme among the old houses of the Loire … high-perched windows and balconies, hanging gardens and dizzy crenellations …* "

Henry James, *A Little Tour in France* (1884)

Azay-le-Rideau

Tourist information: 5 place de l'Europe. Tel: 02 47 45 44 40; fax: 02 47 45 31 46.

Château d'Azay-le-Rideau. Tel: 02 47 45 42 04. Open: daily Apr–Oct 0930–1600; July–Aug 0900–1900; winter 0930–1230 and 1400–1730. ££.

Azay-le-Rideau (1518–27) is a real fairytale castle. The Indre river seeps around it through an English-style park, forming a natural moat and reflecting its turrets and battlements. Inside are a legendary staircase, a gargantuan kitchen and the canopied beds of kings and queens.

> *Infinite love ... I found it expressed by this long ribbon of water that streams in the sun between two green shores, by these lines of poplars that adorn this valley of love with floating lace.*
>
> **Balzac, *Le Lys dans La Vallée* (1848)**

Azay's builder was Gilles Berthelot, an unrivalled social climber who became treasurer to François I. In 1515, he began to replace the small fortified castle that his father had bought. However, like many dream homes, his new château remained unfinished. Berthelot was accused of embezzlement, and died in exile.

Berthelot's wife added elegant little towers to a home that was everyone's idea of a **typical French Renaissance château**, with high roofs, tall watch-turrets, long rows of windows

and majestic Italianate details. The early Renaissance carving above the entrance – dominated by François I's **salamander** – is exceptional. The highlight of the interior is the splendid grand staircase built by an unknown master architect. Tapestries hang in the great hall, where balls and banquets were held, and portraits and historical paintings decorate the apartment that accommodated Louis XIII, as well as the salons, library and dining room. From the richly sculpted loggias, there is a wonderful view of the park.

La Vannerie de Villaines-Les-Rochers

5km (3 miles) from Azay-le-Rideau. Open: daily but closed for lunch 1200–1400.

Visit this basket-weaving co-operative to see weavers at work, and then purchase almost any kind of basket.

Angers

Tourist information: place Kennedy. Tel: 02 41 23 51 11; fax: 02 41 23 51 66.

Château d'Angers. Tel: 02 41 87 43 47. Open: daily Apr–mid-May and mid-Sept–end Oct; June–mid-Sept 0930–1615; Nov–Apr 1000–1230 and 1400–1615; closed Dec–Feb. ££.

The 13th-century château at Angers is best seen at night, looming out of its dry moat, now filled with delicate parterres. The fortress today has no less than 17 circular towers, but the original complex was several times larger. Unbelievably, it was built in just a decade, between 1230 and 1240. Henry Plantagenet was crowned King of England here in 1154. Inside, the château is almost bare except for a few exquisite tapestries. The celebrated **tapestry of the Apocalypse** hangs in a modern annexe.

Blois

Tourist information: 3 avenue Jean Laigret. Tel: 02 54 90 41 41; fax: 02 54 90 41 49; e-mail: blois.tourisme@wanadoo.fr. Château de Blois. Tel: 02 54 78 06 62. Open: daily mid-Mar–Oct 0900–2000; Nov–mid-Mar 0900–1830. ££.

From 1503, the kings of France moved from Amboise to Blois, bringing with them all the finest architects and craftsmen of the day. The former royal château, sitting high on a hill in the centre of town, traces the development of French secular architecture in a mix of styles, from medieval and Renaissance to neo-classical. Its most famous feature is the sumptuously decorated François I external staircase.

No swimming or boating!

The Loire may seem a sluggish river, but its undercurrents, sudden whirlpools and flash floods claim several lives every year. It's no good for boating and don't even think of swimming in it – the locals never do.

Stories of royal intrigue resonate throughout the château. Henri II had the extremist Catholic leader, the Duc de Guise, murdered in the royal bedroom in 1588. (Henri himself would be assassinated in turn nine months later.) After the death of Henri's mother, Catherine de Médicis, her study was discovered to have 237 wooden panels concealing secret cupboards – all opened and shut by a pedal hidden in the floorboards. According to Alexander Dumas, they contained poison.

199

Bourges

Tourist information: 21 rue Victor Hugo.
Tel: 02 48 23 02 60; fax: 02 48 23 02 69.

Bourges is the capital of the ancient province
of Berry – a land of woods and wildlife,
hidden villages, ponds and lakes … and
witches, at least according to people in
the Middle Ages.

The splendid **Gothic cathedral** of St-
Étienne dominates Bourges from the top of
the city's hill. It was built in just 50 years,
and its mismatched towers and rich sculpture make it one of
France's most beautiful cathedrals. The original towers were
built at the beginning of the 12th century but one collapsed
in 1506. The Flamboyant-style replacement is called the **Tour
de Beurre** ('Butter Tower') because its sponsors were allowed
to eat on fast days. Its non-identical twin is known as the
Tour Sourde ('Deaf Tower'). Inside, the stained glass, which
dates from the 12th to the 17th century, rivals that of
Chartres. The tomb of the Duc de Berry is in the double
ambulatory, while the tombs of Bourges' archbishops form
a semicircle in the central part.

Bourges contains many other fine historic buildings. The
palace of Jacques Coeur, chief financier of Charles VII,
is a fine example of a Gothic mansion. The **Hôtel de Ville**,
with its beautiful adjoining garden, and the Renaissance
mansion housing the **Berry Museum** were both built on
Roman foundations.

Sancerre

50km (31 miles) northeast of Bourges. Tourist information: Hôtel de Ville.
Tel: 02 48 54 00 26.

The charming old town of Sancerre stands on a hill surrounded
by vineyards, dedicated to the production of world-famous
wines. A 14th-century keep is all that remains of the château
of the counts of Sancerre.

Chambord

Château de Chambord. Tel: 02 54 50 40 00. Open: daily Apr–
0930–1615; July–Aug 0930–1915; Oct–Mar 0930–1715. Ch
most frequently visited Loire Valley château after Chenonceau,
£££.

François I built Chambord in 1519 to demonstrate the absolute power of royalty, but the end result reflects more his own particular obsessions: Italy and hunting.

He imported an army of Italian craftsmen and provided a pension to an ageing and crippled Leonardo da Vinci. François' other love – hunting – triumphed over everything else. This great masterpiece of Renaissance architecture stands in a vast park alongside the game-rich forest of Sologne and, in his lifetime at least, it was never more than a glorified hunting lodge – despite having 440 rooms and 63 staircases. François I's third obsession had been women, but he seems to have lost the appetite in later life. Graffiti attributed to the king reads: 'Women are fickle; keep away'.

> " *The towers, the turrets, the cupolas, the gables, the lanterns, the chimneys, look more like the spires of a city than the salient points of a single building.* "
>
> **Henry James, *A Little Tour in France* (1884)**

In designing the four-storey staircase for Chambord, Leonardo da Vinci referred to plans for a Milanese villa. One of his first double-stair designs is said to have been drawn up for a brothel, allowing customers to go up the stairs without meeting others on their way out. On the roof, the fantasy forest of chimneys looks like a miniature city of stone and slate. Chimneys have been transformed into towers, and cupolas into belfries. There are panelled pilasters, shell-headed arches and a central lantern with five stages. From the roof, take time to admire the park, 5,440 hectares (13,442 acres) of woods, said to be the largest in Europe.

ıartres

Tourist information: place de la Cathédrale. Tel: 02 37 21 50 00; fax: 02 37 21 51 91. Bring binoculars to see the spectacular stained glass as closely as possible.

No place in France possesses more spiritual and artistic intensity than the **Cathédrale Notre-Dame** in Chartres. It was built in a miraculously short space of time, between 1195 and 1225, and therefore possesses a remarkable unity of style.

An earlier building on the site was destroyed by fire in 1194; the towers, the royal doorway (with its extraordinary sculpted figures) and the crypt survive from this original structure. The façade is a perfect example of Gothic. The 'Old Bell Tower' was built between 1145 and 1165 in soft stone; its surface is decorated with scale-like lines, and it is famous for its 105m (345ft) **spire**. The wooden spire of the 'New Bell Tower' was destroyed by lightning in 1150. The present Flamboyant spire was rebuilt in stone between 1507 and 1513. At 115.18m, it is one of the tallest in France.

The use of flying buttresses and crossed arches made it possible to open up the walls and insert vast windows. The cathedral's huge collection of **stained glass** from the 12th and 13th centuries is superlative and world-famous.

Chenonceau

Tourist information: rue du Château. Tel: 02 47 23 94 45. Open: May–Sept.

Château de Chenonceau. Tel: 02 47 23 90 07. Open: 0900–1900 daily in spring and summer; Dec–Feb 0900–1630/1700; Oct–Nov 0900–1700/1800. £££.

The château of Chenonceau, on its seven stone arches, seems almost to float above the River Cher. It is the most popular and photographed château in France, with a never-ending charm.

Of all the châteaux in the Loire Valley, Chenonceau is probably the one in which most people would choose to live. Perhaps this has something to do with its rather feminine charm, reflected in its nickname, the *Château des Dames*, or 'Château of Women'. Six women oversaw its construction, remodelling and restoration during the course of four centuries.

Catherine Briçonnet, wife of the first owner, Thomas Bohier, supervised much of the building work in his absence. The most famous of Chenonceau's women was Diane de Poitiers, the mistress of Henri II, although she was 20 years his senior, and legendary for her beauty. In 1556, Diane commissioned the flower garden and had the bridge built across the Cher so that she could go hunting on the other side of the river. After Henri's death, in 1559, she was summarily evicted by his widow, Catherine de Médicis, who then built the 60m (200ft) gallery on top of Diane's bridge, and laid out more gardens to the west.

Cross-dressing

Catherine de Médicis' son, Henri III, apparently liked to dress up in women's clothing; his doting mother would organise soirées for him at Chenonceau, inviting all the guests to come cross-dressed.

Cheverny

15km (9 miles) southeast of Blois. Open: daily Apr–May 0915–1200 and 1415–1830; June–mid-Sept 0915–1845; mid-Sept–Mar 0930–1200 and 1415–1730. ££.

The château of Cheverny is rewarding for its amazing interiors. Most châteaux in the Loire Valley look as though they have just completed a moving sale. Cheverny, by contrast, is the sort of place where you trip over family heirlooms. Part of the explanation for this is that Cheverny has remained in the same family since it was built in 1634. In addition to furniture, there is an embarrassment of decorative riches – sculpture gilt, marble ornament and elaborately painted panels and ceilings – and an armoury and trophy room with a forest of antlers completes picture. The aristocratic owners still live there and if you arrive at the right time you might catch them feeding an army of dogs and mounting horses for a day out hunting.

Chinon

Tourist information: 12 rue Voltaire. Tel: 02 47 93 17 85; fax: 02 47 93 93 05; www.chinon.com/tourisme/english.

Château de Chinon. Open: daily mid-Mar–June and Sept 0900–1800; July–Aug 0900–1900; Oct 0900–1700; Nov–Mar 0900–1200 and 1400–1700. ££.

The powerful medieval ensemble of Chinon is little changed since the Middle Ages, or the opening scene of the film *The Lion in Winter*, when Katharine Hepburn (Eleanor of Aquitaine) is released from prison for Christmas and rowed ashore to meet Peter O'Toole (Henry II), who leaps into the River Loire to greet her.

The **château**, much of it ruinous, is a medieval fortress with no Renaissance refinements. It was a **Plantagenet stronghold**, until it was lost by King John. Following Joan of Arc's motivation, it became the base for the final French push in 1429 against the English in the Hundred Years War. It is flanked on one side by vineyards and on the other by a vertiginous, cobbled road that zigzags its way down the hill into the town.

The atmospheric **old town**, Joan of Arc's *Ville-Fort* (fortified town), still consists mostly of tiny medieval stone houses and some Renaissance buildings. Richard the Lionheart is said to have died in 1199 in the Gothic house on the rue Voltaire; it is now a museum. The town's most ancient houses are gathered around the **Grand Carroi** (crossroads).

Chinon is the best-known appellation for red wine in the Loire. Its rocky soil produces an aromatic *cabernet franc*, which can be sampled in the many *caves* at the base of the castle's looming ruins.

Langeais

Tourist information: 9 rue Gambetta. Tel: 02 47 96 58 22.

Château de Langeais. Tel: 02 47 96 72 60. Open: daily. ££.

The Loire flows forcefully around Langeais past many islands, providing a fine sight from the suspension bridge that leads into town. This is one of the oldest settlements in the region. The notorious Fulk Nera, Count of Anjou, built a *donjon*, or keep, here at the end of the 10th century; it is the oldest in France, but is now in ruins in the park of the château.

The rather grim château, which has a delightful interior, was built by order of Louis XI between 1465 and 1470. Its purpose was to keep the Bretons at bay at a time when Brittany was still an independent realm and the French king was residing at Tours. In the end, the fortress was rendered redundant, through the marriage at Langeais in 1491 of Anne of Brittany to Charles VIII of France; some Bretons are still objecting to the alliance today.

The interior of the château has period furnishings and offers glimpses into the daily life of French aristocrats of the early Renaissance. There are fine Flemish tapestries embroidered with *mille-fleurs* and the ubiquitous 'K' and 'A', for Charles and Anne. The great hall is decorated with tapestries depicting the Creation. Best of all on a clear day is the covered gallery – the sentry walk – that runs the length of the castle, and offers fine views of the Loire and the town of Langeais.

" *She was a woman, nothing more. Let's attach a weight to each foot, throw her in the river and think of her the way we would a childhood fairytale.* "

The end of a *grande passion* in Balzac's novel *La Duchesse de Langeais* (1848)

Château de Malmaison

Tourist information: 160 avenue Paul Doumer. Tel: 01 47 32 35 75;
www.rueil-tourisme.com.

15km (9 miles west of Paris. Château de Malmaison. Tel: 01 41 29 05 55.
Open: Mon and Wed–Fri 1000–1200 and 1330–1700/1800; Sat and Sun
1000–1700/1800. ££.

Napoleon and his wife, Josephine, purchased Malmaison and its gardens in 1799. Josephine later bought the neighbouring château of Bois-Préau for its magnificent park. After divorcing his wife in 1809, Napoleon returned to the château only twice: the first time, in 1815, to mourn the death of Josephine, with whom he was still in love; the second time, he stayed here after his defeat at Waterloo, waiting for a passport to the USA.

Tooth trouble

Empress Josephine
apparently had bad teeth
and it is said that she always
carried a rose to raise to her
face when she laughed, to
hide this deformity.

The Bonapartes commissioned an architect in 1800 to transform the château, which they regarded as 'very ordinary', and a Greek–Roman interior was inserted into the 18th-century edifice. The 'Pompeii' style was much in fashion at the time, and the dining room, with its panels of painted stucco, the library and Josephine's boudoir are fine examples. A rich collection of portraits, drawings and clothing completes the almost perfect period interior.

Josephine cultivated more than 250 species of rose for the garden at Malmaison, creating a one-of-a-kind collection. She died in Malmaison on a spring day in 1814, and is buried in the St-Pierre-St-Paul de Rueil church.

The **museums** of the Château de Malmaison and Bois-Préau offer a broad perspective on the art and history of the Napoleonic era, and on Bonaparte's home life and career. Bois-Préau's collection includes the most famous portrait of Napoleon – David's *Bonaparte franchissant le Grand-Saint-Bernard* – which shows Napoleon lashing his rearing horse during a crossing of the Alps.

Nantes

Tourist information: 7 rue de Valmy. Tel: 02 40 20 60 00. Also place du Commerce (tel: 02 40 47 04 51) and outside the château (1 rue du Château).

Although officially in the Pays de la Loire, historically and culturally Nantes is unassailably Breton, and was the residence of the dukes of Brittany during the Middle Ages. Much of the town's later prosperity relied on the slave trade, abolished during the Revolution.

The 15th-century **Cathédrale Ste-Pierre et St-Paul** (*open: daily 0830 until dusk*) was restored following a fire in 1971. Its vaulted nave of gleaming white stone soars to a height of 37m (122ft). The south transept contains a matchless example of Renaissance sculpture.

The formidable medieval **Château des Ducs de Bretagne** (*1 place Marc Elder; tel: 40 41 56 56; open: July and Aug daily 1000–1900, otherwise Wed–Mon 1000–1200, 1400–1800; inner courtyard and ramparts free*), much restored and altered over the centuries, is steeped in history. Anne of Brittany was born here in 1477. In 1598, Henri IV signed the Edict of Nantes here, granting toleration to French Protestants. Bonnie Prince Charlie planned his invasion of England at the castle in 1745.

Nantes' **Musée des Beaux Arts** (*10 rue Georges Clemenceau; tel: 02 40 41 65 65; open: Mon, Wed, Thur, Sat 1000–1800, Fri 1000–2100, Sun 1100–1800; ££*) is one of the best in the country, especially for fans of modern art. Outdoor attractions include the **Jardin des Plantes** (*tel: 02 40 41 98 67*) and regular **boat trips** on the Rivers Erdre and Sèvre.

Orléans

Tourist information: place Albert 1er. Tel: 02 38 24 05 05; fax: 02 38 54 49 84; e-mail: OFFICE-DE-TOURISME.ORLEANS@wanadoo.fr; *www.ville-orleans.fr/html/touroffice.html.*

The capital of the Val-de-Loire region, Orléans has a rich history, much of it destroyed by Second World War bombs. It compensates today for a lack of architectural highlights by being something of a foodie paradise, and remains an important stopover for travellers on the trail of Joan of Arc.

Joan of Arc (1412–31)

Joan of Arc was born in Lorraine and died in Normandy but her soul resides on the Loire. In Chinon, she persuaded a cowardly king to stand up to the English and at Orléans she turned the tide of the Hundred Years War by rallying French forces to rout the English besiegers. For ever after, she became the 'Maid of Orléans'.

Orléans has always been valued for its strategic position on the Loire. In the Middle Ages, its university was one of Europe's most important and in the 10th and 11th centuries it became the royal capital of France. The English besieged the city in 1428 during the Hundred Years War. Within a few days, Joan of Arc, the Maid of Orléans, led the French forces to victory and convinced Charles the Dauphin to accept the crown of France.

Joan of Arc appears everywhere in Orléans. Her statue dominates the place du Martroi, and her profile graces the stained-glass windows of the reconstructed Gothic Cathédrale de Ste-Croix, (*open daily*), which also has beautiful 8th-century carved woodwork. The Maison Jeanne d'Arc museum (*3 place du Général de Gaulle; tel: 02 38 52 99 89; open: Tue–Sun; £*), in the house where Joan stayed during the ten-day siege, recalls her life and times.

The Musée des Beaux-Arts (*place Sainte-Croix; tel: 02 38 53 39 22; open: Tue and Sun 1100–1800, Wed 1000–2200 and Thu–Sat 1000–1800; ££*) is one of the best fine arts museums in the French provinces. The pride and joy of the collection is a series of French masterpieces from the 17th to 19th centuries, including signature works by Le Nain, Watteau, Boucher, Delacroix, and Cogniet. Picasso, Renoir, Monet, Miró, Braque and Dufy are all represented in the modern collection.

Saumur

Tourist information: place de la Bilange. Tel: 02 41 40 20 60; fax: 02 41 40 20 69; e-mail: infos@ot-saumur.fr; www.ot-saumur.fr.

Château de Saumur. Tel: 02 41 40 24 40. Open: daily Apr–Sept 0900–1630; mid-July–Aug 0900–2100; rest of the year 0900–1200 and 1400–1700/1800. ££.

If the high white silhouette of the château of Saumur seems familiar perhaps it is because it appears, easily identifiable, in **Les Très Riches Heures du Duc de Berry**, the most beautiful of French illuminated manuscripts. It overlooks the river and town and the surrounding landscape contributes well to the effect, since it is completely flat.

Built in the 12th century by Geoffrey Plantagenet, the château assumed more princely proportions in the 14th century under Jean le Bon, who equipped the towers with battlements and conical roofs, and added a forest of chimneys, dormers and *fleurs-de-lys* finials. The octagonal staircase at the eastern side of the *corps-de-logis* was built by King René (1409–80), who called Saumur his 'castle of love'.

Saumur has a long association with riding and horse breeding. The **École National d'Equitation** (National Riding School) (*St-Hilaire-St-Florent; tel: 02 41 53 50 60; open: Apr–Sept Mon–Sat, Oct–Mar by appointment; ££*) was opened here in 1972, and the **Musée de la Cavalerie** (Cavalry Museum), in the château, traces the history of horsemanship.

Wine and mushrooms

A wide variety of wines are produced around Saumur, particularly two reds, made from the *cabernet franc* grape, with *cabernet sauvignon* added, and two sparkling wines, Saumur Brut, and the more élite Crémant de Loire. The **Maison du Vin Saumur** (*25 rue Beaurepaire; tel: 02 41 51 16 40; ££*) is the place for information; alternatively, follow the **Route de Vin d'Anjou** from Angers.

The limestone quarries around Saumur provide the ideal conditions for mushroom production. At the Musée du Champignon (*5km (3 miles) northwest in the wine village of St-Hilaire-St-Florent; tel: 02 41 50 31 55; ££*), you can wander around in mushroom caves, and buy fresh, dried or preserved mushrooms, as well as local wines.

St-Benoît-sur-Loire

Tourist information: 44 rue Orléanaise. Tel: 02 38 35 79 00; fax: 02 38 35 79 00. Open: daily 0700–2200; guided tours 1030–1500.

The **abbey** at St-Benoît was built to accommodate the pilgrims who flocked here in their tens of thousands to come near the blessed bones of St-Benoît (St Benedict), the founder of Western monasticism, and of his sister, St Scholastica. The historical details are obscure but the relics seem to have been stolen in a medieval raid on the saint's original resting-place in Monte Cassino, Italy. They were presented to this abbey (then known as Fleury Abbey) in 675.

The **basilica**, constructed between 1067 and 1108, is one of the glories of Romanesque architecture in France. The soaring elegance of the chancel is matched by the energy and the dignity of the biblical sculptures in the porch. As well as its priceless relics, the abbey also acquired a Roman mosaic from Italy, which it used to pave the magnificent choir area. The belfry porch is sculpted with a parable of Paradise, the happy end of St John's Apocalypse, which ranks as one of the finest works of Romanesque art in France.

Tours

Tourist information: 78–82 rue Bernard Palissy. Tel: 02 47 70 37 37; fax: 02 47 61 14 22; e-mail: info@ligeris.com.

The fascinating regional capital of Tours lies behind a circle of busy roads. Already an important river port in Roman times, and prosperous in the Middle Ages (partly because of pilgrims flocking to its holy sites), it has undergone a quiet revival in recent years thanks to its university and a new, fast rail link to Paris.

Many of the half-timbered and crumbling stone buildings in the medieval centre – *Vieux Tours* – have been restored or rebuilt, and much of the old town is now pedestrianised. A series of quaint streets converge on **place Plumereau**, one of the best for people-watching in the region.

The city's **Cathédrale St-Gatien** is an intriguing Gothic pastiche, culminating in a Flamboyant west front. The nearby **Musée des Beaux Arts** (*18 place F Sicard; tel: 02 47 05 68 73; open: daily 0900–1245 and 1400–1800, except Tue; £*) occupies the former Archbishop's Palace. It has a fine collection of French and foreign paintings from the Middle Ages to the 20th century, including a prized Rembrandt and a pair of Renaissance Mantegnas.

There are dozens of excellent and affordable restaurants in Tours, all making use of the region's cornucopia of wine and food, and contributing to the locals' *art de vivre*. The town also has no less than 30 street markets selling fruit and vegetables, antiques, second-hand books, crafts and *charcuterie*.

Vendôme

Tourist information: Hôtel du Saillant – Parc Ronsard. Tel: 02 54 77 05 07; fax: 02 54 73 20 81.

Vendôme lies on the Loir – without an 'e' – a tributary that runs parallel to the more famous river, and enters it near Angers. Although it doesn't have as many châteaux, the Loir is more scenic than its famous neighbour, particularly at Vendôme, where it splits into many channels to flow past the town's old buildings, gardens, and shaded pathways.

The best place to contemplate the river's meanderings is from the terraces of the ruined castle that belonged to the dukes of Vendôme, which lies on a cliff on the south side of town. Although nothing much has happened at Vendôme since the 17th century, it was one of the most important cities in France in the Middle Ages. It was strategically placed, between the counts of Blois and Anjou and the king of France, prospered in many trades – printing, potting, tanning and glove-making – and was a major stop on the pilgrimage route to Santiago de Compostela. The Abbaye de la Trinité is the greatest monument to its medieval history.

The opening of a high-speed TGV railway line has now put Vendôme within 40 minutes of Paris.

Villandry

Tel: 02 47 50 02 09. Château open: daily mid-Feb–mid-Nov; guided tours only. Gardens open: daily 0900–1800/1900. ££.

The château at Villandry was rebuilt in 1536 by Jean le Breton, with unusual features, such as rectangular pavilions and an esplanade, and a surprising, and amazing, Hispano-Moorish (Mudejar-style) ceiling imported from Toledo in 3 000 pieces. A local carpenter worked for 15 years to put it back together.

But the really interesting thing about Villandry is the gardens, which are the most famous in the Loire Valley, and the largest, with more than 80,000 vegetable plants and 60,000 flowers. Fifty-two kilometres (32 miles) of hedges are shaped to create gardens honouring love (in its many different forms,

from tender to passionate), music, herbs and ornamental vegetables. Their design is a happy synthesis of the traditional monastic kitchen garden and the ornamental Italian garden. Three terraces – a water garden, an ornamental garden and a kitchen garden – are superimposed, separated by avenues of lime trees.

The re-creation of these fabulous Renaissance gardens was initiated at the beginning of the 20th century by Dr Joachim Carvallo, founder of the French Historic Houses Association, and his American wife, Ann Coleman.

Versailles

Louis XIV, the Sun King, built the palace of Versailles in the 17th century to show that French kings were second only (and only just) to God. King of France from 1643 until 1715, Louis was the longest reigning monarch in Europe.

The king first started work on transforming his father's hunting lodge in 1668, and ultimately created the largest palace in Europe. To give some impression of the scale of the place, in the late 18th century the palace was home to no fewer than 20,000 servants. The town grew up around the palace, which remained the royal residence for over 100 years. It was here that the seeds of the French Revolution were first sown.

> " *The last balls of Versailles were thrown with an elegant abandon that for generations of nostalgic admirers to come would create the vision of the old monarchy forever moving at the pace of a minuet, while marble fountains threw perfumed water into scalloped bowls.* "
>
> **Simon Schama,** *Citizens* (1989)

The **Galerie des Glaces** (Hall of Mirrors) was built in 1687 and was intended to be the most impressive room in the whole palace. Overseas guests would be brought here to be dazzled by the Sun King's wealth, and court festivities would be held here. The hall is 75m (245ft) long and 12m (40ft) high, with 17 windows facing 17 mirrors, each of which is made up of 34 separate pieces of glass – the largest pieces that could be produced at the time. Other parts of the interior of the palace may be seen on a guided tour (*book in advance at busy times of the year*).

One of Louis' first requests to the architects and designers was for a private pavilion where he could take his mistresses, and this was provided in the form of the Trianon de Porcelaine. In 1687 this was replaced by the **Grand Trianon**, a marble structure that still stands in the grounds. Not far away is the **Petit Trianon**, added by Louis XV in 1762, but better known for its associations with Marie-Antoinette, who loved it and spent a great deal of time there, playing at the rural life.

The **gardens of Versailles** are among the most spectacular in Europe, the masterpiece of Louis XIV's landscaper *extraordinare*, André Le Nôtre. Among the highlights are the famous water parterres, with their ornate bronze statues, immediately behind the main building, the Grand Canal, where royal boating parties would take place, and the Orangerie, where the tender plants were kept. Sadly, more than 10,000 trees in the park were uprooted in a terrible winter storm at the end of 1999, but they are now being replanted.

23km (14 miles) southwest of Paris. Tourist information: 7 rue des Réservoirs. Tel: 01 39 50 36 22. Château de Versailles. Tel: 01 30 84 74 00. Open: daily May–Oct 0900–1900; Nov–Apr Mon–Sat 0900–1230 and 1330–1800. £££.

Getting there: Take the RER train, line C, to Versailles-Rive Gauche, then walk through the town to the château. By car: take the A13 from the Porte d'Auteuil, or the N10 from the Porte de Sèvres. Try to get to Versailles as early as possible, not just to beat the crowds but to allow enough time for your visit – there is a great deal to see.

> " *Successive Ministers of Culture have given priority to saving ancient monuments rather than to encouraging new French styles: ironically, in trying to resist shapeless Americanization, they restored Versailles largely with grants from American philanthropists, organised by the American wife of the curator of that palace. 'It is no longer Versailles,' mourns one of those who think the restoration has been overdone, 'it is Technicolor made in USA'.* "

Theodore Zeldin,
***The French* (1983)**

215

Eating and drinking

Le Blason
1 place de Richelieu, Amboise. Tel: 02 47 23 22 41; fax: 02 47 57 56 18. £.
It would be hard to find a restaurant that offers more for the price of a fixed franc menu. It has also has a range of imaginative à la carte dishes.

Le Manoir St-Thomas
1 mail St-Thomas, between Amboise and Le Clos-Lucé. Tel: 02 47 57 22 52; fax: 02 47 30 44 71. Closed Mon. ££.
Renaissance manor house set in its own small park – a fine setting in which to savour the Loire's regional cuisine from the kitchen of François Le Coz.

Le Grand Monarque
3 place de la République, Azay-le-Rideau. Tel: 02 47 45 40 08. Closed Sun evening and Mon. ££. A former coaching inn that is now a friendly family-run hotel and restaurant almost in the shadow of the château.

Au Rendez-vous des Pêcheurs
27 rue du Foix, Blois. Tel: 02 54 78 05 36. ££. Just a short walk from the Blois château. Fresh fish is king here. Loire Valley *sandre* (a perch-like river fish) and crayfish are usually on the menu.

Café Serpente
2 Cloitre Notre Dame, Chartres. £.
A café right across from the cathedral that serves good simple meals (*coq au vin*, etc).

Nantes

Brasserie La Cigalle
place Graslin. Tel: 02 51 84 94 94. ££.
A beautiful art-nouveau interior which some claim is the finest in France. Breton and Nantais specialities.

La Mangeoire
16 rue des Petits Ecuries. Tel: 02 40 48 70 83. Closed Sun, Mon and for 10 days in May and one week in September. ££. Excellent French cuisine with good-value set meals.

Le Pont Levis
17 rue des États. Tel: 02 40 35 10 20. ££. Outdoor tables facing the château.

Vegetarian restaurants in **Nantes** include **L'Arbre de Vie** (*8 allée des Tanneurs; tel: 02 40 08 06 10; closes towards the end of July and remains closed for most of August; ££*) and **L'Île Verte** (*3 rue S Foucault; tel: 02 40 49 01 26; closed Wed and Sun and through August; £*).

Nightlife

Le Vieux Murier
place Plumereau, Tours. Few towns in the Loire Valley have much nightlife to speak of. The university town of Tours is an exception and this eccentric bar with live music is at its epicentre, at the foot of Gothic houses on place Plumereau.

The larder of France

The valley of the Loire served, historically, as the royal larder of France. Today, the gardens and forests of the region still provide **Paris markets** *with some of their best fish, mushrooms, game, early vegetables and fruit.* **Seafood** *– such as* huitres *(oysters) and* moules *(mussels) – are usually on the menu in the Loire estuary around Nantes. Further inland,* **fish from the river** *dominate the menus; look out for pike in a* beurre blanc *(white wine, shallots and butter) sauce or in* quenelles*, as well as* friture *(tiny fried fish),* sandre *(pike-perch) and* anguille *(eel).*

The regions around Tours and Anjou are, by contrast, more meaty. Here, you'll find delicious *charcuterie* (cold meats) and *rillettes*, a speciality of shredded pork, cooked and preserved in its own fat. It dates back to the Middle Ages, when refrigeration was impossible, and makes a delicious spread, often served in place of pâté. Further upstream, you can savour *boudin blanc* and *boudin noir* (veal and blood sausages) and the smoked *jambon de Sancerre*.

The tradition of **hunting** in the Loire region goes back many centuries and, in autumn, local people eat quail, hare, partridge, rabbit and wild boar with great relish, often accompanied by wild or cultivated mushrooms. You can enjoy good **cheese** any time of year; keep an eye (or nostril!) open for the *crottin de chavignol* goat's cheese. *Crottin* means 'horse dung', and the tiny, crusty cheeses do bear a certain resemblance, but their flavour is so fine that the variety has earned an *appellation contrôlée*. Of all the desserts of the Loire Valley, the single most famous is the *tarte Tatin*, or caramelised apple pie.

Wines of the Loire Valley

For much of its 1 000km (621 mile) length, the Loire provides an ideal climate for **wines**, and more than 80 varieties are produced along its banks. The opportunities for *dégustation* (tasting) along the river are almost limitless, the choices ranging from bone-dry Chenin Blanc to luxuriously sweet dessert wines, from sparkling *crémants* to brisk Cabernet Francs. Pouilly-sur-Loire is perhaps the most famous area, though the vineyards of Sancerre, just across the river, are also renowned. From there, the Loire flows northwest through other regions – Touraine, Anjou-Saumur and Muscadet – which all boast distinctive wines, before it finally reaches the Atlantic. En route, you will see many *vente en direct* signs where you can taste and buy wine from small producers. Otherwise, look out for some of the following wines and winemakers:

Reds

Chinon – producers: Charles Joguet, Couly-Dutheil
Bourgueil – producers: Clos de l'Abbaye, Domaine des Galluches/Jean Gambier

Whites

Pouilly Fumé – producers: Château de Nozet la Doucette, Dagueneau
Sancerre – producers: Alphonse Mellot, Vacheron, Vincent Delaport
Vouvray – producers: Clos Baudoin, Domaine Huet, Château Gaudrelle

Brittany and Normandy

Neighbours, but with very different histories and traditions. Brittany is truly ancient – Carnac may have been continuously inhabited longer than anywhere in the world – and the Celtic Breton culture has survived more than four centuries of French domination.

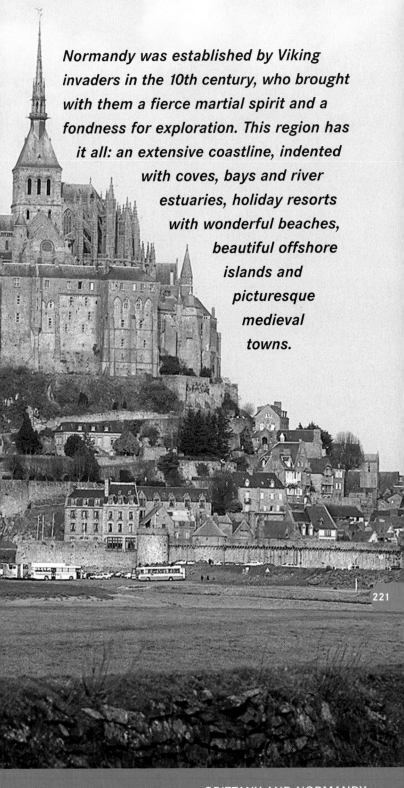

Normandy was established by Viking invaders in the 10th century, who brought with them a fierce martial spirit and a fondness for exploration. This region has it all: an extensive coastline, indented with coves, bays and river estuaries, holiday resorts with wonderful beaches, beautiful offshore islands and picturesque medieval towns.

BEST OF
Brittany and Normandy

Getting there: *From London (Gatwick) there are regular flights to Caen, Deauville, Le Havre and Rouen (Normandy) and to Quimper, Brest, Nantes and Rennes (Brittany).* **Brit Air** *(tel: 01923 502044 (UK), 98 62 10 22 (France)), or* **Air France** *(tel: 020 8742 6600 (UK), 44 08 24 24 (France)). The main rail stations are Rennes, Nantes, Quimper and Brest. For those taking the car, the ferry ports of Le Havre, Calais, Boulogne and Cherbourg are ideal for Normandy, while St-Malo, Roscoff, Brest and Cherbourg are useful gateways to Brittany. The A11 and A81 connect Paris with Nantes, while the A13 and A84 link Rennes with Le Havre. From Cherbourg, the N13 goes direct to Caen and other destinations in Normandy.*

① *The parish closes of the Elorn valley and the Monts d'Arrée*

Marvel at the craftsmanship displayed in the magnificent sculptures of these 'closes' – testament to Breton religious fervour in the 16th and 17th centuries. Some of the best were created by communities that grew rich on the cloth trade. **Pages 232–3**

② *Dinan*

Dinan's medieval port and the cobbled streets around it once echoed to the sounds of a prosperous community, trading in all sorts of commodities, from leather to wax. Today, this perfectly preserved town is more used to the sound of tourists trotting round its many delightful sites and eating places. **Page 237**

③ *Giverny*

See at first hand the charming and colourful subject of Monet's world-famous Impressionist garden paintings – from the Japanese bridge to the water garden, designed by Monet himself. **Page 241**

④ *Mont-St-Michel*

Follow in the footsteps of millions of visitors, who have been coming here for centuries to see this extraordinary ecclesiastical architectural ensemble perched on a granite rock in the swirling and unpredictable sea. **Pages 244–5**

⑤ *Quiberon and Belle-Île*

Coastal walks, white-sand beaches and all sorts of boat trips are the attractions of the beautiful Quiberon peninsula. Enjoy the spectacular coastline around the peninsula, and then jump on a boat to visit the islands of the delightful Gulf of Morbihan. **Page 248**

⑥ *Rennes*

This lively student town has rich architecture, a huge choice of bars and restaurants, and other evening entertainment, beautiful formal gardens and an unmissable Saturday morning produce market. **Pages 250–1**

⑦ *St-Malo*

Originally the island stronghold of fiercely independent privateer sailors, this walled city, one of the busiest of France's northern ferry ports, is now the liveliest town on the Emerald Coast. Wander round its narrow streets, and on the harbour, to find the perfect pavement restaurant or *crêperie*, or a traditional bar full of sea-going Malouins. **Page 254**

⑧ *Vannes*

Historic Vannes is the most convenient departure point for boat trips around the Gulf of Morbihan and its beautiful islands. The town itself is a delight, with 600m of the original ramparts and half-timbered houses nestled behind them. **Page 255**

Avranches

Tourist information: 2 rue du Général de Gaulle. Tel: 02 22 58 00 22.

Avranches, one of the oldest towns in Normandy, has suffered an unusually turbulent history, from the salt-workers' revolt of 1639 to the Second World War. It claims some interesting connections with Thomas à Becket. Its **Musée Municipal** (*place Jean de St-Avit; tel: 02 33 58 25 15; open: daily June–Sept 0930–1200 and 1400–1800, Easter–May closed Tue; £*), housed in the 15th-century bishop's palace, displays a reliquary containing the archbishop's bones. At the end of the palace garden, in **place Thomas à Becket**, a paving stone marks the spot where, in 1172, Henry II publicly repented of the murder of his erstwhile friend and chancellor.

Rue Challemel Lacour has some quaint old houses. From the terraced gardens of the beautiful **Jardin des Plantes** (*open: daily 0830–dark; free*), which once belonged to a Franciscan monastery, there are stunning views over the Baie du St-Michel. The **Bibliothèque du Fonds Ancien** (*Mairie d'Avranches; tel: 02 33 68 33 18; open: daily July–Aug 1000–1800, June and Sept 1000–1200 and 1400–1800; ££, combined ticket with museum*) has a wonderful collection of **illuminated manuscripts** and ancient books, including classical works by Aristotle and Cicero, and outstanding examples of medieval calligraphy.

Basse-Seine

Basse-Seine is the region that lies between Rouen and the sea. Being navigable to large ships, this part of the Seine is lined with factories and refineries and looks, at first sight, rather uninviting. There are, however, many surprises to be found amongst the flatlands of the lower Seine, not least the pastoral countryside, cut by meandering rivers and grazed by dappled brown Normandy cattle. One sight not to be missed is the ancient **Abbaye de Jumièges** (*tel: 02 35 37 24 02; open:*

daily), an atmospheric ruin, built by William the Conqueror and dedicated in 1067, but incorporating the remains of earlier Merovingian and Carolingian churches. It stands in a wooded hollow above the Seine; a ferry below the village takes cars and passengers across the Seine to the dense and extensive beech woodlands of the Brotonne Forest.

Further downstream is the **Abbaye de St-Wandrille** (*tel: 02 35 96 23 11; church always open, and guided tours of the cloister given at 1530 weekdays, 1130 Sun*), another ancient abbey, founded in the 7th century by St Wandrille. This abbey still functions as a living Benedictine community, which was re-established here in 1930. A beautiful 13th-century barn, brought to the site, has been turned into a simple but atmospheric church. At nearby **Caudebec-en-Caux**, the excellent **Musée de la Marine de Seine** provides an account of life in this watery region.

Three road bridges cross the Seine along this stretch, including the spectacular Pont de Normandie (opened 1995), linking Le Havre and Honfleur across the estuary.

Bayeux

Tourist information: Pont St-Jean. Tel: 02 31 51 28 28.

The first French city to be liberated after D-Day, Bayeux alone survived the Second World War with its medieval core almost intact. The **Bayeux Tapestry** is officially the **Tapisserie de la Reine Mathilde** (*Centre Guillaume le Conquérant, rue de Nesmond; tel: 02 31 51 25 50; open: daily May–Aug 0900–1900, 14 Mar–Apr, Sept–15 Oct 0900–1830, 16 Oct–13 Mar 0900–1230 and 1400–1800; ££*). It is exhibited under glass in the Harold Room of a former seminary now known as the William the Conqueror Centre. Its scenes are wonderfully revealing about everyday life in the 11th century, while its border friezes display exuberant depictions of fabulous beasts.

The tapestry's original home was the breathtaking **Cathédrale de Notre-Dame** (*open: July–Aug 0800–1900, Sept–June 0900–1215 and 1430–1900; closed to visitors during services*). The crypt and the towers at the west end are all that survive of the building consecrated by Bishop Odo in 1077, but the Gothic chancel is one of the finest in France.

For broad coverage of the events following D-Day, head for the **Musée Mémorial 1944, Bataille de Normandie** (*boulevard Fabian Ware; tel: 02 31 92 93 41; open: daily; ££*). Directly opposite is the **British War Cemetery**. Just behind the cathedral is the place de la Liberté, a charming little square named after the plane tree known as **L'Arbre de la Liberté** (Liberty Tree), planted here during the Revolution. **Rue Franche** has some of the best examples of Bayeux's well-preserved old houses (15th to 18th centuries).

Brest

Tourist information: 8 avenue Georges Clemenceau. Tel: 02 98 44 24 96; fax: 02 98 44 53 73.

An important naval base since the days of Cardinal Richelieu in the 17th century, Brest was almost totally destroyed by Allied bombing during the Second World War.

The **Rade de Brest** is one of the most impressive natural harbours in the world. A long promenade offers fine views, but a boat cruise from the Port de Plaisance (Pleasure Port) offers a more complete orientation. Look out for the military harbour and shipping lanes, the aircraft carrier *Charles de Gaulle* (still under construction) and the nuclear submarine base.

The port is also the embarkation point for the Crozon peninsula, as well as the site of Brest's one undisputed tourist attraction, **Océanopolis** (*Port de Plaisance du Moulin Blanc; tel: 02 98 34 40 40; open: daily May–Sept 0930–1800, Oct–Apr 0930–1700, closed Mon am; £££*). Created with a view to making oceanology accessible to the general public, this vast scientific theme park sets out to replicate a complete marine environment. With the help of models, 3-D films, computer graphics and a variety of 'hands-on' experiences specifically with children in mind, you'll learn about the movement of the oceans, shipping and navigation, marine pollution, sea birds and coastal flora and fauna. There are fish tanks, the largest open-air aquariums in Europe and a seal pool.

Caen

Tourist information: place St-Pierre. Tel: 02 31 27 14 14.

Caen was heavily bombed during the Second World War but many of its historic buildings have been painstakingly restored. A regional capital and a lively university town, Caen can also offer excellent shopping, late-night bars, a yachting marina and river cruises, with more than 460 hectares (1 137 acres) of green space thrown in for good measure.

Caen was William the Conqueror's favourite town and you can still see the massive ramparts of the **château**, the ducal castle founded in about 1060. Contained within the walls are a 12th-century chapel, the ruins of the keep (added by Henry I of England) and the Great Hall of the duke's palace, known as the **Salle d'Échiquier**. The 14th-century governor's residence is now the **Musée de Normandie** (*esplanade du Château; tel: 02 31 86 06 24; open: daily except Tue, 0930–1230 and 1400–1800, Oct–Mar Wed–Mon 0930–1230 and 1400–1800; £*), a local history museum.

Le Mémorial (*esplanade Dwight-Eisenhower; tel: 02 31 06 06 44; open: daily 0900–1900 (till 2100 between 11 July and 23 Aug), closed Jan; £££*) is a museum dedicated to peace and human rights. Built on the site of the German command centre during the Battle of Normandy, it uses high-tech resources to take visitors on a sombre but compelling journey through the history of Europe in the 20th century.

Falaise

The historic town of Falaise, 29km (18 miles) south of Caen, was the birthplace of William the Conqueror. The château was built on the rocky spur, or 'cliff' from which the town gets its name. The impressive buttressed keep and circular tower are best viewed from the Fontaine d'Arlette beside the River Aute. According to legend, this fountain marks the spot where William's parents, Robert and washerwoman Arlette, first set eyes on each other.

The **Abbaye-aux-Hommes** (*esplanade Jean-Marie Louvel; open: daily*) and the **Abbaye-aux-Dames** (*place de la Reine Mathilde; open: daily*) were founded by William the Conqueror and his consort Matilda, respectively. The **Église St-Étienne** (*open: daily*), completed in the 13th century, contains the tomb of the Conqueror and his mortal remains (perhaps only a thigh-bone after a succession of robberies).

Cancale

Tourist information: 44 rue du Port. Tel: 02 99 89 63 72.

Famous for its oysters since ancient times (archaeologists have found shells in excavated Roman army camps), Cancale harbour is still as busy as ever with fishermen. Six thousand tonnes of oysters, cultivated from year-old 'spats' brought in from the Belon estuary, are produced every year. Sample them from a quayside stall or from one of many restaurants overlooking the sea. The Sentier des Douaniers, a clifftop walk to **Pointe de Grouin**, leaving from the steps at the end of rue de Port, offers views of the oyster beds at the foot of the cliffs. To find out more about the industry, visit the informative museum-cum-oyster farm, **La Ferme Marine** (*L'aurore, St-Kerber; tel: 02 99 89 69 99; tours daily June–Sept (at 1400 in English), Feb–June and Sept–Oct in French only; ££*).

A long cobbled street leads from the port to the old town on the hill. Here, in the former **Église St-Méen**, a museum of the art and traditions of Cancale (*tel: 02 99 89 79 32; open: 1 July–31 Aug 1000–1200 and 1430–1830 except Mon am, June and Sept Fri–Sun 1430–1830; £*) includes an exhibition on the town's historic sailing school.

Carnac

Tourist information: 74 avenue des Druides. Tel: 02 97 52 13 52.

The first humans arrived in Carnac more than 7 000 years
ago and have been here ever since. Carnac is one of the
most important prehistoric sites in the world – and it trades
mercilessly on the fact. The **Alignements**, just outside Carnac
Ville, are parallel rows of about 2 700 monumental menhirs
(stones), spread out over a distance of nearly 4km (2 1/2 miles).
Access is restricted although you can still get quite close to
the Alignements de Kermario on foot. There are views of
the Alignements du Ménec (the largest concentration of
stones) from the **Archéoscope** audio-visual centre. The
D196 road offers another good vantage point. The **Tumulus
de St-Michel** is a large burial mound dating from around
3000 BC with primitive chambers and passageways – not
for the claustrophobic!

To get a proper historical perspective on Carnac and its earliest inhabitants, it's essential to visit the lively and imaginative **Musée de Préhistoire** (Museum of Prehistory) (*10 place de la Chapelle; tel: 02 97 52 22 04; open: Wed–Mon 1000–1200 and 1400–1700, closes 1800 June–Sept, July–Aug 1000–1830, incl Tue; £*). The wonderful finds range from primitive tools to exquisite brooches and necklaces. The voyage of discovery begins 450,000 years ago, and ends with the arrival of the Celts.

The seaside resort of **Carnac Plage** is the town's other face, with many typical resort amenities. The main beach fills up quickly, but there are more secluded alternatives to east and west. Avenue des Druides, behind the seafront, is the place to shop and eat.

Cherbourg

Tourist information: quai Alexandre III. Tel: 02 33 93 52 02.

One of the busiest ports of entry for cross-Channel ferries, unprepossessing Cherbourg is also an important naval base. If you're looking for something to do you could take a stroll along the beach, calling in at the **Basilique de la Trinité**, a 14th- to 15th-century church with lurid medieval bas-reliefs depicting the Dance of Death. Alternatively, for the energetic, there are good views of the harbour and roadstead from the **Fort du Roule** where the **Musée de la Libération** (*Fort du Roule; tel: 02 33 20 14 12; open: daily Apr–Sept 1000–1800, Oct–Mar Tue–Sun 0930–1200 and 1400–1730; £*) takes a look at life in Cherbourg during the Second World War, and the role played by the town in the Allied landings. If you're an art lover, the **Musée Thomas Henry** (*rue Vastel; tel: 02 33 23 02 23; open: Tue–Sat 0900–1200 and 1400–1800, Sun 1000–1200 and 1400–1800; £*) is a real find, with more than 300 paintings and sculptures from the 13th to 19th centuries, including works by Fra Angelico, Murillo and the locally born French artist, Jean-François Millet.

Closes (*Enclos Paroissiaux*)

Brittany's remarkable 'parish closes' date mainly from the 16th and 17th centuries, and bear witness to a religious fervour derived from a twin obsession with death and eternal salvation. Each commune would try to outdo the others in the splendour of its close.

The best examples are concentrated in the Elorn valley and the foothills of the Monts d'Arrée, where towns and villages grew rich on the profits of the cloth trade. The typical close comprises a triumphal arch, to mark the transition from the secular to the sacred world; an ossuary, where the bones of dead parishioners were exhibited; and a calvary decorated with vivid sculptures representing Christ's Passion.

Guimiliau

Guimiliau's extraordinary and memorable calvary dates from 1581 to 1588. It is composed of almost 200 animated granite figures, including St Peter cutting off the ear of the servant Malchus and a spirited rendering of the Breton morality tale of Katherine the Damned, dragged off naked to hell by demons. Miniature stone dramas are crammed into every available recess of the porch. One of the most attractive depicts a drunken Noah. Above the Renaissance pediment is a representation of the local patron saint, Miliau, King of Cornouaille.

La Martyre

La Martyre dates from as far back as the 1450s. In the porch, Ankou (the Celtic representation of Death) appears wielding a mace and a severed head. The Breton inscription reads: 'Death judgement, cold hell: let man think on these things and tremble'. The 15th-century chancel screen is lit by 16th-century stained glass.

Lampaul-Guimiliau

The interior of the church at Lampaul-Guimiliau is ablaze with colour: delicately sculpted groupings of polychrome or gilded figures are surrounded by florid capitals and other ornamentation. The best example is the Passion altarpiece, with a frame of columns wreathed with whorls of vine leaves. Other treasures include – a real rarity – fragments of original medieval stained glass, pieced together and reassembled.

Plougastel-Daoulas

This rather ordinary town is famous for its strawberries, and for one of the finest calvaries in Brittany, commissioned after a devastating outbreak of plague in 1598. It has more than 180 carved figures, including Christ emerging from the tomb and the two thieves, watched over by an angel and a devil respectively. The church is vividly decorated with numerous painted wooden altarpieces.

St-Thégonnec

Behind a highly ornamented triumphal arch, St-Thégonnec's magnificent calvary, built by the stonemasons of Landerneau in 1610, was the last of its kind. The ossuary (1676–82) is a splendid example of late French Renaissance style, with Corinthian columns, alcoves and canopies flanked by caryatids, dragons and other motifs. Inside, don't miss the moving *Entombment* by the Breton sculptor Jacques Lespaignol (1702).

The church was badly damaged by fire in 1998 and most of the statuary, and some altarpieces, have been moved for restoration. The magnificent pulpit, with its detailed carved reliefs, survived intact. St-Thégonnec is the village patron, and images of him abound; in the Holy Sacrament reredos, he appears in typical guise as a bishop, with a wolf harnessed to a cart by his feet. According to legend, the saint forced the wolf to pull the cart after it had eaten his donkey.

Côte Fleurie

The 'Floral Coast' was first developed in the 19th century and most of its resorts have stately seaside promenades and villas of fading elegance. There are racecourses at Cabourg and Deauville, and trotters and racehorses are bred in local stud farms. The area around Lisieux is Camembert cheese country.

Cabourg

Tourist information: Jardin du Casino. Tel: 02 31 91 01 09.

1066

It was just along the coast from Cabourg, at Dives-sur-Mer, that William the Conqueror set sail for England in 1066, changing the course of history.

Cabourg is one of the oldest towns in Normandy but the bathing resort dates only from the *belle époque*. The severely asthmatic writer Marcel Proust was a regular visitor from the 1880s until 1914. He rarely made it to the beach (too draughty!) but was familiar with the golf club and the Casino.

Deauville

Tourist information: place de la Mairie. Tel: 02 31 14 40 00.

Deauville was created in just four years, between 1860 and 1864, and was still thought chic in the 1930s. There are now two **racecourses**, Clairefontaine and La Touques, as well as a superb **beach** and a watersports centre. It's still fashionable – just – to take a stroll on the famous duckboard promenade (*Les Planches*) behind the beach.

Marcel Proust

*Unable to drive, **Marcel Proust** employed one of the first car-hire firms in Cabourg to chauffeur him through the Normandy countryside at reckless speeds, swaddled in overcoats and protected by a leather helmet.*

Honfleur

Tourist information: place Arthur Boudin. Tel: 02 31 89 23 30.

Life in Honfleur revolves around the **Vieux Bassin**, the old port where restaurants and bars now occupy the ground floors of slate-hung houses.

Behind them are the **Greniers à Sel**, huge 17th-century warehouses once used to store salt for the cod fleet. The cobbled quays, twisting alleyways and brightly painted fishing boats proved inspirational to many of the Impressionists.

On the other side of the harbour is the old town and its focal point **place St Catherine**, where the **church** was constructed largely of wood by local shipbuilders in the 15th century.

Lisieux

Tourist information: 11 rue d'Alençon. Tel: 02 31 62 08 41.

Lisieux owes its fame to Thérèse Martin (**St Theresa of Lisieux**), who joined the Carmelite order at the tender age of 15, spent her short life in the local convent and died of TB in 1897. She was canonised by Pius XI in 1925. The vast **Basilique de Ste-Thérèse**, one of the largest churches to be built in the 20th century, was completed in 1954 and is now a place of pilgrimage.

Trouville

Tourist information: 32 quai Fernand Moureaux. Tel: 02 31 14 60 70.

Trouville has all the ingredients of a typical French seaside resort: golden sand, a boardwalk, an **aquarium**, a thalassotherapy centre and a casino. It became fashionable in the 1860s when Napoleon III brought his court here. The **port**, with its narrow, flower-bedecked streets lined with fishermen's houses, is the venue for a traditional fish market every morning.

235

Tip

Bones from St Theresa's right arm are on display in a reliquary in the south transept of the basilica in Lisieux. The rest of her remains (and items of her clothing) can be found in the Chapelle du Carmel

Combourg

Tourist information: Maison de la Lanterne, place Albert-Parent. Tel: 02 99 73 13 93; fax: 02 99 73 52 39.

Rising above the grey-granite town of Combourg are the turreted towers of one of France's most impressive medieval fortresses. In 1761 the **château** (*23 rue des Princes; tel: 02 99 73 22 95; open: daily July–Aug, park: 0900–1200 and 1400–1730; château: Apr–June and Sept–Nov 1400–1730, closed Tue; ££ combined, £ park only*) became the family home of Combourg's most famous son, the Romantic writer François René de Chateaubriand. Not all his memories of the place were happy. In his autobiography, he recounted how his morose father could not tolerate children and would routinely banish François and his sister to their rooms. There, the boy was terrified by a ghost who assumed the form of a cat during his nightly hauntings.

Concarneau

Tourist information: quai d'Aiguillon. Tel: 02 98 97 01 44.

Concarneau's old town, known as the **Ville-Close**, is built on an island, linked to the rest of the town by a bridge. Inside, the narrow streets and alleyways are lined with the predictable mixture of souvenir shops, art galleries and *crêperies*. Escape the mêlée by taking a walk on the massive granite 14th-century **ramparts**, strengthened in the 17th century by master military engineer Vauban. In the excellent **Musée de la Pêche** (*3 rue Vauban (Ville-Close); tel: 02 98 97 10 20; open: daily July–Aug 0930–1930, daily Sept–Dec and Feb–June 1000–1200 and 1400–1700; ££*) you can clamber aboard a trawler for a good insight into the life of an Atlantic fisherman. **Boat excursions** leave from the marina for **Quimper** or the **Îles de Glénan**. There are good beaches to the north and south of the town.

Descriptive Dinan

According to novelist Victor Hugo, Dinan was like 'a house martin's nest cleaving to a precipice'.

Dinan

Tourist information: rue de l'Horloge. Tel: 02 96 39 75 40. Guided themed tours of the town in season (not Sun, holidays); combined museum ticket 'Les Clefs de Dinan' includes entry to castle, Tour de l'Horloge and Maison du Gouverneur.

This perfectly preserved medieval town enjoys a strategic setting high above the Rance valley. This location, coupled with the protection of powerful overlords, enabled Dinan to spawn a prosperous mercantile community trading in wool and cloth, reflected in street names such as rue de la Lainerie (Woolshops Street) and place des Merciers (Haberdashers' Square).

Colourful half-timbered houses, dating mostly from the 14th and 15th centuries, overhang the cobbled streets of the old town. Around **place des Cordeliers** and **place des Merciers**, they were built with arcades, where tradesmen would have sold their wares. The church of **St-Sauveur** has a superb Romanesque porch, with intricate carving, and the heart of the famous Breton knight, Bertrand du Guesclin, under a gravestone in the north transept. The most accessible stretch of Dinan's girdle of ramparts and watch towers connects the neat flower beds of the **Jardin Anglais** (English Garden) with the **du Sillon** tower.

Dinan's most picturesque street, **rue du Petit Fort**, through the monumental **Porte du Jerzual**, is a steep, cobbled roadway leading down to the port. Once an important thoroughfare, echoing to the clatter of carts crammed with ships' timbers, cloth and wax bound for St-Malo, it's now an 'artisans' quarter', with workshops and galleries.

Côte d'Emeraude

The **Emerald Coast** stretches from **St-Malo** to the **Baie de St-Brieuc**. The landscape is rugged for the most part and heavily indented with bays and coves, river estuaries and rocky peninsulas.

The beauty spot of **Cap Fréhel** is a 'must-see', with 160 hectares (395 acres) of unspoilt heath and moorland, sheer cliffs of schist and pink sandstone form a natural barrier to the advancing sea, which lashes the reefs more than 70m (230ft) below. There are panoramic views of the coastline from here, stretching all the way from the **Île de Bréhat** in the west to **Pointe de Grouin** in the east. The fortress of **Fort la Latte** (*open: daily June–Sept, guided tours only; ££*) is perched on a rocky spur overlooking the Cap.

Dinard

Tourist information: 2 boulevard Féart. Tel: 02 99 46 94 12; fax: 02 99 88 21 07.

Once a humble fishing village, Dinard acquired an opulent, even regal air in the late 19th century, when American and British visitors attempted to outdo one another in the grandeur of their cliff-top villas. The French were quick to follow suit and today these neo-Gothic residences are a valued attraction. Dinard still attracts the smart set. Most visitors head straight for one of the three beaches, for swimming, windsurfing, kayaking and other watersports. A pre-dinnner stroll along the Promenade de Clair de Lune (illuminated at night), with its garden backdrop of palm trees, eucalyptus and mimosa, is a good way to savour the atmosphere.

Douarnenez

Tourist information: 2 rue du Dr-Mével. Tel: 02 98 92 13 35; fax: 02 98 74 46 09.

For the perfect photo opportunity visit Douarnenez in the evening as the brightly painted fishing boats return to the haven of **Rosmeur** and dazzling white yachts head for the marina at **Tréboul**. Early in the morning, don't miss the fish auctions in front of the canning factories on the quay, before taking a stroll through the maze of little streets behind the port to the market at **place Gabriel Péri**.

The beaches at Douarnenez are not safe for swimming, but there are sea-fishing trips and boat excursions along the coast. **Vedettes Rosmeur** (*Port de Pêche; tel: 02 98 92 83 83 (Apr–June, tel: 02 06 85 95 55 49)*) run trips to the seabird sanctuary at **Cap Sizun**.

The excellent **Musée du Bateau** (*place de l'Enfer, Le Port-Rhu; tel: 02 98 92 65 20; open: daily 15 June–Sept 1000–1900, Oct–Dec and Feb–mid-June Tue–Sun 1000–1230 and 1400–1800; ££*), housed in a former sardine cannery, has a superb collection of sailing vessels, including flat-bottomed coracles, a Dutch *tjotter* and primitive rowing boats made from animal skins. All sorts of craftsmen are on hand to demonstrate their skills, or you can clamber aboard the steam tug *Saint Denys*, one of 50 boats moored in the **Rhu estuary**. A 19th-century **waterfront** has been re-created on the far side of the harbour.

Évreux

Évreux, capital of the Eure *département*, has done its best to recover from devastating damage caused by wartime bombing by turning the pathways along the banks of the River Iton into a delightful walk. Following the path, you will discover Roman ramparts and glimpse the city's Gothic and Renaissance cathedral, with its imposing 15th-century bell tower.

To the west of Évreux, **Conches-en-Ouche** occupies a dramatic site encircled by the River Rouloir. The **church of St-Foy** is renowned for its Renaissance stained-glass windows on the life of Christ and the life of St Foy, inspired by the engravings of Dürer.

The *département* of **Eure** is at its prettiest further east, where country roads follow the River Eure from Pacy-sur-Eure to Dreux, a region of villages with timber houses and the dense woodland of the Dreux Forest. Further south still is the **Perche** region – famous as the home of the Percheron horse, a huge and beautiful draught horse, bred by Crusaders as battle horses and crossed with Arab blood. Also here is the **Abbaye La Trappe**, isolated in the La Trappe forest and founded by the Cistercians in 1147. The reforming Abbot de Rancé introduced a new strict rule in the 17th century, and those who follow the rule have been known as Trappists ever since – an audio-visual show at the abbey explains exactly what is involved in following the Strict Observance.

Giverny

Fondation Claude Monet, rue Claude Monet. Tel: 02 32
Open: Apr–Nov Tue–Sun 1000–1800. ££.

The village where the renowned Impre.
Claude Monet, made his home for the las
his life (1883–1926) is now a major tourist ...., even
though there isn't a single original canvas by the artist here.
Monet's house and gardens are open to the public as
a museum. The artist's studio is now a gift shop and
reception centre with little to evoke him, besides books,
videos and reproductions of his paintings.

The rest of the house is more atmospheric, especially the rooms
decorated with Monet's wonderful collection of Japanese prints.
The **gardens** will bowl you over. The walled garden to the
rear of the house, known as the *clos Normand*, is a riot of
colour, its shrubs and archways of climbing plants designed by
Monet himself. From here a tunnel leads to the *Jardin d'Eau*
('Water Garden') and the water-lilies that were such a great
source of inspiration to the artist. The famous Japanese bridge

casts shadows on the
pond as wisterias,
azaleas, rhododendrons
and weeping willows
bewitch and dazzle.

A short stroll from
Monet's house is the
Musée Americain
(*99 rue Claude Monet;
tel: 02 32 51 94 65;
open: Apr–Oct Tue–
Sun 1000–1800;
££*), which exhibits
works by leading
American disciples
of Monet, including
Whistler and John
Singer Sargent.

241

...elin

The **château** at Josselin has been in the hands of the Rohan family for more than 500 years already and they're still in residence. Three tent-roofed towers guarding the River Oust and a magnificent façade overlooking the park are all that remain of the original building, which was destroyed on the orders of Cardinal Richelieu in 1629. The **Musée des Poupées** (Doll Museum) in the former stables has a collection of more than 600 dolls and toys from all over the world, the oldest dating back to the 17th century.

Hemmed in between the castle and the hillside is the old town and the ancient basilica of **Notre-Dame des Ronciers**. Founded in the 12th century, the church honours the legend of a peasant who found a statue of the Virgin in a bramble bush – Our Lady of the Brambles. For good views of the château, cross the river to the picturesque little quarter of **Ste-Croix**, with its 11th-century chapel.

The Butcher

The south chapel of Notre-Dame des Ronciers in Josselin houses the tomb of the one-eyed Olivier de Clisson, called 'the Butcher' – his trademark was chopping off the arms and legs of English opponents during battle.

Le Havre

Tourist information: 186 boulevard Clemenceau. Tel: 02 32 74 04 04.

Le Havre was founded in 1517 to replace the silted harbours at Honfleur and Harfleur. Following its almost total destruction during the Second World War, it was largely rebuilt in concrete. Among the controversial buildings are the **Hôtel de Ville**, set in a vast square, the **Église St-Joseph**, with its 106m-high central tower, and the **Espace Oscar Niemeyer**, nicknamed 'the Volcano' on account of its shape.

Among the few reminders of the old town are the **cathedral** (1575–1630) and the house that is now the location for the **Musée de l'Ancien Havre** (*1 rue Jérôme Bellarmato; tel: 02 35 42 27 90; open: Wed–Sun 1000–1200 and 1400–1800; £*).

The **Musée des Beaux Arts André Malraux** (Fine Arts Museum) (*boulevard J F Kennedy; tel: 02 35 42 33 97; open: Wed–Mon 1000–1200 and 1400–1800; £*) occupies a superb site overlooking the sea. It has works by French Impressionists Pissaro and Sisley, as well as canvases by the great 20th-century artist, Raoul Dufy, who was born in Le Havre in 1877.

Locronan

Tourist information: place de la Mairie. Tel: 02 98 91 70 14.

Locronan's **Grand Place** is a stunning ensemble of dormer-windowed Renaissance mansions, built originally for prosperous cloth merchants. **Rue Moal** leads to the delightful 14th-century chapel of Notre-Dame-de-Bonne-Nouvelle, with its small calvary and 17th-century fountain. Locronan's **annual religious** *pardon*, the Petite Troménie, is held every July. The Grande Troménie is a larger-scale version, held every sixth year (next in 2001).

Mont-St-Michel

Mont-St-Michel is France's most popular tourist attraction outside Paris. Perched on the slopes of a remote granite rock, once isolated from the mainland (access today is via a causeway), are rising tiers of churches and fortified towers, founded on a labyrinthine system of crypts and cellars. Since the monastery was founded, the sea has retreated a long way, but it's still hazardous, with quicksands, deceptive currents and tides capable of advancing at speeds of up to 13km (8 miles) an hour.

Hermits were living on the mount as early as the 6th century but it was not until AD 708 that Bishop Aubert of Avranches built the first chapel – supposedly at the command of the Archangel Michael, who appeared to him in a dream. The abbey was founded in the 10th century by Benedictine monks under the special protection of the Dukes of Normandy. From that moment until 1897, when the statue of St Michael brandishing a golden sword was placed on the pinnacle of the church, buildings of unrivalled architectural splendour steadily accumulated.

The ensemble today is breathtaking. Both the abbey and the town frequently came under attack but they never succumbed, not even during the Hundred Years War when the English bombarded the island from a specially constructed wooden *bastille*.

For much of the 18th and 19th centuries the abbey doubled as a prison for royalists, rebels and 'exiled gentlemen', even priests. It was designated a historic monument as long ago as 1874 but a token population of monks and nuns still serves the tiny local community of less than a hundred.

The abbey

Tel: 02 33 89 80 00.
Open: daily May–
Sept 0900–1730;
Oct–Apr 0930–
1700. Optional
guided tours. For
a more atmospheric
visit, the abbey
reopens Mon–Sat
May–Sept 2200–
2400. ££.

The focal point of the abbey complex and its crowning glory is the **church**. The Romanesque nave, completed early in the 12th century, was constructed over an earlier chapel. The chancel collapsed in the 15th century; its sleek rib-vaulted replacement, Flamboyant Gothic in style, is supported by its own **Crypt of the Mighty Pillars**. The church also required plenty of external support in the form of flying buttresses and a spectacular *chevet*.

Early in the 13th century new accommodation for the monks was built on the north side of the mount. This stupendous structure, one of the finest examples of Gothic architecture in France, is known appropriately as **La Merveille** ('The Marvel'). In the magnificent **cloisters**, the spaces between the arches are filled with ingenious limestone carvings of plants and other motifs. The Abbey's formidable **defences**, an elaborate network of ramparts, watch towers, gatehouses and fortified courtyards are also impressive.

The town

There's not much to the town besides the touristy **Grande Rue**, which winds tortuously around the base of the mount. Crammed with souvenir shops and eating places, this is where medieval wayfarers would have bought their pilgrims' badges before booking in at a hostelry.

Tourist information: Corps de Garde des Bourgeois (Guard Room).
Tel: 02 33 60 14 30.

Pont-Aven

Tourist information: 5 place de l'Hôtel de Ville. Tel: 02 98 06 04 70.

American artists began arriving in Pont-Aven as early as the 1860s but it was Paul Gauguin and his French disciples – urged to 'paint what you see, not what is there' – who really put the town on the map. Gauguin founded the 'Pont-Aven School' in the 1880s, and the town today trades mercilessly on its links with the artists. The scenery that inspired them has changed little over the last hundred years. The *Route des Peintres en Cornouaille* brochure will guide you to these landscapes and settings and to the galleries and museums.

Synthetism

Gauguin and his Pont-Aven School artists rejected Impressionism in favour of Synthetism – a daring neo-Primitivist style of bold, flat outlines and brilliantly contrasting colours, toned down with a dull, matt finish.

Pont-Aven is charming, with its granite bridge, rushing water bubbling and foaming over the smoothed stones of the bed of the Aven, its old watermill, and its delicious butter biscuits (*galettes de Pont-Aven*). Follow the banks of the river past derelict mills, manicured river gardens and old wash-houses to the sleepy port at the head of the tidal estuary – no longer trading in wine and cereals but a haven for pleasure craft.

To follow in the footsteps of the artists, climb the wooded hillside of the **Bois d'Amour** ('Wood of Love') to the **chapelle de Trémalo**. Inside is the gaunt Christ figure that inspired Gauguin's *Le Christ Jaune* (1889).

The **Musée de Pont-Aven** (*place de l'Hôtel de Ville; tel: 02 98 06 14 43; open: daily; ££*) opened in 1986 to coincide with the centenary of Gauguin's first visit. There are surprisingly few works here by the master himself (most have gone abroad), but there are paintings, prints and drawings by other leading members of the group.

Parc Régional d'Armorique

The Parc Régional d'Armorique is a land of woods and flat granite moorland, but it also includes the dramatic windswept cliffs of the Crozon peninsula. The lakeside town of **Huelgoat** makes a good base if you enjoy walking. The tourist office (*rue des Cendres*) has details of paths in the surrounding forest that will take you to the **Café du Chaos** (so-called because of the boulder-strewn valley in which it sits) and the **Camp d'Arthus** Roman fort. Further west, the **Crozon peninsula** is covered in defensive works from the 17th century and is today the base for France's nuclear submarine fleet. It was at **Camaret**, a quiet fishing port noted for its good seafood restaurants, that Robert Fulton, inventor of the submarine, conducted early trials – the story is told in the local naval museum. Further west, the **Pointe de Penhir**, marked by a monument to the Breton Resistance Movement, stands on a breezy clifftop, which is a popular spot for walks and sea views.

Pont l'Évêque

Tourist information: 16 bis rue St-Michel. Tel: 02 31 64 12 77; fax: 02 31 64 76 96; www.normandy-tourism.org.

Pont-l'Évêque has been a **centre of cheese-making** since the 17th century. Its cheese is made from the milk of pure-bred Norman cows and can be sampled at the dairy east of the town on the D162. Pont-l'Évêque also has some splendid half-timbered houses in the neighbourhood of rue Vaucelles, as well as an old Dominican convent with its original wooden balcony still intact. The town makes a good base for exploring the delightfully pastoral **Pays d'Auge**, a land of cider orchards and timber-framed manor farms.

Quiberon and Belle-Île

Presqu'Île de Quiberon

Tourist information: rue de Verdun. Tel: 02 97 50 07 84.

'The most beautiful peninsula in Europe'? Certainly, this skeletal finger of land has much to recommend it. The lively seaside resort of **Quiberon** town is the embarkation point for **boat excursions**. Stroll to **Pointe-de-Conguel** for splendid views of the Gulf of Morbihan and the islands.

The peninsula's west coast, known as the **Côte Sauvage** ('Wild Coast'), is awesome in rough weather. Shipwrecks and drownings are commonplace in its treacherous waters. See the spectacle from the promontory at **Beg-er-Goalennec** or further north at **Pointe-du-Percho**. The sheltered **east coast** has the best beaches for swimming, notably the *sables blancs* ('white sands') near Penthièvre and the mini-resort of **St-Pierre-Quiberon**.

Belle-Île

Tourist information: quai Bonnelle, Le Palais. Tel: 02 97 31 81 93.

The 'Beautiful Island' is renowned for its scenery, but it also offers a huge range of activities, from golf to sea fishing.

The island's fortifications included the magnificent **Citadelle Vauban** (*Le Palais; tel: 02 97 31 84 17; open: daily 0930–1200; ££*), begun early in the 16th century. The fort was abandoned long ago but it's been well preserved.

The port of **Sauzon**, at the mouth of a long estuary, is arguably the prettiest spot on Belle-Île. Bathing is safest in the vicinity of Locmaria; the five beaches include **Port-An-Dro** and **Grandes Sables**, 2km (1 mile) of pure white sand. The footpath from the **Grotte de l'Apothicairerie** cave to the harbour at **Port Goulphar** follows the most impressive stretch of Belle-Île's 100-km (62-mile) coastline.

Quimper

Tourist information: place de la Résistance. Tel: 02 98 53 04 05. The passeport culturel *is an inclusive ticket to the main museums and the H-B Henriot* faïence *showrooms, and a free guided tour of the town.*

The ancient capital of Cornouaille, Quimper derives its name from the Celtic word *kemper*, meaning 'the confluence of rivers' (the Steir and the Odet). The town is most famous for its *faïence* ceramic ware, but it also has a cathedral and a picturesque Old Town with lively waterside cafés. Hop on a pleasure boat leaving for the Odet estuary, or take a stroll along the riverbank.

Quimper's impressive Gothic **cathedral** is the largest in Brittany. To see the heart of **old Quimper**, head from the cathedral towards the **River Steir**. In this pedestrianised area, feudal mansions, decorated with statues and caryatids, rub shoulders with half-timbered tradesmen's houses. A little watch tower at the end of **rue Kéréon** is a reminder that Quimper was once a fortified city.

The **Musée de la Faïence** (*14 rue Jean-Baptiste-Bousquet; tel: 02 98 90 12 72; open: Mon–Sat 1000–1800; ££*), in an old pottery factory, gives the low-down on the local ceramics industry that is still thriving today. Find out which minerals are used to create the distinctive blue, green and yellow pigments, then have a browse in the showrooms of the H-B Henriot *faïencerie* next door.

July's **Festival de Cornouaille** is one of the liveliest celebrations of Breton culture in the region.

249

Rennes

The regional as well as the historic capital of Brittany, Rennes is a prosperous go-getting town with a rich architectural heritage. A fire in 1720 led to the rebuilding of part of the city in an elegant classical style, creating a pleasing contrast with the chevron-patterned timber houses of the Old Town or Ville Rouge.

Breton is still taught at Rennes' two universities and the separatist movement has strong roots here. The presence of nearly 40,000 students gives Rennes an extra vitality. Entertainment here includes the annual *Tombées de la Nuit* music festival, which takes place in August, as well as year-round arts performances and many fine eating places.

In medieval times the Duke of Brittany processed through the **Portes Mordelaises**, the ceremonial gateway to the city, on the way to his coronation. The two machicolated towers date from the 15th century and were once joined to the ramparts; a small stretch of these can be seen to the right. The gateway leads into the **place des Lices**, where jousting would have taken place. These days, the square is the site of Rennes' extensive Saturday morning market.

The fire that swept through Rennes in 1720 caused extensive damage to more than 30 medieval streets. Subsequently, two new squares were created. The focal point of **place de la Mairie** was the **Hôtel de Ville** (Town Hall). Across the river, the monumental **Palais du Commerce** is now the main post office. The **Vilaine** was not canalised until the 19th century but the elegant houses lining the quays date from the period after the fire. They were designed in the Paris fashion with granite arcades, limestone upper stories and mansard roofs. The arcades are now occupied by shops.

On the **place du Parlement**, the magnificent **Palais de Justice** was the first building in Rennes to be made of stone and consequently one of the few to escape the 1720 fire. Ironically, a mysterious fire (attributed by some to the Breton fishermen's dispute) seriously damaged the roof in 1994.

Up the hill from the river, the former Benedictine **Abbey of St-Mélaine** became a hospital during the Revolution. The orchard was transformed in the 19th century into a splendid 10-hectare (25-acre) green space (the **Jardins du Thabor**), part formal French garden, part English landscaped park, planted with roses, camellias and rhododendrons.

In the old town, the 19th-century **Cathédrale St-Pierre** (*rue de la Monnaie; open: 0930–1200 and 1500–1800; free*) has a sumptuous interior, with more than enough paintings and gilded stucco.

Tourist information: 11 rue St-Yves. Tel: 02 99 67 11 11. Guided tours.

Roscoff

Tourist information: 46 rue Gambetta. Tel: 02 98 61 12 13; fax: 02 98 69 75 75.

There's a lot more to this versatile port than the car-ferry terminal. The ships' nails and miniature galleons carved on the walls of the 16th-century parish church are reminders of the town's colourful maritime past. The ornamental cannons on the tower point towards England, the old enemy, which burnt the original settlement to the ground in the 1400s.

Roscoff has always made its living from the sea. By the 17th century, many of the town's merchants were moonlighting as buccaneers, frustrating English customs officers with an illegal traffic in wine and brandy. Clustered around the church are the former **corsairs' houses**, magnificent granite mansions with monumental chimneys, elaborate skylights, fanciful gargoyles and transom windows. One of the best examples is the so-called **Maison de Marie Stuart**, although the house has no connection with the Queen of Scots who visited Roscoff as a five-year-old in 1548.

From the garden of the 17th-century **Chapelle Ste-Barbe** there are good views of both the old port and the deep-water harbour at Bloscon.

Vegetables are almost as plentiful in Roscoff as shellfish. One of the town's streets, **rue des Johnnies**, honours those local entrepreneurs who used to travel to England to sell onions from their bicycles. The practice died out in the 1930s, but Roscoff has a **Musée des Johnnies** (*Chapelle Ste-Anne; tel: 02 98 61 12 13*).

Rouen

Tourist information: 25 place de la Cathédrale. Tel: 02 32 08 32 40. Bureau de change, guided tours and accommodation booking.

Delightful Rouen is famous as the place where Joan of Arc was tried for witchcraft and later burnt at the stake. Allied bombing raids destroyed more than 40 per cent of the town's centre, as well as its bridges, but restoration has been almost total. Rouen's manageable old town, with its tortuous streets, half-timbered houses and ethereal towers and spires has much appeal.

Joan of Arc

On 30 May 1431, Joan was burned at the stake on **place de Vieux-Marché** after being proclaimed a heretic and excommunicated. A large plain cross marks the site. The starkly modern **Église Ste-Jeanne-d'Arc** was completed in 1979. Joan was taken for interrogation to the still-intact **Tour Jeanne d'Arc**, where she refused to confess, despite being shown the implements of torture. After her trial, Joan was led to the blackened **Abbatiale St-Ouen** to make a public recantation of her heresy. This church is one of France's finest Gothic monuments. After her death, Joan's heart and ashes were cast into the Seine near the **Pont Boïeldieu**

Cathédral de Notre-Dame

Place de la Cathédrale. Open: Mon–Sat 0800–1900, Sun 0800–1800. Guided tours of the crypt, etc, hourly 1000–1700.

The magnificent **west front** of this venerable ensemble was made famous by Monet's timeless studies. The 151m (495ft) spire on the **lantern tower** is the tallest in France. Equally impressive are the stone filigree of the portals and the 14th-century stained glass. King Richard's 'lion' heart is actually buried here.

St-Malo

Tourist information: esplanade St-Vincent. Tel: 02 99 56 64 48. Closed Sun except during July and Aug; no accommodation booking service.

There's lots to do in this lively Channel port. See the château and the walled citadel, enjoy the miles of beaches, go on a tour of the late-night bars and restaurants, or take the children to the Grand Aquarium – actually 40 aquariums, and hugely popular.

The island fortress of the fiercely independent, sea-going Malouins is now joined to the mainland by a causeway. The building of its formidable castle began in 1395, and continued well into the 18th century, when the barracks, now the **Hôtel de Ville** (Town Hall), were added. The walls of the massive keep are 7m (23ft) thick in places. It's a steep climb (169 steps) to the top of the tower but worth it for the view.

Île du Grand Bé and Fort National

There are great views from these two island outposts of St-Malo, accessible only at low tide. To the French, Grand Bé is virtually synonymous with one of the nation's great literary figures (and a Malouin by birth), François René de Chateaubriand. The trek to see his grave is so popular that queues sometimes form on the causeway. There's little else to do here but admire the view – of the entire Emerald Coast on a clear day.

Tip

Visitors should take care to start back to St-Malo from the Île du Grand Bé before the tide comes in, or they may suffer the indignity of being rescued by the coastguard in full view of the locals, who gather on the beach to witness precisely this spectacle.

Fort National (*tel: 02 45 75 11 21; open: daily 15 June–30 Sept for guided tours; £*) was constructed from the hardiest Chausey granite by Louis XIV's military engineer, Vauban (*see pages 75 and 100*), in 1689 to give added protection to the town. From the ramparts you can see as far as Dinard and the Rance estuary.

Vannes

Tourist Information: 1 rue Thiers. Tel: 02 97 47 24 34.

Historically important, and still one of the liveliest towns in Brittany, Vannes likes to promote its maritime image. The port is the gateway to the Gulf of Morbihan, but there is also much of interest in the town itself.

Tip

Vannes' cathedral has two special treasures: an exquisite 13th-century wedding chest decorated with painted scenes of knightly romance, and the mummified finger of Blessed Pierre Rogue, guillotined for his beliefs during the Revolution.

Vannes was originally a fortified city and a 600m (1 969ft) stretch of the ramparts remains, complete with gates and machicolated watch towers. Behind the walls are clusters of brightly painted 15th- and 16th-century half-timbered houses, with slated overhangs and gabled windows; **place Henri IV** has some of the best. There's a lively market on Wednesday and Saturday mornings in and around **place des Lices**, originally a space used for tournaments and executions. The medieval market took place indoors at the wonderful 13th-century building of **la Cohue**

Vannes is the most convenient base for exploring the **Gulf of Morbihan**. Boats leave from the Gare Maritime to many of the offshore islands.

Vitré

Tourist information: place St-Yves. Tel: 02 99 75 04 46.

A market town with a beautifully preserved medieval core, Vitré is synonymous with its formidable **château**, founded in the 11th century on a rocky outcrop, with pointy towers and machicolations. Climb the Tour de Montafilant for good views. The streets of the old town are twisting and cobbled; start with **rue de la Baudrairie**, the old leather-workers' quarter. Many of Vitré's half-timbered granite mansions were built by wealthy cloth merchants – look out for unusual balustraded wooden staircases. The **Promenade du Val** follows the line of the 13th-century town walls to offer panoramic views of the Vilaine valley.

Buying your way out

The name of Vitré's medieval suburb Rachapt means 'repurchase'. When the castle was under siege during the Hundred Years War, the defenders paid the English to go away.

Eating and drinking

Le Petit Normand
35 rue Larcher, Bayeux. Tel: 02 31 22 88 66. Closed Wed and Sun pm. ££. Restaurant with traditional Norman dishes such as *jambon à l'os au cidre*.

Saint-Jean
19 rue St-Jean, Bayeux. Tel: 02 31 22 45 58. ££. Crêpes and *galettes* are the mainstay of this restaurant with a terrace.

Alcide
1 place Courtonne, Caen. Tel: 02 31 44 18 06. ££. Traditional French cooking. Good-value set menus.

L'Insolite
16 rue du Vaugueux, Caen. Tel: 02 31 43 83 87. Closed Sun pm and Mon. ££. Terrace restaurant serving fish and seafood specialities.

Côte d'Emeraude

Restaurant de la Fauconnière
Cap Fréhel. Tel: 02 96 41 54 20. £. A lunch spot offering superb views from its cliff-edge site.

L'Aventur
78 rue du Petit Fort, Dinan. Tel: 02 96 39 56 34. ££. Grilled meat and fish dishes as well as excellent seafood.

Le Jacobin
11 rue Haute-Voie, Dinan. Tel: 02 96 39 47 05. ££. Near the Jardin Anglais. Traditional French cuisine.

Printania
5 avenue George-V, Dinard. Tel: 02 99 46 94 00. Open: all day. ££. Views of St-Malo from the terrace. Fish specialities include stuffed clams and grilled salmon.

La Mère Poulard
Grand Rue, Mont-St-Michel. Tel: 02 33 60 14 01. ££. Famous throughout the island for its (overpriced) omelettes.

St-Pierre
Grande Rue, Mont-St-Michel. Tel: 02 33 60 14 03. ££. Atmospheric half-timbered building with restaurant.

L'Âtre
7 esplanade Commandant Menguy, St-Servan, St-Malo. Tel: 02 99 81 68 39. Closed Wed, and Tue evenings out of season. ££. Restaurant offering *fruits de mer* and fish specialities.

Crêperie Chez Chantal
2 place aux Herbes, St-Malo. Tel: 02 99 40 93 97. Closed Mon out of season. £. Crêperie in the old town serving a large range of sweet and savoury pancakes at attractive prices.

Côte Fleurie

Eating out in **Deauville** is expensive.

Restaurant Pizza Morny
39 rue Olliffe, Deauville. Tel: 02 31 81 46 46. ££. Serves fish dishes as well as the usual pizza/pasta options.

L'Hippocampe
44–46 quai St-Catherine, Honfleur. Tel: 02 31 89 98 36. ££. Restaurant over-looking the Vieux Bassin, serving *fruits de mer* and fish specialities.

Pont-Aven

Le Moulin du Grand Poulguin
quai Théodore Botrel, Pont-Aven. Tel: 02 98 06 02 67. ££. Crêperie, also selling pizzas.

Tahiti
rue de la Belle Angèle, Pont-Aven. Tel: 02 98 06 15 93. Closed Mon. ££. Chinese and 'exotic' specialities.

Quiberon and Belle-Île

La Belle Époque
42 rue Port-Maria, Quiberon. Tel: 02 97 50 17 68. ££. Small seafront restaurant with reasonably priced set menus.

Contre Quai
rue St-Nicolas, Sauzon, Belle-Île. Tel: 02 97 31 60 60. ££. Good-value fish restaurant in a lovely coastal setting.

Rennes

Rennes offers a variety of dining experiences. In half-timbered houses in the old town, **Ti-Koz** (*3 rue St-Guillaume; tel: 02 99 79 33 89; ££*) and **Auberge St-Sauveur** (*6 rue St-Sauveur; tel: 02 99 79 32 56; £££*) specialise in classic French cooking. *Crêperies* in equally good locations include **Maison de la Galette** (*6 place Ste-Anne; tel: 02 99 79 01 43; £*) and **Crêperie St-Georges** (*31 rue St-Georges; tel: 02 99 38 87 04; closed Sun; £*). The pavement cafés and pizzerias on rue St-Michel and the adjoining square are good for people-watching.

Rouen

Place du Vieux Marché is the best place to start looking for restaurants in Rouen. Duckling (*caneton*) is the local speciality. **La Couronne** (*31 place du Vieux-Marché; tel: 02 35 71 57 73; £££*) claims to be the oldest hostelry in France (1343), with traditional Norman cooking. The **Café de Rouen** (*rue du Gros Horloge; £*) upholds the traditional French values of courtesy and prompt service.

Vannes

Restaurants cluster in Vannes' pedestrianised streets off place Henri IV and down by the port (*place Gambetta and rue St-Vincent*). In July and August if you see somewhere you like during the day, book a table.

Breizh Café
13 rue des Halles, Vannes. Tel: 02 97 54 37 41. ££. Thoroughly Breton, even down to the mineral water. Try the beef *brochette* in cider.

Les Seychelles
11 rue de Closmadeuc, Vannes. Tel: 02 97 42 51 08. ££. Bright and breezy, serves creole specialities and inventive salads.

Nightlife

St-Malo is the liveliest town on the Emerald Coast and, festivals aside, there's quite a bit to do in the evenings. Facilities at the **Casino** (*Chausée du Sillon; £££*) include bars, a brasserie and a disco. There are several other good night spots: **Hiss et Oh** (*7 rue de Chartres; tel: 02 23 18 17 21; ££*) caters for all musical tastes, from reggae and funk to salsa, Celtic and jazz, with regular live performances and free entry.

Regional food

Both Normandy and Brittany are heavily agricultural, and the rolling farmland of the region is studded with historic châteaux, half-timbered manor houses and farm buildings constructed from local granite or Cotentin stone. Many of these buildings have been converted – in Brittany, a number of them are cider museums, while in Normandy there are places where you can find out about Calvados and cheese-making.

Eating and drinking in Brittany and Normandy, as elsewhere in France, is an undiluted pleasure. In the coastal villages, early risers can watch the day's catch being brought ashore on its way to the dining table. Seafood is available everywhere in super-abundance. Oysters are a speciality of Cancale, the resorts of the Baie du St-Michel and the villages of the Belon estuary; Courseuilles is known for shellfish; Honfleur for shrimps; and Camaret and Douarnenez for lobster (served *Armoricaine* in a rich hot sauce). A bowl of steaming *moules marinières* (mussels in wine sauce), often served with *frites* (chips), makes an appetising lunch. Sole, turbot, bass and mackerel, sardines and tuna also appear regularly on menus; other treats include salmon from the River Aulne and trout from the Monts d'Arrée.

When you've had your fill of oysters, mussels, crab and fish, there are other specialities to enjoy: *pré salé* lamb, raised on the salt-marshes, and with a distinctive 'ready-salted' tang; *andouilles* (chitterlings); *canard à la Rouennais* (duck); and *poulet vallé d'Auge* (chicken), not forgetting the ubiquitous crêpes and the nourishing traditional Breton stew *kig ha farz*. In Normandy, meat is traditionally served in a creamy sauce; pork in cider is also a popular dish. Look out for *tripe à la Mode* and the strong-flavoured Morlaix ham. Normandy produces excellent cheeses, too, including Camembert, Livarot and Pont-l'Évêque. Crêpes (thin pancakes) and *galettes* (the same made with buckwheat) are served throughout Brittany and Normandy with every conceivable filling, from cider, yoghurt and jam, to cheese, ham and eggs.

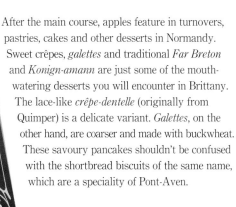

After the main course, apples feature in turnovers, pastries, cakes and other desserts in Normandy. Sweet crêpes, *galettes* and traditional *Far Breton* and *Konign-amann* are just some of the mouth-watering desserts you will encounter in Brittany. The lace-like *crêpe-dentelle* (originally from Quimper) is a delicate variant. *Galettes*, on the other hand, are coarser and made with buckwheat. These savoury pancakes shouldn't be confused with the shortbread biscuits of the same name, which are a speciality of Pont-Aven.

The traditional Breton desserts have one ingredient in common: butter. *Far Breton* is a richly textured flan made with a creamy batter and filled with prunes or raisins (sometimes the flavour is enhanced with a dash of rum or cinnamon). *Konign-amann*, literally 'butter-cake', was invented in Douarnenez in 1865. This flaky pastry made with sugar and almonds is served warm – crisp on the outside, it should melt in the mouth.

Lifestyles

Shopping, eating, children and nightlife in France

les fleurs
ées à
a botte

Shopping

Food and wine

Even if you can't always take it home, food comes high on anyone's shopping list in France. There are **markets** every day of the week in many French cities and towns; in Paris, you can visit nearly 60 street markets in any given week. Anyone who can walk by the stalls of a typical French market and fail to want to fill a shopping basket doesn't have eyes to see or a nose to smell. And French food shops are equally tempting; the mouth-watering chocolates and *pâtisseries* in the window displays taste even better than they look, and it's easy to understand why the French refer to window-shopping as '**window-licking**' (*lèche-vitrine*).

Even if you genuinely don't want to buy, take a look anyway at the best goods that France – and the seas around it – can provide: oysters, mushrooms, cheeses, wines, bread and rainbows of fruit and vegetables. Food in France often costs more than in the UK, but you should find it easier to buy produce of **exceptional quality**. For fruit and vegetables, markets are best. The lettuces alone – frilly, curly, smooth, glossy, red, every shade of green – are a feast for the eyes. *Saucisson sec* (salami) and other cold meats, *foie gras*, the cheese of your choice and, of course, the ubiquitous *baguette*, provide the ingredients for a memorable **picnic lunch**. The French eat more **cheese** than any other people in the world

and, at the last count, produce approximately 400 different kinds. If you want to buy **wine**, the *caviste* (cellarman) in any wine shop will happily give advice.

Hypermarchés

Despite the rising numbers of huge hypermarkets (*hypermarchés*) in the past couple of decades, small French towns, in dramatic contrast to the British, still have their bakery, butcher's shop, *pâtisserie*, and so on. These specialist shops are usually family-run and sell top-quality produce, but it is definitely worth checking out the hypermarkets, too. **Carrefour**, **Leclerc**, **Auchan** and **Mammouth** are just some of the names you'll see on enormous roadside signs, guiding you to their vast complexes. Inside the supermarkets, you'll find a huge range of French-manufactured items for the kitchen and house – from classic Duralex glasses to Le Creuset cast-iron pots and pans. The French are leaders in the cosmetic industry, and you'll find well-known brands such as Clarins, Garnier, L'Oréal and Nivea at relatively low prices. Other products to look out for are olive-oil soaps, perfumed with almond, lavender, apricot and other traditional fragrances, as well as French aperitifs (Dubonnet, Pastis, Suze), which are very cheap.

Paris fashion

❝ *If you want to establish an international presence you can't do so from New York. You need the consecration of Paris.* **❞**

Oscar de la Renta, fashion designer, *International Herald Tribune* (26 Feb 1991)

Paris is, always has been, and seemingly always will be, the undisputed **world centre of fashion**. No other city can boast

263

such close associations with so many famous designers or fashion houses: Coco Chanel, Christian Dior, Givenchy, Schiaparelli, Guy Laroche, Pierre Cardin, Hermès, Agnès B, Sonia Rykiel, Louis Vuitton, Jean-Paul Gaultier, Christian Lacroix, Yves Saint-Laurent … the list goes on and on. Saint-Laurent remains the superstar of the Paris scene, despite young Brits such as John Galliano, Alexander McQueen and Stella McCartney being appointed to head up long-established French houses. With foreign names such as Vivienne Westwood, Issey Miyake, Kenzo and Armani all having showcase outlets in Paris, there's no doubt about the city's continuing supremacy. The world's

eyes are on Paris during its fashion weeks in January and July (for the prestigious, high-fashion *haute-couture* shows) and March and October (for *prêt-à-porter*, or ready-to-wear). Even if you can only afford to window-shop, don't miss out – those windows are spectacular!

Although fashion generally doesn't come cheap, it can be good value in Paris. At the beginning of January and during July the **sales** are on, and you'll find discounts of 30 to 50 per cent on clothing, shoes, accessories and fabrics. In no other country in the world will you have the chance to see so many designer clothes for sale in the same place, from cool Kenzo to flamboyant

Gaultier. Even the top-of-the-range items might be in your price bracket in the shops that sell second-hand designer goods; often, the clothes have only been worn once for some special event.

Some of the more distinctive shops are in the *passages*, the arcaded galleries that run through elegant 19th-century buildings in Paris, mainly in the 2nd and 9th *arrondissements*. You'll find the **Galerie Vivienne** and **Galerie Colbert** off rue Vivienne, and the *passages* of the Palais Royal off Rue de Monpensier; the *Passage des Panoramas* is the oldest, dating from about 1800. The historical 'shopping malls' often house small shops, ideal for the specialist trader, and you're likely to find hat designers, toy shops, leather specialists and antiquarian bookshops, as well as quirky little cafés.

The **department store** is a Parisian speciality, and the perfect place to shop for fashion – and many other lovely things. **Galeries Lafayette** (*40 boulevard Haussmann; tel: 01 42 82 34 56*) is known as the 'Louvre of department stores', providing shoppers with the kind of service and entertainment that the Louvre provides to art lovers. It is actually three stores in one, with one devoted to women's fashions, one to men's and another to items for the home. Its women's fashion department sells names such as Dior, Chanel, Alexander McQueen and Dolce e Gabbana. **Le Printemps** (*64 boulevard Haussmann; tel: 01 42 82 50 00*) is the city's other huge department store; its women's shop now has the biggest accessories department in Paris. The **BHV** (*52–64 rue de Rivoli; tel: 01 42 74 90 00*) is DIY heaven, stocking an estimated 350,000 hardware items. The shop is so big that a visitor welcome centre on the ground floor often has to give directions, although half the fun is in browsing.

265

Eating out

*Eating is a **national pastime** in France, a country where chefs have the same status as physicists or poets. At a more mundane level, it is still a passion. Only passion can account for the aromas and array of pastries and breads that overpower you in a tiny village bakery or the creative nuances of a meal in a humble bistro. France (and particularly Paris) has its share of mediocre and overpriced restaurants but it is still a gourmet's paradise, because eating here is a question of culture rather than convenience and fuel. **Brillat-Savarin**, 18th-century philosopher of the culinary arts, summed it up thus: 'Animals eat. Only human beings dine.'*

" *Tell me what you eat; I'll tell you what you are.* "
Brillat-Savarin, *Physiologie du Goût* (1825)

Tips for eating out

Make **reservations** if possible – and pay the hard-working chefs the simple courtesy of cancelling if you cannot come. Many restaurants in France are small, and mealtimes are long – they don't push people out the door after they finish – so each table is important.

If you haven't booked a table, the best strategy is to arrive promptly at **opening time**. The French (but not Parisians) begin lunch at 1200–1230, dinner at 1900–1930. In Paris, they eat at least 30 minutes to an hour later. If you want to eat at 1500, your choice of restaurants will be few and far between. In Paris, at least, you can usually find a brasserie, which, by definition, is supposed to stay open. If you're in a hurry, don't eat in a restaurant – they are simply not the place to rush through a meal. Try a café, wine bar or tea *salon* instead; if you want to eat on the run, step into a bakery or *pâtisserie* for a sandwich.

If saving money while eating well is your object, consider making **lunch** the day's main meal. Many restaurants serve a lunchtime menu for 25 to 40 per cent less than the evening version; this is a good tactic if you fancy eating in some of France's more celebrated and multi-starred establishments, but funds are limited. If a restaurant or café is good, its *vin de table* or *vin ordinaire* (table wine) should be good, too, and perfectly adequate to accompany a meal. Order a jug of tap water – *une carafe d'eau* – instead of bottled water.

Tipping

Normally, a menu will say *service compris*, meaning the price of service is included. Sometimes, service is added to the prices indicated (*service non compris*). In any case, service is always added to the final bill before it is presented. You can leave extra if you want to, but an additional tip should never exceed 5 per cent.

Drink

The French drink more alcohol (and bottled water) per head than any other nation, but you will rarely see French people drunk in public. Drinking in France tends to be social and spread over a substantial lunch or dinner. Simple bingeing on booze,

267

while not unheard of, is unusual.
There are no universal licensing
hours, as each establishment applies
for its own licence and hours. Some
may stop serving drinks and close as
early as 2200, others may continue
selling alcohol up to 0200, and others
have round-the-clock licences.

In a café, customers drink coffee,
soft drinks, beer or perhaps, as
an aperitif, a *kir* (white wine and
blackcurrant liqueur). If you're in
a hurry, it's perfectly acceptable
to **stay standing at the bar** to
consume your order; doing this is
the cheapest way of using a café, at
least in Paris and some other cities.
Sitting down at a table normally

means that you intend to take your
time. The café or bar will charge you
more, but you won't be pressurised
to move on, or to buy more drinks.

Water in French bars and cafés
costs almost the same as a beer.
Bottled water is either *gazeuse*
(fizzy), or *non-gazeuse* (still). It is
typical to order water by brand
name: Evian, for example, is
always still and Badoit is
effervescent and a little more
mineral-rich. Coca Cola (*un coca*)
and Sprite are common soft
drinks, as is bottled and sugary
jus d'orange. If you want freshly
squeezed orange juice, ask for
an *orange pressée*.

Beer is normally ordered as *une pression* or *un demi* – a third of a litre of light draught lager. In really touristy areas, you will be offered *une grande*, a half-litre or the rough equivalent of a pint. Many bars have something stronger on tap, such as Belgian beers Leffe or Grimbergen. Spirits and whisky are two to three times as expensive as beer, as is an aperitif in a restaurant.

The French paradox

Despite their apparently reckless consumption of cream and butter, the French have a surprisingly **low rate of cardiac disease**. Medical research has pointed to the regular, moderate consumption of red wine as one of the reasons. However, other studies suggest that the French attitude towards eating, so different from the approach in Anglo-Saxon countries, could also be a factor. The French, it seems, rarely experience guilt while eating.

France with children

In general, the French adore babies and children. They are welcome in most places, including cafés and restaurants (although parents might worry about the effect the cigarette smoke could have on them) – but a Parisian is more likely to bring a dog than a child to a really classy restaurant. Outside holiday resorts, few restaurants offer special children menus – French children are expected to eat the same food as their parents – but most will readily serve up children's portions. High chairs are few and far between.

Settling in and seeing the sights

Renting a **house (*gîte*)** or **apartment** in the region you are visiting is not only more affordable if you're travelling with children, but also offers other advantages. It gives a family the chance to meet French neighbours, explore local parks and playgrounds, shop at local markets and cook their own French meals. Most hotels will happily accommodate children with an extra bed or cot and only charge a modest supplement. Under-4s ride for free on SNCF trains and buses, and get into museums for free. Parents pay half-fare for 4 to 11 year olds. Museums will probably charge half-price for 5 to 18 year olds.

Many of the country's paintings, sculptures and architectural landmarks that interest adults might be an eye-opener for children as well, although little ones will probably have less patience with a structured approach. France is full of **specialist museums** devoted to folklore, popular traditions, transportation, magic, and so on, as well as **castles**, many of which will seem like a fairytale come true to young ones. **War memorials** in Caen and Verdun can teach older children and teenagers more about history in an afternoon than they might learn in school in a year. Younger children will be delighted by French **circuses**. In France the circus is regarded as an art form and the French have no qualms about seeing animals performing in them.

Paris: science, sewers and skeletons

Paris is celebrated as a city for lovers but it can also be a fun place for children. The **Cité des Sciences** has many exciting interactive exhibits, with a planetarium, a weather station and the chance to try landing a plane or watch a nuclear explosion. Two special sections cater for younger and older children, both in the aptly named **Cité des Enfants**. Also in the park are playgrounds, a cinema, a submarine and a flight simulator.

If the grimy and ghoulish appeals to your children, take them on a visit to the Paris **sewers** or to see the **catacombs**, which contain a few million skeletons (bring a torch). The catacombs are beneath place Denfert-Rochereau in Montparnasse.

After dark

*Between Paris and the provinces, France has more than a dozen major **opera houses** and a dozen **orchestras**, many attracting top international talent. Chamber music and sacred music are performed regularly all over the country in some of the most beautiful venues imaginable (churches, abbeys, Roman amphitheatres, baroque theatres). France has an interesting experimental music scene, too, thanks to the efforts of composer Pierre Boulez who founded the IRCAM centre in Paris.*

French **rock music** is not quite up to the standards of its cheese. The central figure is the middle-aged Johnnie Halliday. The tacky 1970s pop icon François Claude is an eternal hit and the French will insist that his *Comme d'habitude* is vastly superior to Frank Sinatra's *I did it my way*. The French are true connoisseurs of **jazz** and have offered many American jazz greats a home from from home – and sometimes a more sympathetic one at that. Violinist Stéphane Grappelli and guitarist Django Reinhardt are the best-known French jazz exponents. French *chansons* are still alive and kicking, even though there is no one of the stature of Edith Piaf, Jacques Brel or Serge Gainsbourg.

World music

World music is hot in France, particularly the quarter-tone funk of Algerian Rai (*Rai* in Arabic means 'opinion'). Rai musician Khaled is the Michael Jackson of the Arabic world, and hugely popular in France. He blends traditional Algerian music with western styles such as soul, reggae and rock. Caribbean Zouk is a rhythmic form of music, tracing its roots to the Caribbean, Africa and Europe. *Zouk* means 'party' and the songs are sung in the Creole language of the French Antilles. The music is characterised by driving tempos, layered percussion, lots of brass and the juggling of melodic elements from around the world.

Son et Lumière

In 1952, the curator of the **Château de Chambord** hit upon the idea of making this glorious Loire Valley Renaissance château the star of a theatrical entertainment. The building became both stage and protagonist, with light being synchronised with sound – music and narration – to tell the history of the location. Smoke bombs or fireworks provided a fitting climax. The idea began a trend for 'Sound and Light' shows, which have been a huge success throughout France, particularly in the Loire Valley and at Versailles. For better or for worse, the idea has gone around the world, and now the Parthenon, the Pyramids, the Forum in Rome

273

and the Taj Mahal all star in their own sound and light shows. Although it wasn't part of the original idea, some shows now include the participation of local actors and/or musicians.

Festivals

Most French villages lower the shutters at 2100. However, everyone turns up when there's a festival on. Many are purely local events, celebrating a region's traditions, wine and food, and offering the perfect chance to eat, drink and make merry with the French. Some of the seasonal festivals in France, although adapted to Christianity, have their origins in pagan ritual. Big official festivals, while based on folklore or historic events, often mix tourist hype with tradition. Music, theatre and art festivals fall into a third category. The one with the most cachet is the **Avignon Festival**, but there are many others.

The local tourist office is always a good source of information about festivals and special events; this is just a small selection:

February
Mardi Gras in Nice
Carnaval in Nîmes
Fête du Citron (Lemon Festival) in Menton

May
53rd Cannes Film Festival in Cannes
Gypsy Festival in Les-Saintes-Maries-de-la-Mer
La Fête des Mais (Feasts of May) in Nice

July
Bastille Day (Fête Nationale) in Paris
Aix en Musique in Aix-en-Provence
International Festival (dance and drama) in Avignon
International Dance Festival in Aix-en-Provence
International Jazz Festival in Juan-les-Pins
New Morning Jazz Festival in Paris
Flamenco Festival in Mond-de-Marsan

August
Inter-Celtic Festival in Lorient, Brittany
International Piano Festival in Roque d'Anthéro
International Mime Festival in Périgueux
La route du Rock (rock music) in St-Malo
International Folklore Festival in Murat

September
Festival d'Automne (theatre, dance and music) in Paris
International Festival (food and wine) in Dijon

November
International Mime and Clown Festival in Strasbourg

December
Christkindlmarkt (Christmas market) in Strasbourg and other Alsatian towns.

Tickets for performances and major festivals are available at FNAC book and record shops. Tickets for smaller festivals can usually be obtained from the tourist office.

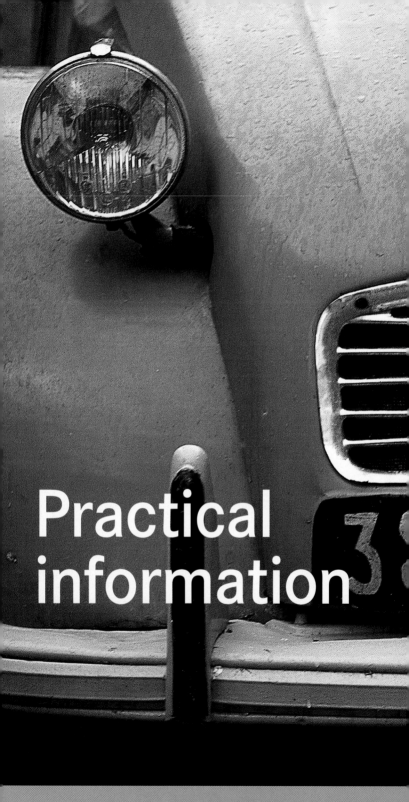

Practical
information

Practical information

Airports

Flying is the fastest option for getting to France, although the Eurostar is almost as fast to Paris from London (*see page 281*). The major gateways in Paris are Charles de Gaulle (Roissy) Airport (*tel: 01 48 62 22 80*) in Paris and Orly Airport (*tel: 01 49 75 52 52*). Flying time is 50 minutes from London.

Airlines
Air France *Tel: 020 8742 6600; www.airfrance.fr.*
Britair *Tel: 020 8742 6600.*
British Airways *Tel: 0345 222 111; www.britishairways.com.*
EasyJet *Tel: 0158 702 900; www.easyjet.com.*
KLM UK *Tel: 08705 074074; www.airuk.co.uk.*

Discount air tickets
STA Travel *86 Old Brompton Rd, London SW7. Tel: 020 7361 6161.*
Trailfinders *194 Kensington High Street, London W8. Tel: 020 7937 5400.*

Climate

France has an Atlantic maritime climate in the west with mild winters and cool summers. The middle of the country is continental – winters are colder and summers are hotter. It gives way to a Mediterranean climate in the south with hot, dry summers and low rainfall.

Communications

To ring France from the UK, dial 00, then 33 and omit the zero of the area code. To call the UK from France, dial 00, then 44 and omit the first zero. The Paris city code is 01. The majority of telephones are now card-only, the pre-paid cards being available from the ubiquitous *tabacs* (tobacconists) or the post office. International calls are cheaper Mon–Fri 2230–0800, and from 1400 Sat to 0800 Mon. You can use some British mobile phones in France.

Currency

The French franc, written as FFr, FF, or sometimes just F, is divided into 100 centimes. Notes are in denominations of 500, 200, 100, 50, 20 and 10 francs. Coins are in denominations of 10, 5, 2 francs and 1 franc, and 50, 20, 10 and 5 centimes.

Disabled travellers

French people will go out of their way to be welcoming and helpful to disabled travellers but, in terms of infrastructure, France still has far to go in addressing the needs of disabled travellers. Progress is, however, being made in giving all people access to historical monuments, resorts, recreational facilities and festival events. Furthermore, newer museums, and hotels in Paris and the provinces, and older buildings that have recently been remodelled, will usually have wheelchair access.

Further information:

Comité National Français de Liaison pour la Réadaptation des Handicappés (CNFLRH) *38 boulevard Raspail, 75007 Paris. Tel: 01 45 48 98 90; fax: 01 45 48 99 21.*

Association des Paralysés *17 boulevard Auguste-Blanqui, 75013 Paris. Tel: 01 40 78 69 00; fax: 01 45 89 40 57.*

Union Nationale des Associations de Parents d'Enfants Inadaptes (UNAPEI) *15 rue Coysevox, 75018 Paris. Tel: 01 42 63 84 33; fax: 01 42 63 08 45.*

Electricity

The French electricity supply is 220V – sufficient to work with British appliances. The plugs have two pins, which are large for heavy-duty items and small for the small devices most visitors are likely to bring with them, so an adaptor will be needed. If you forget to pack one, French hardware stores stock them.

Emergencies
Police *Tel: 17.*
Ambulance *Tel: 15.*
Fire *Tel: 18.*

Entry formalities

British citizens do not require a visa, but visitors who have retained their Commonwealth passports may need one.

Getting there

By air
The best travel deals require planning ahead – or waiting until the last minute. An APEX (Advance Purchase Excursion) fare is 30 to 40 per cent cheaper than the full economy fare for a cross-Channel or trans-Atlantic flight but is subject to restrictions: purchase 21 days ahead of time, a stay of at least two weeks, return in 90 to 120 days. APEX fares are not fully refundable so cancellation insurance is advisable. Some cross-Channel operators now offer an 'APEX'-type discount for advance bookings.

The internet is an excellent source of information for flight information,

whether you plan to travel in six months' time or tomorrow. However, it is worth checking the details with a travel agent.

www.cheapflights.co.uk
www.lastminute.com
www.flightline.co.uk
www.previewtravel.com
www.expedia.com
www.thetrip.com
www.travelocity.com

By car
The advantages of bringing your own car are obvious. Aside from saving on air or train fares, you have a great deal of flexibility. In addition to the price of crossing the Channel, tolls and petrol, you need to factor in the stress of driving but it will probably be worth it for people travelling as a group of three or more. The fastest way is through the **Eurotunnel** (*Customer Services Centre tel: 0990 353535*).

Crossing the Channel
By ferry, the main gateways from the UK are: Calais, served by Hoverspeed, P&O Stena and SeaFrance; Dieppe, served by P&O Stena from Newhaven; Le Havre, by P&O European ferries from Portsmouth; Cherbourg, by P&O from Portsmouth and Brittany Ferries from Poole; and Ouistreham, by Brittany Ferries from Portsmouth.

Brittany Ferries *Tel: 0990 360360.*
Hoverspeed *Tel: 0990 240241 or 0990 595522.*

Rail Europe (*tel: 08705 848848*) offers cut-price fares for cities in provincial France – you must book a week in advance and stay away for at least one Saturday night.

Health

Standards of health care are high in France and hazards few. A well-stocked *pharmacie* (chemist) – a green cross marks the spot – is never far away. French pharmacists have high professional standards and can offer advice and minor first aid. Much of France is hot in the summer, so take precautions to avoid dehydration. Dogs can be a problem in the countryside and walkers should carry a stick. *La rage* (rabies) is still fairly common so, if you are bitten, seek medical advice immediately. There are two types of poisonous viper in the south of France but they are very rarely seen.

P&O European Ferries *Tel: 0990 980555.*
P&O Stena Line *Tel: 0990 980980.*
SeaFrance *Tel: 0990 711711.*

By rail
The Eurostar train has reduced the travelling time between London and Paris to three hours – including an underground ride through the 'Chunnel'.

Eurostar UK *Eurostar House, Waterloo Station, London SE1 8SE. Eurostar Ticket Office: 102–104 Victoria St, London SW1 (open: Mon–Fri 0900–1730, Sat 0900–1545). Reservations: tel: 0990 186 186.*

Information

French Travel Centre *178 Piccadilly, London W1V 0AL. Tel: 0891 244123 (premium rate); fax: 020 7493 6594; www.franceguide.com. Open: Mon–Fri 0900–1700.*

Paris Tourist Office (main branch) *127 avenue des Champs-Élysées, 75008. Tel: 01 49 52 53 54; fax: 01 49 52 53 00; www.paris.org.*

Maison de la France (Tourist Information Agency) *8 avenue de l'Opéra, 75001 Paris, France. Tel: 01 42 96 10 23; fax: 01 42 86 8052.*

Direction du Tourisme *2 rue Linois, 75740 Paris, Cedex 15, France. Tel: 01 44 37 37 44; fax: 01 44 37 38 39.*

French Consulate General (Visa Section) *PO Box 57, 6A Cromwell Place, London SW7 2EW. Tel: 020 7838 2000; fax: 020 7838 2046. Information Service: 0891 887733 (calls charged). Open: Mon–Fri 0900–1130 (and 1600–1630 for visa collection only) (except French and British national holidays).*

Consulate in Scotland *Tel: 0131 225 7954; fax: 0131 225 8975.*

French Embassy (Cultural Section) *23 Cromwell Road, London SW7 2EL. Tel: 020 7838 2055; fax: 020 7838 2088. Open: Mon–Fri 0930–1300 and 1430–1700.*

British Embassy *35 rue du Faubourg St-Honoré, 75383 Paris, Cedex 08, France. Tel: 01 42 66 91 42; fax: 01 42 66 95 90.*

Insurance

The standard of medical facilities in France is high but so are the fees for health care, and a large amount of paperwork is involved in obtaining refunds. There is a reciprocal health agreement with the UK, so you should obtain a Form E111 from the Post Office before you go. On presentation of this at an office of the Caisse Primaire d'Assurance Maladies (Sickness Insurance Office), UK citizens are entitled to a refund of 70 to 80 per cent of the cost of dental and medical treatments, and of prescribed medicines.

Opening times

Shops: department stores are open Mon–Sat 0900–1830. Most shops are closed 1200–1430. Food shops are open 0700/0800–1830/1930 (but closed for lunch in small towns and villages). Some food shops such as bakers and *pâtisseries* are open on Sunday

mornings, in which case they will probably close on Monday. Many shops close all day or half-day Monday.

Banks: generally open Mon–Fri 0900–1200 and 1400–1600. Some close on Monday. Banks close at about noon on the day before a public holiday.

Business: offices are generally open Mon–Fri 0900–1200 and 1400–1800.

Bars and restaurants: opening hours vary enormously depending on the proprietor. Some bars/cafés open early in the morning and stay open until the early hours of the next day. Restaurants generally open about 1200–1500, although some open and close a little later. Evening openings start at about 1900/1930 through to about 2200 for

last orders. Many restaurants close on Sunday and public holidays.

Churches: generally open from dawn until dusk, but, as is happening elsewhere in the world, many are increasingly being locked for security reasons.

Museums: usually open about 0900–1800, and closed on either Monday or Tuesday. Reduced or free admission is often available on Sunday. Many museums stay open late one evening in midweek, so check each museum for details.

Public holidays

1 January, Easter Sunday, Easter Monday, Feast of the Ascension (40 days after Easter), Whit Sunday (seventh Sunday after Easter), Whit Monday, 1 May, 8 May (VE Day), 14 July (Bastille Day), 15 August (Feast of the Assumption), 1 November (All Saints), 11 November (Armistice Day), 25 December.

Reading list

John Ardagh *France in the New Century*. A portrait of a changing French society by a journalist with decades of experience.

Julian Barnes *Flaubert's Parrot* and *Metroland*. Brilliant, soul-searching mix of lit-crit and biography.

M F K Fisher *Two Towns in Provence*. Better written and more insightful

283

than Peter Mayle's *A Year in Provence* and published decades earlier.

Alistair Horne *The Fall of Paris, The Price of Glory* (Verdun) and *To Lose a Battle* (1940). A trilogy that explores the three disastrous wars that have shaped recent French history.

Hugh Johnson and Hubert Duijker *The Wine Atlas of France*. Everything you need for a lifetime of wine tasting in the French countryside.

Nancy Mitford *The Sun King*. Evocative summing-up of the reign of Louis XIV.

Tobias Smollett *Travels Through France and Italy*. The ultimate Francophobe's guide to France. However, a few things have changed since 1763.

Barbara Tuchman *A Distant Mirror*. Anatomy of the 14th century – its chivalry, the Hundred Years War, plagues and crusades.

Patricia Wells *Food Lover's Guide to Paris*. Perfect for people who love both Paris and food.

Theodore Zeldin *France 1858–1945* and *The French*. Intimate look at French history and character.

Safety and security

There is a fair amount of petty crime in Paris, Marseilles and other big cities. Cars with foreign number plates and rental cars are often targeted by criminals for break-ins, sometimes from scooters. Thefts should be reported at the *commissariat de police*. Even if you have no hope of getting back your possessions, you should fill out a *constat de vol* (theft report) to back up any insurance claim.

Time

France is one hour ahead of Greenwich Mean Time and uses the 24-hour clock.

Tipping

Tip taxi drivers 5 to 10 per cent by rounding up the bill. Although tipping hotel staff such as chambermaids is not expected, a small appreciation of good service won't go amiss. In restaurants, service charge of 15 per cent is normally included and indicated on the bill (*service compris*). Again, extra good service might be rewarded with an additional small tip.

Toilets

A few years ago the phrase 'a French toilet' would have summoned up the image of an unappealing hole in the ground, but this is no longer the truth. French toilets are as good as any others in Europe, although the 'unisex' principle is stronger and even in Paris you must be prepared to find a row of cubicles used by both men and women. More common is a split loo, where you pass the attendant and go left or right, but be prepared to put a franc or two in the saucer when you leave.

PRACTICAL INFORMATION

Index

Editorial, design and production credits

Project management: Dial House Publishing Services

Series editor: Christopher Catling

Copy editor: Jane Franklin

Proof-reader: Lucy Thomson

Series and cover design: Trickett & Webb Limited

Cover artwork: Wenham Arts

Text layout: Wenham Arts

Cartography: Polly Senior Cartography

Repro and image setting: Z2 Repro, Thetford, Norfolk, UK

Printed and bound by: Artes Graficas ELKAR S. Coop., Bilbao, Spain

Acknowledgements

We would like to thank the following for the photographs used in this book, to whom the copyright belongs:

J Allan Cash: page 182

Bob Battersby: pages 15, 118–19, 129A, 129B, 139, 140, 144 and 145

Michael Busselle: pages 99B and 109

Côtes Vues Picture Library: pages 95, 96, 101, 103, 106, 107, 110, 112, 114–15 and 117

Chris Fairclough: pages 16, 20–1, 24, 25, 26, 27, 29, 30, 33, 34, 37, 38, 39, 40, 41, 42, 48–9, 146–7, 151, 153, 154, 157, 158, 160, 162, 163, 168, 169, 170–1, 175, 176, 177, 185, 186, 187, 190, 191A, 191B, 200–1, 224, 225, 226, 228, 230–1, 232, 235, 237A, 237B, 239, 240–1, 243, 244, 245, 246A, 246B, 249, 250, 253, 254, 258A, 258B, 259A, 259B, 264–5, 273 and 280–1

Fred Gebhart: pages 104 and 105

D'Herouville: page 275

John Heseltine: pages 126, 136, 137, 138 and 141

Jacques Lebar: page 36

Neil Setchfield: pages 4–5, 7, 8–9, 11, 12–13, 19, 50–1, 54, 55, 56, 59, 60, 62, 65, 66, 67, 68, 70, 71, 72–3, 75, 76, 77, 79, 80, 82, 85, 86–7, 88, 89, 90–1, 99A, 123, 125, 127, 131, 132, 134, 192–3, 196, 198, 200, 202, 204, 206, 208, 211, 213, 214, 215, 217, 219, 260–1, 262, 263, 266, 267, 268, 269, 271, 272, 274, 276–7, 278, 282–3 and 285

Spectrum Colour Library: pages 179 and 180

Gillian Thomas: pages 155 and 164.